European Multiculturalisms

EUROPEAN MULTICULTURALISMS

CULTURAL, RELIGIOUS AND ETHNIC CHALLENGES

Edited by Anna Triandafyllidou, Tariq Modood
and Nasar Meer

EDINBURGH UNIVERSITY PRESS

EUROPEAN
COMMISSION

CITIZENS AND GOVERNANCE IN A
KNOWLEDGE-BASED SOCIETY

This volume is published thanks to the support of the Directorate General for Research & Innovation of the European Commission, 6th Framework Programme, Socio-Economic Sciences and Humanities, under the auspices of the EMILIE Specific Targeted Research Project (Contract no. CIT5-CT-2005-028205). The volume is solely the responsibility of its editors and authors; the European Commission cannot be held responsible for its contents or of any use which may be of it.

© editorial matter and organisation Anna Triandafyllidou, Tariq Modood and
Nasar Meer 2012
© the chapters their several authors 2012

Edinburgh University Press Ltd
22 George Square, Edinburgh
www.euppublishing.com

Typeset in 11/13 Sabon by
Servis Filmsetting Ltd, Stockport, Cheshire, and
printed and bound in Great Britain by
CPI Group (UK) Ltd, Croydon CR0 4YY

A CIP record for this book is available at the British Library

ISBN 978 0 7486 4452 0 (hardback)
ISBN 978 0 7486 4451 3 (paperback)

The right of the contributors to be identified as author of this work has been asserted in accordance with the Copyright, Designs and Patents Act 1988.

Contents

Notes on the Contributors vii
Acknowledgements xi

1 Introduction: Diversity, Integration, Secularism and
   Multiculturalism 1
   Anna Triandafyllidou, Tariq Modood and Nasar Meer

PART I Theoretical Developments in a Comparative European
   Perspective

2 Framing Contemporary Citizenship and Diversity in Europe 33
   Tariq Modood and Nasar Meer

3 The Multicultural States We're In 61
   Nasar Meer and Tariq Modood

4 Beyond Post-national Citizenship: Access, Consequence,
   Conditionality 88
   Per Mouritsen

5 Islamic Difference and the Return of Feminist Universalism 116
   Nilüfer Göle and Julie Billaud

PART II Cultural Diversity and Policy Responses in the European
   Union

6 Religious Diversity and Education: Intercultural and
   Multicultural Concepts and Policies 145
   Ruby Gropas and Anna Triandafyllidou

7 Active Immigrants in Multicultural Contexts: Democratic
   Challenges in Europe 167
   Ricard Zapata-Barrero and Ruby Gropas

8 Not a One-way Road? Integration as a Concept and as a Policy 192
Frauke Miera

9 Ethnic Statistics in Europe: The Paradox of Colour-blindness 213
Angéline Escafré-Dublet and Patrick Simon

Index 239

Notes on the Contributors

Julie Billaud is a postdoctoral research fellow in anthropology at the University of Sussex. Her doctoral thesis is an ethnographic exploration of women's public visibility in post-war/reconstruction Afghanistan. From January 2009 to July 2010 she was part of the 'Islam in the making of the European Public Sphere' research project, directed by Professor Nilüfer Göle from the École des Hautes Études en Sciences Sociales (Paris). Her most recent area of research is social theory and the practice of rights in relation to culture and religion.

Angéline Escafré-Dublet is a postdoctoral fellow in the Center for International Studies and Research (CERI) at Sciences Po, Paris. She obtained a PhD in history from Sciences Po in 2008, prior to which she was a Visiting Fellow for two years at the University of Chicago Center for the Study of Race, Politics and Culture. From 2008 to 2010 she was a postdoctoral fellow in the research unit on International Migration and Minorities at the National Institute for Demographic Studies (INED), Paris. Her research interests focus on migration and how this relates to matters of politics and culture in Europe and North America.

Nilüfer Göle is a professor of sociology at the École des Hautes Études en Sciences Sociales in Paris. She works on Islamic visibility in European public spaces and the debates it engenders on religious and cultural difference. Her sociological approach aims to open up a new reading of modernity from a non-Western perspective and a broader critique of Eurocentrism in the definitions of secular modernity. She is the author of *Islam in Europe: The Lure of Fundamentalism and the Allure of Cosmopolitanism* (2010, Marcus Weiner).

Ruby Gropas is Lecturer in international relations at the Law Faculty of the Democritus University of Thrace (Komotini), Research

Fellow at the Hellenic Foundation for European and Foreign Policy (ELIAMEP) and Visiting Scholar at Stanford University (2011). Her research concentrates on European integration and foreign policy, migration and multiculturalism, transatlantic relations and human rights. She was Managing Editor of the *Journal of Southeast European and Black Sea Studies* (Taylor and Francis, 2006–9) and Southeast Europe Policy Scholar at the Woodrow Wilson International Center for Scholars in Washington, DC (2007, 2009), and is currently Vice-President of the Alexander S. Onassis Public Benefit Foundation Scholars' Association. She holds a PhD in history from Cambridge University.

Nasar Meer is a senior lecturer in the School of Arts and Sciences, University of Northumbria, and was previously a lecturer in sociology at Southampton University and a research fellow at the Centre for the Study of Ethnicity and Citizenship, Bristol University. His publications include *Citizenship, Identity and the Politics of Multiculturalism* (2010, Palgrave) and *Race & Ethnicity* (forthcoming, Sage). He is guest editor of a special issue of *Ethnic and Racial Studies* comparing anti-Semitism and Islamophobia, and (with S. Thompson and W. Martineau) editing special issues of both *Ethnicities* and *Respublica* on theorising misrecognition. He is also a Palgrave book series editor (with V. Uberoi and T. Modood) on the politics of identity and citizenship (www.palgrave.com/products/series.aspx?s=CaI).

Frauke Miera is a political scientist whose PhD dissertation was on Polish migration to Germany. She has worked as a researcher and lecturer on migration and integration issues at the Social Science Research Centre in Berlin; the temporary International Women's University in Hanover; the Department of Political Science at the Free University, Berlin; the University of Southampton; and the European University Viadrina in Frankfurt (Oder). Her fields of interest include integration policies, theories on multiculturalism and the representation of migrant minorities in the 'master narrative'. She has also worked at the Museum of History of the Federal Republic of Germany in Bonn and at the German Historical Museum in Berlin. She is currently working as a curator at the Berlin District Museum of Friedrichshain-Kreuzberg. She is a founding member of Network Migration in Europe (www.network-migration.org).

NOTES ON THE CONTRIBUTORS

Tariq Modood is Professor of Sociology, Politics and Public Policy and the founding director of the Centre for the Study of Ethnicity and Citizenship at the University of Bristol. He has held more than forty grants and consultancies (UK, European and US), and has (co-)authored or (co-)edited more than thirty books and reports and over one hundred articles or chapters in political philosophy, sociology and public policy. He is the co-founding editor of the international journal *Ethnicities*. His recent publications include *Multiculturalism: A Civic Idea* (2007, Polity), *Still Not Easy Being British: Struggles for a Multicultural Citizenship* (2010, Trentham Books) and, as co-editor, *Multiculturalism, Muslims and Citizenship: A European Approach* (2006, Routledge) and *Secularism, Religion and Multicultural Citizenship* (2009, Cambridge University Press). He is a regular contributor to media and policy debates in the UK, was awarded an MBE for services to social sciences and ethnic relations in 2001 and was elected a member of the Academy of Social Sciences in 2004.

Per Mouritsen is a professor of political theory and citizenship studies in the Department of Political Science at Aarhus University, Denmark. He is the author of many articles and book chapters on citizenship and migration and recently co-edited *Constituting Communities: Political Solutions to Cultural Conflict* (2008, Palgrave Macmillan) and *The Muhammad Cartoons Controversy in Comparative Perspective*, a special issue of *Ethnicities* (2009). He directs a comparative project on civic integration in Europe (CiviTurn), participates in the EU 7th Framework Programme ACCEPT Pluralism and is writing a book on the concept of citizenship.

Patrick Simon is director of research at INED in Paris and is a research fellow at the Centre of European Studies (CEE) at Sciences Po. He studies ethnic and racial divisions, anti-discrimination policies and the integration of ethnic minorities in European countries. In 2010 he edited, with C. Beauchemin and C. Hamel, the preliminary findings of a large survey on immigrants and second generations in France: *Trajectories and Origins. Survey on Population Diversity in France. Initial findings* (Documents de Travail no. 168, INED, Paris).

Anna Triandafyllidou is a part-time professor at the European University Institute, Robert Schuman Centre for Advanced Studies, in Florence, Italy and Senior Research Fellow at the Hellenic

Foundation for European and Foreign Policy (ELIAMEP) in Athens. She has been Visiting Professor at the College of Europe in Bruges since 2002 and has held teaching and research positions in the UK, Italy, the USA and Greece. She has published more than one hundred articles in refereed journals and chapters in collective volumes on migration, nationalism and European integration. Her most recent books include *Migration in 21st Century Greece* (2010, Kritiki, in Greek), *Muslims in 21st Century Europe* (2010, Routledge), *Irregular Migration in Europe: Myths and Realities* (2010, Ashgate), *What is Europe?* (with R. Gropas, 2012, Palgrave) and *Migrant Smuggling. Irregular Migration from Asia and Africa to Europe* (with T. Maroukis, 2012, Palgrave).

Ricard Zapata-Barrero is Associate Professor of political theory at the Department of Social and Political Science, Universitat Pompeu Fabra in Barcelona, Spain. His main lines of research deal with contemporary issues of liberal democracy in contexts of diversity, especially the relationship between citizenship and immigration. He is Director of the GRITIM (Interdisciplinary Research Group on Immigration, www.upf.edu/gritim). He is a regular contributor to media and policy debates, and has served on a number of commissions and government committees. His recent publications include (with L. E. Lindkilde and P. Mouritsen) *The Muhammad Cartoons Controversy in Comparative Perspective*, a special issue of *Ethnicities* (2009), and *Immigration and Self-government of Minority Nations* (2009, Peter Lang). For more information see http://dcpis.upf.edu/~ricard-zapata/

Acknowledgements

European Multiculturalisms reflects the culmination of findings from the EMILIE research project (A European Approach to Multicultural Citizenship. Legal, Political and Educational Challenges) which was generously funded by the European Commission Research Directorate (6th Framework Programme, Socio-Economic Sciences and Humanities) between 2006 and 2009. The book took shape during the year following the end of the project, and each chapter has undergone several revisions before reaching its present form. During this process we have had the opportunity to benefit from comments and discussions not only among the EMILIE consortium but also with other colleagues external to the project. In particular we would like to thank Varun Uberoi and Dita Vogel for their comments on earlier drafts of chapters of this book. A big thanks goes also to our families for their ongoing support and for the price paid in terms of less personal and family time. Many thanks also to our European Commission project officer Alessia Bursi for her continuous support throughout the project and to Nicola Ramsey at Edinburgh University Press for her support in getting this book onto the bookshelves. Any errors and omissions are of course our responsibility.

1
Introduction: Diversity, Integration, Secularism and Multiculturalism

Anna Triandafyllidou, Tariq Modood and Nasar Meer

The upsurge of international terrorism during the past decade and the global financial crisis of the last couple of years have provided fruitful ground for the securitisation of migration and integration agendas on the one hand, and the condemnation of previous 'multicultural integration' approaches as harmful to social cohesion on the other. In this context of pronounced social and economic insecurity, European countries find themselves divided in their approaches, with different policy priorities as regards migrant integration. The governments of several 'old' immigration hosts, such as France, the Netherlands or Denmark, have turned to civic assimilation approaches as the way forward. Even in the UK, where policies on the ground remain pluralist and multiculturalist in their orientation, Prime Minister David Cameron declared in February 2011 that multiculturalism had failed. He did so soon after the German Chancellor Angela Merkel declared that 'multiculturalism has failed, completely failed', even though Germany had never adopted a multicultural policy agenda. Within this climate, 'new' hosts in southern Europe, such as Greece, Italy and Spain, are hesitant to open up towards their immigrants and the ethnic and religious diversity that these minorities bring to their societies. At the same time these countries are increasingly preoccupied with irregular migration and its impact on both labour markets and social cohesion. Central Eastern European countries, for their part, remain concerned with emigration (towards other EU member states) rather than immigration, even if diversity challenges from established minorities and other groups also persist.

This book contributes to the debate on the presumed crisis of multiculturalism in Europe by offering new theoretical and empirical insights on the issue. The first part of the book discusses the varieties of multiculturalism that we find in different European countries and assesses them against the existing theoretical literature. It also addresses issues of diversity and gender with special reference to Muslim women, and to the challenges of post-national citizenship. The second part of the book includes four chapters that discuss how diversity is dealt with in education, at the political level, with regard to integration policies and in relation to ethnic statistics, through a systematic comparative analysis of policy approaches in different European countries.

In the following sections of this introductory chapter, we introduce the different characterisations of integration provided within different policy and theoretical perspectives concerning the accommodation of ethnic diversity, and we explain our focus on the varieties of European multiculturalism. Section 1.4 presents the methodological basis of the comparative chapters while Section 1.5 gives a brief explanation of the book structure and contents.

1.1 Integrating diversity, secularism and multiculturalism

The fact of pluralism, to borrow a phrase from Rawls, emerges as self-evident in a world comprising at least 600 languages, 500 ethno-cultural groups and innumerable religions spread across nearly 200 recognised sovereign states. By definition, therefore, 'diversity' is an inescapable feature of human societies and 'can neither be wished out of existence nor suppressed without an unacceptable degree of coercion, and often not even then' (Parekh 2000: 196). A large part of human history reflects the implications of coming to terms with this diversity throughout cycles of migration and patterns of settlement, where the intermingling of diverse cultural, religious and ethnic mores renews and/ or unsettles established social and political configurations.

History, of course, does not stand still and so it is unsurprising to find it difficult to imagine a modern polity that is not faced with challenges of social and political integration. The twenty-seven member states of the European Union are no exception. As Gutmann (1994: 3) declared nearly two decades ago, 'it is hard to find a democratic or democratising society these days that is not the site of some significant controversy over whether and how its institutions should better recognize the identities of cultural and disadvantaged minorities'. Such contestations might concern the separation of public and private spheres, a reconfiguration in the constituents of incorporation in the country's self-image or the emergence of what can either be conceived as mundane or politicised calls for dietary or uniform changes in places of school and work. What is common to each of these scenarios is the view that conceptions of integration cannot ignore the internal diversity of societies that are host to cultural, religious and ethnic 'difference'. Not ignoring diversity, however, is certainly not the same as recognising or accommodating it.

In the Asylum and Migration Glossary issued by the European Migration Network, integration is defined as a 'dynamic, two-way process of mutual accommodation by all immigrants and residents of member states'. The glossary also adds that 'the promotion of fundamental rights, non-discrimination and equal opportunities for all are key integration issues at the EU level'. Integration policy in the EU follows a set of common basic principles, although integration issues are the prerogative mainly of member states, in line with the principle of subsidiarity. This formal definition provided at the EU level leaves a lot of questions unanswered, however, most notably as to how far a country should go in accommodating diversity.

Indeed, how different European states pursue integration can vary widely. One view is that integration should proceed on the grounds of established configurations into which diverse cultural, religious and ethnic minorities should assimilate. That is to say that where minorities 'insist on retaining their separate cultures, they should not complain if they are viewed as outsiders and subjected to discriminatory treatment' (Parekh 2000: 197). A more nuanced and elaborate version of this position limits the comprehensiveness of assimilation to the public sphere, into which minorities should assimilate in order to participate in the political cultures of a society, but not be prevented from retaining their diversity at the level of the family and of some parts of civil society. The insistence here is upon a prescribed 'political culture, which includes its [society's] public or political values, ideals, practices, institutions, modes of political discourse, and self-understanding' (ibid. p. 200).

Some perceive this mode of integration – comprising at least partial assimilation – as presently ascendant, perhaps buoyed as a short-term panacea (and longer-term prophylactic) to the sorts of societal disunity allegedly associated with ethnic minority separatism in general, and Muslim alienation and estrangement (and ultimately violent extremism) in particular (see Meer, de Witte, Faas, Mouritsen and Brigstocke forthcoming). For example, according to Kostakopoulou (2010: 830), integration as partial assimilation is observable across Europe in:

> Policies for 'social cohesion', 'integration' and 'assimilation', including the official promotion of national identity, official lists of national values,

language [and clothing] prohibitions in public transport, schools, universities and hospitals, compulsory language courses and tests for migrants, naturalisation ceremonies and oaths of loyalty.

Such normative prescriptions for integration comprising full or partial assimilation have not gone unchallenged. Until relatively recently, however, there were some instances where any assimilation was viewed as less favourable than other modes of integration. This would include approaches deemed as multicultural and which recognise that social existence consists of individuals and groups, and that both need to be provided for in the formal and informal distribution of powers; not just in law, but in representation in the offices of the state, public committees, consultative exercises and access to public forums. This means that while individuals have rights, mediating institutions such as trade unions, churches, neighbourhoods, immigrant associations and so on may also be encouraged to be active public players and forums for political discussion (and may even have a formal representative or administrative role to play in the state).

One implication of this multicultural mode of integration is the re-forming of such things as national identity and citizenship, and offering an emotional identity with the whole to counterbalance the emotional loyalties to ethnic and religious communities (Modood 2007a). Of course, multiculturalism as a concept for promoting integration is – like very many others – 'polysemic', such that multiculturalist authors cannot be held entirely responsible for the variety of ways in which the term is interpreted. This point is noted by Bhabha (1998: 31), who addresses the tendency for multiculturalism to be appropriated as a '*portmanteau* term', one that encapsulates a variety of sometimes contested meanings (cf. Meer and Modood 2009a). In this respect the idea of multiculturalism might be said to have a 'chameleonic' quality that facilitates its simultaneous adoption and rejection in the critique or defence of a position (Smith 2010). This may be illustrated by how multiculturalism is simultaneously used as a label to describe the fact of diversity in any given society and as a moral stance that cultural diversity is a desirable feature of a given society (as well as the different ways in which the state could recognise and support it).

Moreover, in both theoretical and policy discourses, multiculturalism means different things in different places. In North America, for example, multiculturalism encompasses discrete groups with territorial claims, such as the Native Peoples and the Québecois, even though these groups want to be treated as 'nations' within a multinational state, rather than merely as ethno-cultural groups in a mono-national state (Kymlicka 1995). In Europe, while groups with such claims, like the Catalans and the Scots, are thought of as nations, multiculturalism has a more limited meaning, referring to a post-immigration urban mélange and the politics it gives rise to. One outcome is that while in North America language-based ethnicity is seen as the major political challenge, in Western Europe the conjunction of the terms 'immigration' and 'culture' now nearly always invokes the large, newly settled Muslim populations. Sometimes, usually in America, political terms such as multiculturalism and 'rainbow coalition' are meant to include all groups marked by 'difference' and historic exclusion, such as women and gays (Young 1990).

Nevertheless, the term multiculturalism in Europe came to mean, and now means throughout the English-speaking world and beyond, the political accommodation by the state and/or a dominant group of all minority cultures defined first and foremost by reference to race, ethnicity or religion, and additionally but more controversially by reference to other group-defining characteristics such as nationality and aboriginality. The latter is more controversial not only because it extends the range of the groups that have to be accommodated, but also because of the larger political claims made by such groups, who resist having these claims reduced to those of immigrants. Hence, despite Kymlicka's attempt to conceptualise multiculturalism-as-multinationalism, the dominant meaning of multiculturalism in politics relates to the claims of post-immigration groups (Modood 2007a).

This provenance of multiculturalism has bequeathed to its contemporary instantiations the importance of reconciling ideas of multiculturalism to ideas of citizenship, within a reciprocal balance of rights and responsibilities, assumptions of virtue and conceptions of membership or civic status (Meer 2010). While there is agreement that the membership conferred by citizenship should entail equal opportunity, dignity and confidence, different views remain about the proper ways, in culturally diverse societies, to confer this civic status. Those engaged in the 'multicultural turn' still maintain that conceptions of integration can frequently ignore the sensibilities of minorities marked by social, cultural and political differences (May, Modood and Squires 2004).

Hence the political multiculturalism of Modood, for example, insists that 'when new groups enter a society, there has to be some education and refinement of ... sensitivities in the light of changing circumstances and the specific vulnerabilities of new entrants' (Modood 2006: 61). As such, a widely accepted contemporary thrust of what multiculturalism denotes includes a critique of 'the myth of homogeneous and mono-cultural nation-states' (Castles 2000: 5), and an advocacy of the right of minority 'cultural maintenance and community formation, linking these to social equality and protection from discrimination' (ibid). Yet in recent years, the appeal of multiculturalism as a mode of integration has suffered considerable political damage, such that the argument that multiculturalism is a valuable means of the 'remaking of public identities in order to achieve an equality of citizenship that is neither merely individualistic nor premised on assimilation' (Modood 2005: 5) is not being embraced as broadly as it once might have been.

The reasons for this are various, but they include how for some multiculturalism has facilitated social fragmentation and entrenched social divisions (Policy Exchange 2007; Malik 2007) while for others it has distracted attention away from socio-economic disparities (Barry 2001; Hansen 2006) or encouraged a moral hesitancy amongst 'native' populations (Caldwell 2010; Prins and Salisbury 2008). Some even blame it for international terrorism (Phillips 2006; Gove 2006; cf. Vertovec and Wessendorf 2005: 10–11). While these political positions are the instigators of anxieties over multiculturalism, other beneficiaries have included a number of competing political orientations concerned with promoting unity, variously conceived, alongside or to a greater degree towards recognising diversity (Modood and Meer, this volume). Some observe this focus on promoting unity in the discovery or rediscovery of national identity (Orgad 2009); others point to its evidence in notions of civicness (Mouritsen 2008) or in a resurgent liberalism that allegedly proves, in the final analysis, to be 'neutral' (Joppke 2008). To this we could also add perhaps the most salient term in contemporary political discussion concerning migration-related diversity, that of social or community cohesion (Dobbernack 2010).

Most notably, it also includes the view that 'the Muslim presence challenges the liberal secular state and condemns the liberal multicultural state' (Levey 2009: 3), in a manner that brings together different sides of the political spectrum. For example, the first part of what Levey points to is an assessment prominent in the accounts of various bestselling authors including the late Italian intellectual

Orianna Fallaci (2003), the German economist Thilo Sarrazin (2010), the British historian Niall Ferguson (2004) and the polemicist Melanie Phillips (2006), among many others. This assessment allows Mark Steyn (2006) to maintain that 'much of what we loosely call the Western world will not survive this century, and much of it will effectively disappear in our lifetimes, including many, if not most Western European countries'. That is to say that Islam in Europe is unique because:

> Since its arrival half a century ago, Islam has broken – or required adjustments to – a good many of European customs, received ideas, and state structures with which it has come into contact. Sometimes the adjustments are minor accommodations to Muslim tradition – businesses eliminating the tradition of drinks after work, women-only hours at swimming pools, or prayer rooms in office buildings, factories and department stores . . . occasionally what needs adjusting is the essence of Europe. (Caldwell 2010: 11)

The second part of Levey's assessment finds expression in the view that Muslims in Europe are exceptional in not following path-dependent institutional opportunity structures of minority integration. That is to say that, taken as an aggregate, accommodating Muslims will be more difficult because Islam is more publicly confessional than other faiths, refuses to be privatised and instead advances into the public realm of politics in collective and exceptional ways (see Meer 2012). Different exponents of this view include Joppke (2009a and b) and Koopmans et al. (2005), as well as O'Leary (2006) and Hansen (2006), among others. In Joppke's (2009b: 108) account

> if one considers that explicit Muslim claims did not emerge in earnest before 1989, the year of the Rushdie controversy in Britain and of the first Foulard affair in France, the speed and depth of accommodating Muslims have been breathtaking, up to the point that 'laicist' France is now providing state financed Imam education.

The explanation for this sustained and rapid claims-making may be found in the force with which 'in pious Muslims there reverberates the archaic power of religion, which is not merely subjective belief, but objective truth, which cannot leave room for choice' (2009a: 111). The presence of Muslims in Europe has therefore resurrected religious disputes from an earlier age, potentially unstitching secularism's peace compacts in a manner that may be unacceptable where Muslims are promoting a way of life that is antithetical to liberal democratic norms and conventions. As Levey (2009: 3) summarises:

On this account, the 'Muslim question' requires an ever more resolute insistence on 'core' liberal values and the established liberal settlements governing religion and politics, while multiculturalism is blamed for encouraging cultural relativism and social segregation, and for sowing confusion about the appropriate boundaries of the tolerable.

Kymlicka (2005b: 83) narrows down this observation further in his conclusion that 'if we put Western democracies on a continuum in terms of the proportion of immigrants who are Muslim, I think this would provide a good indicator of public opposition to multiculturalism'. As Bhikhu Parekh (2006: 180–1) notes, this can be traced to a perception that Muslims are 'collectivist, intolerant, authoritarian, illiberal and theocratic', and that they use their faith as

> a self-conscious public statement, not quietly held personal faith but a matter of identity which they must jealously guard and loudly and repeatedly proclaim ... not only to remind them of who they are but also to announce to others what they stand for.

This is something that has arguably led some commentators who may otherwise sympathise with religious minorities to argue that it is difficult to view them as victims when they may themselves be potential oppressors (Meer and Modood 2009b).

As a matter of fact, in most if not all European countries there are points of symbolic, institutional, policy and fiscal linkage between the state and aspects of Christianity. Secularism has increasingly grown in power and scope, but a historically evolved and evolving compromise with religion is the defining feature of European, especially north-western European secularism, rather than the absolute separation of religion and politics. Secularism today enjoys hegemony in Western Europe, but it is a moderate rather than a radical secularism (Modood 2010). The presence of Muslims and Islamic claims-making upon European societies and states, however, has resulted in a (temporary?) reversal of aspects of secularisation and the decline of public religion. In reaction there are increased assertions of Enlightenment secularism and of (cultural) Christianity.

Hence, there seem to be three visible trends. While exploratory accommodations of Muslims, often highly visible, such as the *Conseil Français du Culte Musulman* and the *Islamconferenz* are apparent in some countries (Cesari 2004; Modood and Kastoryano 2006; Bowen 2010), there are also negative reactions to these trends. Some of these reactions are populist and Islamophobic, but two in particular relate to the changing nature of religion and secularism; the first relates to Christians and the second to radical secularism.

The emergence of a new, sometimes politically assertive cultural identification with Christianity has been noted in Denmark (Mouritsen 2006) and in Germany; in fact, Chancellor Merkel has asserted that 'those who don't accept [Christian values] don't have a place here' (2010). Similar sentiments were voiced in the EU Constitution debate and are apparent in the ongoing debate on Turkey as a possible future EU member (Casanova 2009). Some of the exponents of the EU Constitution debate wanted a declaration to include a reference to Christianity as the religion of Europe. Even some of those who did not favour this openly rejected Turkey as a possible EU member because it was not a Christian country, and worse, would bring a massive 70 million Muslims into the EU.

These assertions of Christianity are not necessarily accompanied by any increase in expressions of faith or church attendance, which continue to decline across Europe. Giscard d'Estaing, the former President of France, who chaired the Convention on the Future of Europe, the body which drafted the (aborted) EU Constitution, expresses nicely the assertiveness in question: 'I never go to Church, but Europe is a Christian continent'.

It has to be said, however, that the political views about Europe referred to are held not just by cultural Christian identitarians, but also by many practising Christians, including the Catholic Church. It has been argued that Pope John Paul II 'looked at the essential cleavage in the world as being between religion and non-belief. Devout Christians, Muslims, and Buddhists had more in common with each other than with atheists' (Caldwell 2010: 151). Pope Benedict XVI, the same author contends, 'thinks that, within societies, believers and non-believers exist in symbiosis. Secular Westerners, he implies, have a lot in common with their religious fellows' (Caldwell 2010: 151). The suggestion is that secularists and Christians in Europe have more in common with each other than they do with Muslims. That many secularists do not share Pope Benedict's view is evident from the fact that the proposed clause about Christianity was absent from the draft of the EU Constitution.[1] While there is little sign of a Christian Right in Europe of the kind that is strong in the USA, there is to some degree a reinforcing or renewing of a sense that Europe is 'secular Christian'. This is analogous to the term 'secular Jew' to describe someone of Jewish descent who has a sense of Jewish identity but is not religiously practising and may even be an atheist.

Besides this secular Christian identity assertiveness which is to be found (albeit not exclusively) on the centre-right of the political spectrum, there is also a more radical secularism that is more characteristic of the Left. It is an ideology that goes back to the Enlightenment (though more the French rather than the British or German Enlightenment) and is not only non-religious but often anti-religion. It has been most epigrammatically captured by Karl Marx's famous 'religion is the opium of the masses' and Nietzsche's 'God is dead'. The post-9/11 period has seen the emergence of a radical discourse referred to as 'the new atheism' (see Beattie (2007), who has bestselling authors such as Richard Dawkins, Sam Harris and Christopher Hitchens in mind). Such authors interpret political secularism to mean that religious beliefs and discourse should be excluded from the public sphere and/or politics and certainly from activities endorsed or funded by the state. Thus these authors argue, for example, for the disestablishment of the Church of England, the removal of the Anglican bishops from the House of Lords and the withdrawal of state support for faith schools in the UK.

This is a position which fully chimes with the reassertion of *laïcité* in France, as in the banning of the headscarf in state schools in 2004 and of the burqa in public spaces in 2010 – a ban that is proliferating across Western Europe. With groups like Muslims, Sikhs and Hindus pressing for institutionalisation (which to a large extent has already happened in the case of the Jews), and religious groups more involved in the delivery of welfare and urban renewal, it is clear that this radical political secularism is not only a break with the inherited status quo secularism in most parts of Western Europe, but is also at odds with the current institutionalisation of religious pluralism.

1.2 *European multiculturalisms*

This interdisciplinary book proposes an intellectual framework to evaluate recent developments in European multiculturalisms. If we take the view that there has been an observable 'retreat' in northwestern Europe from relatively modest approaches of multicultural citizenship across a variety of citizenship regimes, this does not necessarily mean that the desirability of recognising minority cultural differences as a means of cultivating an inclusive citizenship has been eliminated. More specifically, the rise of competing intellectual and policy agendas emphasising the requirements of minority integration, in order to strengthen broader social solidarity and bonds of common community (variously conceived in terms of national identity, active citizenship, social cohesion and so forth), may not expunge what has preceded it.

These are empirical questions, and while the fact of these tendencies remains constant across different national contexts, the very forms they take and the implications they herald can vary radically across different European citizenship regimes. Namely, what are states actually doing and not doing? Is this repeated as a pattern across different countries? Moreover, can an intellectual framework be developed for conceptualising what 'post-multicultural' citizenship regimes in Europe may resemble? The key elements or ideas in the retreat of multiculturalism are therefore far from established or widely understood, while at the same time the empirical basis (as opposed to surface rhetoric) informing this 'retreat' has already been shown to be a more complicated and mixed affair (Jacobs and Rea 2007; Meer and Modood 2009a; Modood and Meer, this volume).

Any cross-national understanding of contemporary citizenship therefore needs to capture and explain the permutations in these developments. This requires some notion of a political community in which individuals have rights and correlative duties enforced by law but are likely to also have a sense of shaping and being shaped by a public space that goes beyond law and politics. Only when we have a sufficient understanding of this kind of citizenship will we be able to assess the recent developments in relation to post-immigration multicultural citizenship.

In some respects this is also a question of socio-economic integration and full social citizenship, but it is not merely that. During most of the twentieth century there was a left–right struggle about the extent to which citizenship should or should not entail social welfare and economic rights, illustrated in Marshall's well-known typology (1950). In the 1990s, citizenship was being qualified by international human rights norms and conventions (Soysal 2002), while in the early twenty-first century it was the dilemma between citizenship as shared values (Joppke 2008) and citizenship as a common public space for dialogue and a negotiated identity (Modood 2007a; Parekh 2000) that had moved to the top of political agendas. This indeed is the fundamental question raised by post-immigration diversity for a variety of nation-states: what is the identity of citizenship itself and what does it imply for other identities that citizens may have or want to have?

Questions about citizenship as membership, entitlement and social expectations, including the question of civic identity, are not about merely vertical (state to citizen) but also horizontal (citizen to citizen) relationships (Gagnon and Iacovino 2007: 125). So to address the questions of citizenship, especially those concerning social expectations, one has to ask how the state and citizens should relate to individual and group diversity.

In this book we will trace the implication of these questions thematically, taking applied examples and cases spanning across, rather than narrowly focused in, five northern European states (Belgium, the UK, Denmark, France and Germany) and two southern European states (Spain and Greece) that have been host to a variety of multicultural citizenship and diversity integration debates and policies. These include: the national and multinational political orientations in which cultural, religious and ethnic diversity in Europe proceeds, particularly in the public sphere and the contemporary re-emergence of integration as a concept and as a policy solution across Europe. The role of gender relations, the status of women and the tensions between ethnic, cultural and religious diversity and gender equality are also an important issue that we look at as well as the interaction of religious diversity in education, and the rise of interculturalism as a policy solution. Last but not least, this book discusses the significance of cultural, religious and ethnic diversity for equality and anti-discrimination policies; assesses the challenge of political representation and participation of a diverse citizenry into a common political community; and, finally, examines the implication of this diversity for statistics and data gathering oriented toward social policy.

A prevailing feature of these debates is that contemporary European multicultural challenges relate mainly to the successful integration and participation of Muslim citizens and residents into European societies (Modood, Triandafyllidou and Zapata-Barrero 2006). We therefore detail empirical and theoretical inquiries on immigrant minority claims, with a special focus on Muslim immigrants, the value issues entrenched in them and the related policy challenges and measures adopted to address them. Indeed, the 'crisis of multiculturalism' comes at a time of heightened security awareness as a result of the events of 9/11 and the London and Madrid bombings, and their aftermath. However, nearly a decade after 9/11 and five years after the London and Madrid bombings, it is time for a more sober discourse on the renewed challenges that multiculturalism is facing today.

The upsurge of international terrorism has led to the increasing securitisation of migration and integration agendas. Even though suspected terrorists are apparently to be found among the educated, middle-class, legal immigrants – the 'good' kind of immigrants for whom Western societies and economies have been competing in the past decade – the issue of terrorism is now used in the policy debate to justify tougher controls of migration in general. In this context, many existing models and policies of immigrant integration and the accommodation of cultural, religious and ethnic diversity have been questioned. We shall therefore pay special attention to the religious dimension and the religious values debated in relation to the concrete legal, political and educational challenges investigated.

At the theoretical level, this book argues that the debate on integrating diversity, multiculturalism and citizenship has to be context-oriented to develop new theoretical insights related to the specific European context. At the empirical and policy levels, this collection highlights some of the weaknesses, the ambivalence and the major challenges of immigrant integration policy in Europe today. The collection has an emphasis both at national and European level. We shall emphasise national debates and approaches to accommodating diversity but also describe to what extent some debates, policy challenges and best practices have a European currency. We detail to what extent there are common value conflicts to be found in the different European countries, or possibly common values that underpin feasible policy solutions.

This book adopts a constructivist perspective. It does not treat values or religions as static objects but rather seeks to address their dynamic and interactive character. For this reason, while the book investigates, analyses and as far as possible evaluates concrete policy issues and measures, it also pays special attention to the debates that develop with regard to these policies, the ways in which issues and policy approaches are discursively constructed and the ways in which value discourses are organised and values made relevant for policy decisions. The authors engage with both a 'hard fact' policy approach, which will provide for some concrete policy analysis and recommendations, and a 'soft fact' approach that will unveil the underlying normative and value constellations, and the ways these are organised in public and political debates. We consider the two perspectives as complementary and equally necessary for the study of immigrant diversity and integration.

The collection pays particular attention to the question of religion and more particularly to the claims made by Muslim residents/

citizens in the countries studied. Indeed, there is a widespread perception that Muslims are making politically exceptional, culturally unreasonable or theologically alien demands upon European states. It is our contention that the logic of Muslim claims-making is contemporary but also particularly European (Modood, Triandafyllidou and Zapata-Barrero 2006). The challenges that Muslims raise expose the fact that secularism is taken for granted in most European countries. They press politicians and intellectuals to rethink their secular values, whether secularism has ever truly characterised modern European societies and most importantly why and in what versions it is still desirable. These questions lie at the heart of the philosophical and political discourses of European modernity and may be considered as peculiarly European even if generally modern.

1.3 Methodological background and selection of countries

This book originates from an EU-funded research project entitled *A European Approach to Multicultural Citizenship. Legal, Political and Educational Challenges (EMILIE)*. EMILIE (see also http://emilie.eliamep.gr) was a three-year project funded within the 6th Framework Programme of the European Commission in the Socio-Economic Sciences and Humanities area, that brought together nine universities and research centres from nine European countries: five from northern European states (Belgium, the UK, Denmark, France and Germany), two located in southern Europe, namely Spain and Greece, and two located in Central Eastern Europe (Poland and Latvia). The overall aim of the EMILIE research project was to analyse the multicultural citizenship and diversity integration debates and policies developed in these countries.

This book brings together the theoretical and comparative insights that this project has generated. Thus, the first part of the book (Chapters 2 to 5) presents new theoretical insights regarding the accommodation of diversity within citizenship discourses and policies, paying special attention to Muslims and women. The second part of the book (Chapters 6 to 9) reviews the policy responses addressing cultural diversity in the nine countries studied from a comparative perspective. Each chapter concentrates on one dimension, thus Chapter 6 looks at religious diversity in education, Chapter 7 at migrant political participation in multicultural contexts, Chapter 8 at the concept and policies of integration in different EU countries and Chapter 9 at the role and use of ethnic statistics in social policy

DIVERSITY, INTEGRATION, SECULARISM AND MULTICULTURALISM

in the different countries. This volume has a truly comparative focus to the extent that we have deliberately avoided country chapters but rather opted for a thematic focus and a critical comparative analysis of the policies in the different countries.

The choice of the countries under study has been based on the wish to compare 'old' migrant hosts such as Belgium, France, the UK, Denmark and Germany with new immigration countries such as Spain and Greece, and also countries that are still predominantly faced with emigration (towards other EU countries) rather than immigration, such as Latvia and Poland. The scope is to identify policies, issues and discourses with European currency that extend to countries with very different past and present migration and diversity realities.

Countries such Belgium, France and the UK have a relatively long experience in developing institutions and policies related to immigrant integration. This process has also evolved, in differing degrees and directions, into a re-elaboration of national identity with a view to incorporating cultural and religious diversity (Brubaker 1992; Bryant 1997; Favell 1998; Koopmans and Statham 2000; Kastoryano 2002; Modood 2005). France and the UK may be considered ideal-typical cases of different models of immigrant integration. The former privileges individual integration into a civic culture, leaving religion and ethnicity to the private realm and following a relatively open citizenship policy (Brubaker 1992). The latter has also adopted a relatively liberal citizenship policy but followed a community-based integration model where not only individual but also collective rights and claims of ethnic and religious groups are recognised and accommodated (Favell 1998; Modood 2005). The case of Belgium, however, is complicated by its internal divisions and federal structure. Immigrant claims and rights are enmeshed in complicated federal politics and risk disturbing the sensitive balance between the two Belgian communities, the Francophones and the Flemish.

Denmark and Germany, on the other hand, have taken more time to develop deliberate processes of integration, despite their strong welfare system models. In Denmark the relevant public and political discourses emphasise a universalistic public self-conception as a highly egalitarian welfare state, at the expense of Muslim immigrants' claims framed as particularistic and ethically inferior (Mouritsen 2006). Germany's closure to long-term immigrant residents has been related to its predominant understanding of German society as mono-national and mono-cultural, despite a large immigrant population present in the country for several decades (Brubaker 1992). Although citizenship laws and naturalisation processes have recently been liberalised, many are worried about cultural and political changes related to a growing number of naturalised immigrant residents. Such changes are seen to threaten the cultural 'authenticity' of German society as well as the established power structures.

The two southern European cases under study in this volume are Greece and Spain, two countries that have been transformed from sending to receiving societies since the early 1990s. Their immigration populations have rapidly risen in the course of the last twenty years and currently account for approximately 10 per cent of their total resident population. The arrival of legal and undocumented immigrant workers has been given high visibility in the Greek and Spanish media (Penamarin 1998; Perez Diaz et al. 2001; Zapata-Barrero 2003; Triandafyllidou 2000; González-Enríquez 2009), becoming a contested issue in the political debate. The newcomers have largely been perceived by both lay people and politicians as threats to the host country security, cultural authenticity and affluence. Only in the last few years has the issue of immigrant integration, and more particularly the accommodation of cultural and religious claims raised by Muslims, acquired more prominence as a legitimate objective of national immigration policy.

The two Central Eastern European countries investigated are also new hosts, but with a different background from their southern European counterparts. Since 1989, Poland has become both a major sending country in Europe and a host of legal and undocumented migrants from Eastern Europe and the Third World. While striving to accomplish its political and economic transition successfully, the country has had to face significant outflows towards other EU countries, temporary and seasonal migration from East Eastern Europe (notably Ukraine) and small but socially 'visible' numbers of Chechen refugees. The current notion of multiculturalism competes with the historical, pre-World War II idea of Polish multiculturalism that involved quasi-colonial ties with Ukraine and Belarus, and was open to diversity brought in the country through immigration. Since the year 2000, Polish citizenship laws have allowed third-generation descendants of Polish citizens to reacquire Polish citizenship, leading to a steep rise in applications in remote locations, such as Latin America. These factors might influence further the diversification of the Polish homogeneous post-communist society.

Latvia, on the other hand, is a very interesting case because while it has experienced increasing emigration in recent years, current immigration remains low. However, over one-fifth of the country's population consists of stateless persons, who since 1991 have been considered as long-term migrants. This stateless population includes mainly former Russian citizens or people from other former Soviet Republics (Belarus, Ukraine and to a lesser extent Poland) who had migrated to Latvia during communist times, often several decades ago, and who did not qualify automatically for Latvian citizenship or were not able to pass the naturalisation test (mainly because of their poor Latvian language skills) and thus were eventually left to their own devices. Although legally speaking this population may not be defined as immigrants, from a sociological point of view their situation, their claims and the policy challenges related to their successful integration into the Republic of Latvia resemble those concerning other immigrant populations in Europe.

Taking into account the above similarities and differences, this book offers new theoretical and empirical insights into the realities of multiculturalism in Europe.

1.4 Contents of the book

The book is organised into two parts. In Part I, each author engages with a distinct theoretical and conceptual question and highlights how it can be further developed by examining the policies and debates developed in a range of European Union countries. In Part II, individual chapters engage with specific policy areas (education, political representation, anti-discrimination, social policy and statistics) and discuss the conceptual and implementation challenges that arise in different countries seeking to highlight the European dimension in the analysed issues and concepts.

Tariq Modood and Nasar Meer, in Chapter 2, formulate a framework in which to conceive twenty-first-century European political orientations that seek to address contestations over citizenship as identity. The twentieth century witnessed a left–right struggle over the extent to which citizenship should or should not entail social welfare and economic rights. By the end of the century it was citizenship as identity that had moved to the top of political agendas. This is the contemporary question in relation to post-immigration diversity in a variety of European states: what is the identity of citizenship itself and what does it imply for other identities that citizens may have or want to have?

This chapter proposes a typology to theoretically map the responses to minority diversity, associated with immigration from outside Europe, in prevailing conventions of citizenship across seven European Union member state countries (five northern and two southern). This comprises political orientations of (1) National Cohesion; (2) Liberal Neutrality; (3) Multiculture; and (4) Multicultural Citizenship. It is argued that each orientation encompasses a variety of distinct elements in relation to the following eight criteria: anti-discrimination legislation; an emphasis on national identity; recognition of 'difference'; the issue of neutrality; the sphere of rights; relationship to the state; the emphasis on minority nation identities; and the emphasis on interaction between groups. Taken together, this formulation can help us make sense of the varieties of present responses to migration-related diversity across European Union member states.

In Chapter 3, which is a complementary chapter to Chapter 2, Meer and Modood empirically apply the theoretical formulations proposed in Chapter 2 by exploring how, if at all, citizenship conventions concerned with (1) membership; (2) entitlements; and (3) social expectations are incorporating minority identities in seven European Union countries. It details permutations in movement, to differing degrees and from different starting points, in conceptions of nationhood as *ius soli*, the valorisation of national identities, and the enactment of anti-discrimination legislation, amongst other criteria. For example, the chapter will show how within north-western Europe, France provides an illustration of a political orientation geared towards national cohesion, specifically in the assertion of civic nationhood and the placing of social cohesion as a goal above the recognition of group 'difference'. Yet there is movement too – illustrated by the creation of a Parisian consultation body for third country nationals (TCNs) and some regional innovation exemplified by how the City Council of Paris does allow for group-based claims. Perhaps equally significant is the development of a form of 'colour consciousness' that is increasingly being mobilised as a means to combat discrimination. Germany, meanwhile, after decades of pursuing an ethno-national citizenship, has seen significant changes in the management of immigration, integration and its very conception of citizenship with the introduction of *ius soli*. This has been followed by further amendments geared toward integration strategies, as well as the invitation to migrants and civil society actors to take part in the National

Integration Summits. Denmark is perhaps set apart by the very content and 'tone' of popular discourse, particularly around cultural diversity and Islam. The situation of our two cases from southern Europe, meanwhile, is related to the resilience of ethnic conceptions of nationhood, which means that the recognition of minority difference remains low and the location of minority identity remains restricted to the private sphere (with the exception of historically established minorities or autonomous regions). The chapter shows how in other countries the developments are different again, including how the UK is closer to multicultural citizenship than national cohesion, even while matters of national unity assume a greater prominence than they previously have, and where a securitisation of ethnic relations has emerged over fears of Muslim extremism.

In Chapter 4, Per Mouritsen goes deeper into current discourses and practices of citizenship, assessing the gap between norms and reality. Indeed, with the political crisis of multiculturalism as a progressive idiom, a shift towards citizenship discourse has taken place in many countries, including some that never saw much multiculturalism in legal and policy terms. Citizenship discourse does not replace the normative vocabulary of recognition so much as offer alternative versions, drawn from older sources – liberal, republican and social democratic – but imbuing each with new meaning and controversy, above all in relation to Islam. Citizenship recognition is a feature of its identity and status, as distinct from (but also related to) a legal aspect of rights and duties, the very access to polity membership and a participatory aspect. It concerns the subjective feelings of self-esteem, worth and belonging as full membership in a polity, feelings and orientations which in turn depend upon the public affirmation of membership eligibility and worthiness on behalf of significant others: other citizens of the polity.

While early multiculturalism held that the facile universality and equality of liberal and republican citizenship was blind to difference, the claims of the latter are nowadays constituted against such difference – aspects of which negatively define the terms of recognition as something difficult which require change and should be earned. This corresponds to a development whereby citizenship as full membership, despite being non-exclusive in terms of many specific rights, immunities and entitlements, is increasingly recaptured and repoliticised by nation-states – contra post-nationalism hopes in the 1990s.

Based on a short reflection on the very structure of citizenship recognition as closely related to the other dimensions of citizenship, as noted above, this chapter outlines four generic modalities: (1) citizenship as a right to have rights and be a subject of law; (2) citizenship as autonomy and partnership in liberal justice; (3) citizenship as good citizenship (participation/loyalty); and (4) citizenship as welfare state membership. On each count, the chapter offers a brief discussion of the normative promises and customary criticisms of such promises, and analyses how each aspect is currently politicised in the context of ostensibly 'un-civic' Islamic religion. The chapter offers empirical illustration from three northern European countries – Denmark, Germany and the UK – drawing on findings on civic integration programmes, citizenship acquisition policy and tests, anti-discrimination, conceptions of civicness and secularism, and the semantics of citizenship discourse more broadly.

Part I of the volume concludes with a focused reflection on multiculturalism and feminism. Thus in Chapter 5 Julie Billaud and Nilüfer Göle discuss the shortcomings of multiculturalism and feminism as models that originally aimed at avoiding the marginalisation of minorities. It is an attempt to discuss the reasons for the failure of the feminist movement and the limits of multiculturalism in producing appropriate frameworks for thinking through Islamic difference. One of the reasons that can be advanced is the secular and universalist assumptions that underpin the European traditions of feminism and multiculturalism, especially under their liberal versions. Within the liberal frame of mind, modernity is coupled with secularism and the critiques of modernity can only emerge from within. Islam appears as a relic from the past, deemed to disappear with progress. This teleological version of history describes Islam as an anachronism and denies Muslim actors' capacity to exercise agency and be part of modernity. Other multiculturalists have underlined the limitations of such an approach to understand difference. They have shown how contemporary liberal philosophies tend to perceive 'irrationality' in actors whose way of inhabiting the world is guided not by liberal ethics but by moral values inspired by religion. As such, this chapter largely focuses on the liberal and exclusionary tendencies of some trends of multiculturalism. It does not aim to reject multiculturalism as a whole, but rather seeks to identify some elements of its foundations that have contributed to the erosion of its inclusive potential.

Part II of the book concentrates on the specific policy responses developed in the nine countries under study in this volume to deal with ethnic, cultural and religious diversity. In this chapter we identify common issues and policies across Europe and compare the challenges faced by each country and the ways in which they have dealt with them.

In Chapter 6, Anna Triandafyllidou and Ruby Gropas concentrate on education policies. Indeed, the education sector is probably one of the most sensitive and politically charged areas of public policy where issues of cultural, religious and ethnic diversity are addressed. There is a pressing need for education policies to respond to the multiple challenges posed by today's diverse and dynamic European societies. This chapter is based on extensive empirical research undertaken in the context of the EMILIE project in nine European countries. The chapter addresses a set of value and policy issues in the area of education and education policy by highlighting and critically discussing the responses given to them in these nine countries.

After briefly reviewing the methodology adopted in the empirical country studies, Section 6.3 discusses the difference between intercultural and multicultural education, how they are reflected and/or implemented in education policies and what kind of representations of difference or ethnic/cultural diversity they carry with them. Section 6.4 looks at how intercultural or multicultural education can lead to the recognition of minority differences with a view to pluralising national identity. A particular issue that is addressed here is that of faith-based schooling. To what extent can this be, or is it perceived to be, in conflict with citizenship education or secular/ republican principles? In the current context where modern societies appear to be perceived as secular yet are indicating signs of being increasingly multi-faith, some of the issues that need to be debated are how anti-racist principles can be rendered compatible with faith-based schooling and how it is possible for faith-based schooling not to become an expression of separatism. Section 6.5 looks at wider exclusion–inclusion challenges and the ways in which education policies can help balance the promotion of social cohesion and common, civic values on the one hand, and the pursuit of implicit or explicit assimilationist approaches on the other.

In Chapter 7, Ricard Zapata-Barrero and Ruby Gropas discuss the challenges that migration brings for European societies as regards the quality of their democracy. The diversity that characterises today's European societies is a reality that should be neither ignored nor bypassed when attempting to conceptualise European multicultural democracy. Democracy and multiculturalism have been approached in recent literature in a rather theoretical and normative way. There is still very limited context-based research that comprehensively tries to identify commonalities and differences among European states in order to envisage a European multicultural democracy line of research.

Chapter 7 examines this democratic challenge from the perspective of three main dimensions: participation, representation and naturalisation. Our purpose is to explore the extent to which TCNs are able to participate in the political process in various EU member states, and the criteria according to which they are either granted political rights or are excluded from these. EU member states present very different political structures and opportunities, and this is reflected in the very different ways and degrees in which ethnic minorities or newer immigrant populations participate in the respective political systems. Equally important, however, is the fact that for political rights to be actively and effectively exercised, and for political opportunities to be able to be translated into actual influence, resources are essential. Language competence, access to relevant information, social networks, financial means and education are among these key resources. The extent to which these resources exist within a society's different communities may affect the level of their participation and representation. Finally, access to citizenship is one of the defining dimensions of political participation and representation. Citizenship policies constitute a core instrument that governments have at their disposal to further democratise their increasingly diverse societies. Drawing from the above, this chapter provides an overview of the democratic challenges posed in seven European countries, namely Belgium, Denmark, France, Germany, Greece, Spain and the UK. In particular, it explores the political engagement of migration-related minorities by examining the remit of political rights and the extent of their political participation.

In Chapter 8, Frauke Miera concentrates on the concept and practice of integration across Europe. In several European countries, multiculturalism as a political programme is considered as having failed or even as the cause of social and cultural segregation. Departing from different historical national contexts such as the French republican assimilation model, the German ethno-national non-acting or exclusive model, or countries with a relatively short history of immigration, several states seem to disallow the idea of managing cultural pluralism in the sense of respecting equal group rights and openly negotiating how a culturally diverse society is shaped and changing. Instead, the concept of integration appears as dominating the immigration-related discourse. If we look at integration programmes we should therefore ask what is meant by the postulated mutuality of the integration process? Who are the agents of the integration process? Who is addressed? Who has the willingness or capability to move on this road or the power to change its course? Who sets the agenda? How is the process managed on this road? Is there any space for negotiation and change? What is the institutional setting of integration and how is it reflected upon? The chapter seeks to address these questions regarding the integration concept as it is agreed upon in the 'common basic principles for immigrant integration policy in the European Union'.

The second part of the chapter starts with a discussion of the German conceptualisation and practice of integration but it also includes examples from the other countries under study in this book, with the aim of showing that current conceptions of integration differ from simple assimilation models. Nevertheless, in a more complex way they also tend to focus on the individual migrant/member of ethnic minorities demanding their adaptation to major society. At the same time the state initiates a 'dialogue with migrants', especially Muslims, thus symbolising acknowledgement of group identities and opening up new forms of participation. Yet the integration discourse and related policies show a general suspicion of Muslims, who seem to have to be disciplined and 'normalised' according to the liberal norms and values of the host society.

The final chapter of this book focuses on the question of ethnic statistics in the EU. The authors of this chapter, Angéline Escafré-Dublet and Patrick Simon, note that in its first General Policy Recommendation of 1996, the European Commission against Racism and Intolerance (ECRI) defined its position on the question of collecting 'ethnic' data for the purpose of combating racism, xenophobia, anti-Semitism and intolerance (ECRI (96) 43 rev). Believing that 'it is difficult to develop and effectively implement policies ... without good data', it recommends collecting

> in accordance with European laws, regulations and recommendations on data-protection and protection of privacy, where and when appropriate, data which will assist in assessing and evaluating the situation and experiences of groups which are particularly vulnerable to racism, xenophobia, anti-Semitism and intolerance.

The same holds for the CERD (Committee for Elimination of Racial Discrimination) and for most of the international organisations striving to tackle racism and discrimination, including the European Commission.

Data on the situation of ethnic and racial minorities is required to assess discrimination, increase awareness and implement anti-discrimination policies. The production of ethnic statistics, however, remains contentious and, in the context of the anti-discrimination legal framework put in place by the EU Race Directive of 2000, members have had contrasting responses on the matter. While the UK has been producing ethnic statistics as a necessary tool for the implementation of effective equality policies, in France ethnic statistics are perceived to foster racism and are thus highly controversial. Finally, in countries such as Germany or Spain the notion is absent from the debate.

With a view to charting the different stages of where each member state stands in its implementation of anti-discrimination policies, the chapter analyses how countries take up the challenge of measuring diversity. First, it explores how the official production of statistics reflects the process of differentiation at play in each national context. Second, it investigates the implementation of anti-discrimination policies and the opportunity to collect ethnic data as introduced by European policies. Third, it discusses why debates on ethnic data emerged in some countries but are absent in others. The authors examine one of the strongest criticisms against ethnic data, which claims that it stigmatises individuals and favours racism. This chapter argues that the various processes of differentiation at play in each country pre-existed the debate on ethnic statistics. The construction of comprehensive monitoring systems to measure diversity does not constitute a return to past occurrences of racial prejudices, but rather a move forward, creating new methods to combat discrimination and providing new opportunities for the empowerment of minority groups.

Notes

1. This was not ratified by the Council of Ministers and so was missing from the final document and the Lisbon Treaty.

References

Barry, B. (2001), *Culture and Equality: An Egalitarian Critique of Equality*, London: Polity Press.
Beattie, T. (2007), *The New Atheists: The Twilight of Reason and the War on Religion*, London: Darton, Longman and Todd.
Bhabha, H. K. (1998), 'Culture's in between', in D. Bennet (ed.), *Multicultural States: Rethinking Difference and Identity*, London: Routledge.

Bowen, J. (2010), *Can Islam be French? Pluralism and Pragmatism in a Secularist State*, Princeton, NJ: Princeton University Press.

Brubaker, R. (1992), *Citizenship and Nationhood in France and Germany*, Cambridge, MA: Harvard University Press.

Brubaker, R. (2001), 'The return of assimilation? Changing perspectives on immigration and its sequels in France, Germany, and the United States', *Ethnic and Racial Studies*, 24(4), pp. 531–48.

Bryant, C. (1997), 'Citizenship, national identity and the accommodation of difference: Reflections on the German, French, Dutch, and British Cases', *New Community*, 23(2), pp. 157–72.

Caldwell, C. (2010), *Reflections on the Revolution in Europe: Can Europe be the same with different people in it?*, London: Penguin.

Calhoun, C. (ed.) (1994), *Social Theory and Politics of Identity*, Oxford: Blackwell.

Casanova, J. (2009), 'Immigration and the new religious pluralism: A European Union – United States comparison', in G. B. Levey and T. Modood (eds), *Secularism, Religion and Multicultural Citizenship*, Cambridge: Cambridge University Press, pp. 139–63.

Castles, S. (2000), *Ethnicity and Globalization: From Migrant Worker to Transnational Citizen*, London: Sage.

Cesari, J. (2004), *When Islam and Democracy Meet: Muslims in Europe and in the United States*, Basingstoke: Palgrave Macmillan.

Commission on the Future of Multi-Ethnic Britain (CMEB) (2000), *The Future of Multi-Ethnic Britain*, London: Profile Books.

Dobbernack, J. (2010), '"Things fall apart". Social imaginaries and the politics of cohesion', *Critical Policy Studies*, 4(2), pp. 146–63.

Fallaci, O. (2003), *The Rage and the Pride*, New York: Rizzoli International Publications.

Favell, A. (1998), *Philosophies of Integration: Immigration and the Idea of Citizenship in France and Britain*, London: Macmillan.

Ferguson, N. (2004), 'The end of Europe?', American Enterprise Institute Bradley Lecture (1 March 2004).

Gagnon, A. G. and R. Iacovino (2007), *Federalism, Citizenship and Quebec: Debating Multinationalism*, Toronto: University of Toronto Press.

González-Enríquez, C. (2009), 'Spain, the cheap model. Irregularity and regularisation as immigration management policies', *European Journal of Migration and Law*, 11, pp. 139–57.

Goodhart, D. (2004), 'Too Diverse?' *Prospect Magazine*, February 2004.

Gove, M. (2006), *Celsius 7/7*, London: Weidenfeld and Nicolson.

Gutmann, A. (1994), 'Introduction', in A. Gutmann (ed.), *Multiculturalism. Examining the Politics of Recognition*, Princeton, NJ: Princeton University Press.

Hansen, R. (2006), 'The Danish cartoon controversy: A defense of liberal freedom', *International Migration*, 44(5), pp. 7–16.

Jacobs, D. and A. Rea (2007), 'The end of national models? Integration courses and citizenship trajectories in Europe', *International Journal on Multicultural Societies*, 9(2), pp. 264–83.
Joppke, C. (2004), 'The retreat of multiculturalism in the liberal state: Theory and policy', *British Journal of Sociology*, 55(2), pp. 237–57.
Joppke, C. (2008), 'Immigration and the identity of citizenship: The paradox of universalism', *Citizenship Studies*, 12(6), pp. 533–46.
Joppke, C. (2009a), *Veil: Mirror of Identity*, Cambridge: Polity Press.
Joppke, C. (2009b), 'Limits of integration policy: Britain and her Muslims', *Journal of Ethnic and Migration Studies*, 35(3), pp. 453–72.
Kastoryano, R. (2002), *Negotiating Identities: States and Immigrants in France and Germany*, Princeton, NJ: Princeton University Press.
Kivisto, P. and T. Faist (2007), *Citizenship: Discourse, Theory, and Transnational Prospects*, London: Blackwell.
Koopmans, R. and P. Statham (eds) (2000), *Challenging Immigration and Ethnic Relations Politics: Comparative European Perspectives*, Oxford: Oxford University Press, p. 433.
Koopmans, R., P. Statham, M. Giugni and F. Passy (2005), *Contested Citizenship: Immigration and Cultural Diversity in Europe*, Minneapolis, MN: University of Minnesota Press.
Kostakopoulou, D. (2010), 'Matters of control: Integration tests, naturalisation reform and probationary citizenship in the United Kingdom', *Journal of Ethnic and Migration Studies*, 36(5), pp. 829–46.
Kymlicka, W. (1995), *Multicultural Citizenship*, Oxford: Oxford University Press.
Kymlicka, W. (2005a), *Testing the Bounds of Liberal Multiculturalism*. Draft paper presented at Toronto, 9 April 2005.
Kymlicka,W. (2005b), 'The uncertain futures of multiculturalism', *Canadian Diversity*, 4(1), pp. 82–5.
Kymlicka,W. (2007), 'The new debate on minority rights' (and postscript), in A. S. Laden and D. Owen (eds), *Multiculturalism and Political Theory*, Cambridge: Cambridge University Press, pp. 25–59.
Levey, G. B. (2009), 'Introduction', in G. B. Levey and T. Modood (eds), *Secularism, Religion and Multicultural Citizenship*, Cambridge: Cambridge University Press.
Malik, K. (2007), 'Thinking outside the box', *CRE: Catalyst*, January–February. Available at www.kenanmalik.com/essays/catalyst_box.html, accessed on 19 June 2008.
Marshall, T. H. (1997 [1950]), *Citizenship and Social Class and other Essays*. Cambridge: Cambridge University Press.
May, S., T. Modood and J. Squires (2004), *Ethnicity, Nationalism, and Minority Rights*, Cambridge: Cambridge University Press.
McGhee, D. (2008), *The End of Multiculturalism? Terrorism, Integration*

and Human Rights, Milton Keynes: Open University Press and McGraw-Hill Education.

Meer, N. (2010), *Citizenship, Identity and the Politics of Multiculturalism*, Basingstoke: Palgrave.

Meer, N. (2012), 'Misrecognising Muslim consciousness in Europe', *Ethnicities*, forthcoming.

Meer, N. and T. Modood (2009a), 'The multiculturaul state we are in: Muslims, "multiculture" and the "civic re-balancing" of British multiculturalism', *Political Studies*, 57(3), October 2009, pp. 473–97.

Meer, N. and T. Modood (2009b), 'Refutations of racism in the "Muslim question"', *Patterns of Prejudice*, 43(3/4), pp. 332–51.

Meer, N., N. de Witte, D. Faas, P. Mouritsen and J. Brigstocke (forthcoming), 'Delineating the emergence of the civic and "post-multicultural" turns in the Netherlands, Britain, Denmark and Germany'.

Modood, T. (1992), *Not Easy Being British: Colour, Culture and Citizenship*, London: Runnymede Trust/Trentham Books.

Modood, T. (2005), *Multicultural Politics*, Edinburgh: Edinburgh University Press.

Modood, T. (2006), 'The Danish cartoon affair: Free speech, racism, islamism, and integration', *International Migration*, 44(5), pp. 3–62.

Modood, T. (2007a), *Multiculturalism, a Civic Idea*, London: Polity Press.

Modood, T. (2007b), 'Multiculturalism's civic future: A response', *Open Democracy*, 20 June. Available at www.opendemocracy.net/faith_ideas/Europe_islam/multiculturalism_future, accessed on 19 June 2008.

Modood, T. (2010), 'Moderate secularism, religion as identity and respect for religion', *The Political Quarterly*, 81, pp. 4–14.

Modood, T. and R. Kastoryano (2006), 'Secularism and the accommodation of Muslims in Europe', in T. Modood, A. Triandafyllidou and R. Zapata-Barrero (eds), *Multiculturalism, Muslims and Citizenship: A European Approach*, London: Routledge.

Moore, C. (2006), 'How Cromwell gave us Joan Collins and other luminaries', *Daily Telegraph*, 17 June. Available at www.telegraph.co.uk/opinion/main.jhtml?xml=/opinion/2006/06/17/do1702.xml&sSheet=/opinion/2006/06/17/ixop.html, accessed on 13 July 2008.

Mouritsen, P. (2006), 'The particular universalism of a Nordic civic nation,' in T. Modood, A. Triandafyllidou and R. Zapata-Barrero (eds), *Multiculturalism, Muslims and Citizenship: A European Approach*, London: Routledge.

Mouritsen, P. (2008), 'Political responses to cultural conflict: Reflections on the ambiguities of the civic turn', in P. Mouritsen and K. E. Jørgensen (eds), *Constituting Communities. Political Solutions to Cultural Conflict*, London: Palgrave, pp. 1–30.

O'Leary, B. (2006), 'Liberalism, multiculturalism, Danish cartoons: Islamist fraud and the right of the ungodly', *International Migration*, 44(5), pp. 22–33.

Orgad, L. (2009), '"Cultural defense" of nations: Cultural citizenship in France, Germany and the Netherlands', *European Law Journal*, 15(6), pp. 719–37.

Parekh, B. (2000), *Rethinking Multiculturalism: Cultural Diversity and Political Theory*, London: Palgrave.

Parekh, B. (2006), 'Europe, liberalism and the "Muslim question"', in T. Modood, A. Triandafyllidou and R. Zapata-Barrero (eds), *Multiculturalism, Muslims and Citizenship: A European Approach*, London: Routledge.

Penamarin, C. (1998), 'El analisis de textos en una nueva clave. Discursos e imagenes sobre la inmigracion en *El Pais*', *Cuadernos de Información y Comunicación*, 3. Available at www.ucm.es/info/per3/cic/index.htm, accessed on 3 November 1998.

Perez Diaz, V., M. Berta Alvarez and C. González-Enríquez (2001), *Espana ante la inmigracion*, Barcelona: Fundacion La Caixa (available in Spanish and English). Available at www.estudis.lacaixa.comunicacions.com/webes/estudis.nsf/wurl/pfes008cos_esp, accessed on 22 April 2002.

Phillips, M. (2006), *Londonistan: How Britain Created a Terror State Within*, London: Gibson Square Books.

Policy Exchange (2007), *Living Apart Together: British Muslims and the Paradox of Multiculturalism*, London: Policy Exchange.

Presseurop (2010), 'Mutti Merkel handbags Multikulti'. Available at www.presseurop.eu/en/content/article/364091-mutti-merkel-handbags-multikulti, accessed on 28 March 2011.

Prins, G. and Robert Salisbury (2008), 'Risk, threat and security – the case of the United Kingdom', *RUSI Journal*, 153(2), pp. 22–7.

Rocher, F., G. Rocher and M. Labelle (1995), 'Pluriethnicité, citoyenneté et intégration: de la souveraineté pour lever les obstacles et les ambiguités', *Cahiers de Recherche Sociologique*, 25.

Sarrazin, T. (2010), *Deutschland schafft sich ab*, Munich: DVA.

Smith, K. E. (2010), 'Research policy and funding – academic treadmills and the squeeze on imaginative spaces', *British Journal of Sociology*, 61 (1), pp. 176–95.

Statham, P., R. Koopmans, M. Giugni and F. Passy (2005), 'Resilient or adaptable Islam? Multiculturalism, religion and migrants' claims-making for group demands in Britain, the Netherlands and France', *Ethnicities*, 5(4), pp. 427–59.

Steyn, M. (2006), 'European population will be "40 percent Muslim" by 2025', *Wall Street Journal*, 4 January 2006.

Triandafyllidou, A. (2000), 'The political discourse on immigration in southern Europe: A critical analysis', *Journal of Community and Applied Social Psychology*, 10(5), pp. 373–89.

Vertovec, S. (2007), 'Super-diversity and its implications', *Ethnic and Racial Studies*, 30 (6), pp. 1024–54. Available at www.informaworld.com/smpp/title%7Edb=all%7Econtent=t713685087%7Etab=issueslist%7Ebranches=30-v30, accessed on 10 December 2010.

Vertovec, S. and S. Wessendorf (2005), 'Migration and cultural, religious and linguistic diversity in Europe: An overview of issues and trends', Centre on Migration, Policy and Society (COMPAS), Working Paper no. 18, University of Oxford. Available at www.compas.ox.ac.uk/publications/papers/Vertovec%20Wessendorf%20WP0518.pdf, accessed on 10 December 2010.

Young, I. M. (1990), *Justice and the Politics of Difference*, Princeton, NJ: Princeton University Press.

Zapato-Barrero, R. (2003), 'Spain', in J. Niessen and Y. Schibel (eds), *EU and US Approaches to the Management of Immigration*, Brussels: Migration Policy Group.

Part I

Theoretical Developments in a Comparative European Perspective

2

Framing Contemporary Citizenship and Diversity in Europe

Tariq Modood and Nasar Meer

Introduction

The EMILIE project, as stated in Chapter 1, was an investigation into the current nature and extent of multicultural citizenship in nine European countries. Such an investigation, however, has to be conducted in a climate where it is commonly asserted that multiculturalism is or should be dead or dying. A cursory glance at the pages of the popular press or academic texts will reveal that critics of multiculturalism are to be found across Europe and are arguably much greater in number today than a decade or so ago. While preparing this chapter, two European premiers, German Chancellor Angela Merkel and UK Prime Minister David Cameron, made high-profile, internationally discussed speeches which declared respectively that 'multi-kulti has utterly failed' and 'multiculturalism is dead' (Weaver 2010; Cameron 2011). For some, multiculturalism has facilitated social fragmentation and entrenched social divisions (Policy Exchange 2007; Malik 2007). For others, it has distracted attention from core socio-economic disparities (Barry 2001; Hansen 2006) or encouraged a moral hesitancy amongst native populations (Caldwell 2009; Prins and Salisbury 2008). Some even blame it for international terrorism (Phillips 2006; Gove 2006). Independently of whether or not these criticisms are valid, there appears to be a certain consensus amongst scholars and commentators that multiculturalism as a public policy has been and continues to be in retreat (Brubaker 2001; Joppke 2004). What remains much less clear, however, is what this retreat of multiculturalism in Europe actually consists of, and particularly so in Western Europe. For example, does it entail the same thing in different countries? What are states actually doing and not doing? And is there a comparative framework for addressing these questions? The key elements or ideas in the retreat of multiculturalism are therefore far from established and widely understood.

33

Perhaps on one level, however, the answers to some of these questions can be found in the widespread view that a variety of European nation-states are 're-nationalising' (Orgad 2009; Mouritsen 2009). That is to say that while in the 1980s and 1990s it was argued that there was a trend of denationalising, and that this was the way of the 'post-national' future, from our present vantage point at the beginning of the second decade of the twenty-first century, it appears that many central promises contained within ideas of post-national citizenship and post-war cosmopolitanism have not come to fruition, or at least are not obviously visible across citizenship regimes. This is particularly true of those accounts that saw as the future of citizenship in Europe a retention and administration of citizenship rights in cross-national human rights covenants that would be materially supported by international law (Soysal 1994). Others simultaneously anticipated a diminution in the 'particularistic' content of political communities, such that the boundaries between nations, states, cultures or indeed societies might become empirically porous and even morally irrelevant (Archibugi et al. 2005; Archibugi et al. 1998).

Each of these positions has arguably had something to grapple with, for in recent years there has indeed been a spectre stalking Europe, but this has not been of the historical-materialist kind. Instead, we can witness today something of a trend in the valorisation of national identities in nation-state citizenship across Western Europe, characterised as a re-nationalisation of various citizenship regimes (Kiwan 2008). In the next section we briefly survey this terrain before critically engaging with one scholarly characterisation of it. Following this, we begin to offer our alternative reading and then we step back to register some competing normative frameworks before returning to the empirical discussion in the final section of the chapter. We conclude that a normative conception of multiculturalism remains a resilient means of explicating empirical developments in fields of contemporary nation-state citizenship in Europe. We specifically argue that it is striking how, in interpreting and evaluating a new emphasis on national identities, some authors ignore how some degree of particularity is both pragmatically necessary and justifiable within a variety of ideational and empirical political orientations.

2.1 The terrain

The chronology of 're-nationalising' in the context of post-immigration ethno-religious diversity varies between countries and in several cases has been evident since the 1990s. In the case of the UK it came from the centre-left, beginning with New Labour's invocation of an Orwellian-style patriotism and proposals to modernise and remake Britishness under the terms of 'Cool Britannia' and 're-branding Britain' (Leonard 1997). Not only was this a strand within what is probably the most multiculturalist government the UK has had (1997–2001), but the ideas of rethinking and remaking Britishness in response to ethnic diversity were stimulated by ethnic minority intellectuals (Gilroy 1987; Modood 1992; CMEB 2000[1]). That a concern for making national identities more explicit was widespread across Europe is evidenced by the European Council agreement in 2004 on 'common basic principles' supporting nation-states in educating immigrants on 'the host society's language, history, and institutions'.[2] The European Union Pact on Immigration and Asylum 'maintains that it is for each Member State to decide on the conditions of admission of legal migrants to its territory and, where necessary, to set their number'.[3] As such, it facilitates member states with the means to regulate admission criteria. Here we might include the Danes' requirement of Danish language competencies at 'level 3', which 'bars most non-Europeans from ever gaining citizenship' (Mouritsen 2009: 6) and which goes hand in hand with the introduction of a citizenship test that is notable for its emphasis upon questions of a difficult nature concerning historical-national Danish culture. These developments have arisen in a wider political context in Denmark in which the very content of popular discourse, particularly around cultural diversity and Islam, has taken a notably nationalistic tone (Meer and Mouritsen 2009). This is especially true of the ways in which conceptions of commendable political subjectivity and forms of civic association have become related to national identity (Mouritsen 2009).

Similar developments are evident in the debate over a German *Leitkultur*, and which seeks the promotion of a German 'leading culture' in a more explicit way than in its traditional conception of ethnic citizenship. Indeed, this is despite, or perhaps because of, significant movement away from the latter, at least in law. Following decades of pursuing an ethno-national citizenship, Germany has since the late 1990s undergone significant changes in its management of immigration and integration, and in its conception of citizenship. Thus, and after federal policies had previously focused almost entirely on the control and return of migrants (Schönwälder 2001), in 1998 the Red-Green government characterised Germany as an 'immigration country' and amended the Citizenship Law (2000) to introduce the principle of *ius soli*. These developments have been accompanied by others such as the introduction of the Immigration Law (2005), which encourages the cultivation of 'integration strategies', and which in turn was followed by the invitation to migrants and civil society actors to take part in a National Integration Summit (2006). Yet the content of this 'integration' has also included a nationalist imperative, whereby newcomers are expected to undertake 300 to 600 hours of German language classes and lessons on German society and history (Jacobs and Rea 2007).

Simultaneously in the UK, the Nationality, Immigration and Asylum Act (2002) explicitly introduced a test (implemented in 2005) for residents seeking British citizenship. Thus, applicants should show 'a sufficient knowledge of English, Welsh or Scottish Gaelic' and also 'a sufficient knowledge about life in the United Kingdom' (Home Office 2004: 11). Those immigrants seeking to settle in the UK (applying for 'indefinite leave to remain') equally have to pass the test which has been effectively implemented since 2 April 2007. If applicants do not have sufficient knowledge of English, they are required to attend English for Speakers of Other Languages (ESOL) and citizenship classes. The government has, however, insisted that 'it would be unfair for migrants to have to answer questions on British history that many British people would have difficulties with' (McNulty quoted in Kiwan 2008: 69). Accordingly, the emphasis is on the experience of living in the UK rather than an attempt to test Britishness in terms of scholastic knowledge.

What this brief summary shows is that despite important variations, it is evidently the case that in north-western Europe there is presently a renewed emphasis and explicitness regarding national identities among countries that have not always prioritised this, for example the UK and Denmark, and increasingly Germany. In some cases, the turn to national identities by governments appears to involve a confused means of encouraging forms of social and political unity (cf. Uberoi 2008), whereas in other cases national identities are viewed as a means of engendering a kind of value consensus that may act as a prophylactic against forms of (Muslim) radicalism (MGhee 2008; Uberoi and Modood 2009). In other cases still, it would be hard not to view the turn to national identities as little more than a means of pursuing an assimilationist project. The 'drastic break with multiculturalism' (Entzinger 2007: 201) made by the Dutch has been widely recorded; it has seen the Netherlands discontinue some emblematic multiculturalist policies while introducing others specifically tailored to ignore ethnic minority differences. These include the large-scale abandonment of dual-citizenship programmes; a withdrawal of national-level funding for minority group organisations and activities supporting cultural difference; reallocating the small percentage of public broadcasting time dedicated to multicultural issues; and a cessation of ethnic monitoring of labour market participation (Entzinger 2007; 2003; Van De Vijver et al. 2006).

In the 1990s, various European states began 're-nationalising' and reforming access to citizenship and the status of citizens just at the point that some scholars were discerning an international trend towards denationalisation. This movement accelerated and 'hardened' as states reacted to 9/11 and the threat of international networks involving citizens or residents in their country, and even more so to an alleged 'failure to integrate' on the part of Muslims, which stood alongside perceptions of Muslims as a cultural threat and demographic projections of Muslim numbers growing at a much faster rate than non-Muslims (cf. Caldwell 2009). The post-national trend has also been deflected by how migrants and subsequent generations have asserted not so much their right to not be citizens in the countries in which they have settled, but various kinds of transnational political identities, especially a solidarity with an imagined global Muslim community (the *ummah*) together with or having primacy over civic solidarities (Mandaville 2009).

In this chapter we are only interested in the first of these developments, namely the policies and discourses of European states and opinion-makers in relation not to issues of war and security but rather to integration. While we note that these two issues can overlap, and have indeed been doing so in some national contexts, we focus much more on the anxieties over perceived failures in minority, and particularly Muslim, integration (Brubaker 2001; Bauböck et al. 2006; Mouritsen 2009). Here, interestingly, a forcefully presented argument by a leading scholar seems to salvage something of the post-national argument, namely Christian Joppke's (2008) claim that re-nationalisation is not what it appears to be.

2.2 Joppke's paradox and alternative readings

Joppke (2008) has argued that present discourses of national identity in Europe are both normatively and practically strengthening liberalism at the expense of nationalism. He argues, for example, that even while some politicians and states talk of national identities as a means of privileging majority cultures as *Leitkultur*, for example in Germany and Denmark, such movements are structurally bound to fail. When states try to incorporate content into their national identities they invariably end up listing universal principles such as liberty, equality, fairness, human rights, tolerance and so on. This means that while many states are appealing to a national identity, the content they give it will be neither ethnic nor cultural (language, history or religion) but rather one comprised of liberal principles. In this view while the symbolic form may be particularistic, the content is necessarily universal, because if it were more particularistic (for example, Christian) it would fail in its purpose to integrate immigrants, especially Muslims. Joppke maintains, therefore, that 'the typical solution to the problem of collective identity across Europe today is the one pioneered by republican France, according to which to be national is defined in the light of the universalistic precepts of human rights and democracy' (Joppke 2008: 541).

An important feature of Joppke's argument is that where some politicians and states do emphasise particularistic aspects of national identity, such as Lutheranism or Christianity more generally, their own constitutional courts, he maintains, are required to uphold universalist principles. They especially rule in favour of non-discrimination, which is interpreted as the non-privileging of one culture over another. The outcome is that the courts strike down particularistic legislation and support appeals of discrimination from minority individuals and groups, something frequently supported in Joppke's view by the European Court of Human Rights (ECHR).[4] Of course, Joppke acknowledges that a discourse exists in several countries, typified by Germany and Denmark, in which universalist liberalism is used in an exclusionary particularistic way by arguing that liberalism is 'our culture' and that some others, such as Muslims, cannot become part of the 'We' because they are not sufficiently liberal (Joppke 2008: 541–2; Mouritsen 2008: 21–2, believes that this may be more widespread than Joppke suggests; cf. Müller 2007). Joppke maintains, however, that these exclusionary uses of liberalism have to appeal to the liberal principle of non-discrimination between cultures (as long as liberal norms are observed) and so he believes they cannot be sustained. This means that while some liberals may aggressively enforce liberal norms (this is his reading of the ban on the headscarf in state schools in France) they must do so within liberal constraints (in a non-discriminatory way by not targeting an ethnic group or a religion but by applying universal rules) and so they must promote liberal principles and not a specific national culture. Thus he argues that 'the decoupling of citizenship and nationhood is the incontrovertible exit position for contemporary state campaigns for unity and integration, especially with respect to immigrants' (Joppke 2008: 543).

Joppke sees these developments in the perspective of a 'retreat of multiculturalism' (Joppke 2004; for critiques see Jacobs and Rea 2007; Meer and Modood 2009) and so it is not surprising that, in interpreting and evaluating the new emphasis on national identities, Joppke ignores the potential theoretical contribution of multiculturalism. That is to say, the ways in which some degree of particularity is both pragmatically necessary but also justifiable within a variety of ideational and empirical political orientations. Where we are currently witnessing various political projects of remaking and updating national identities, they are not being departicularised. There are cases, such as Spain and Greece, that retain a strong orientation toward *ius sanguine*, but in which an opposing trend would not have to empty out the historical-cultural character of nationality but instead would include minority ethnicities. The latter, therefore, need not be about being blind to minority ethnic groupness but, on the contrary, seeking to pluralise, and not empty out, cultural content. In other words, for the dominant ethnicity to demonopolise the state and the citizenship by not making cultural assimilation a condition of full citizenship and of full social acceptance is to respect, not wipe out, the varied ethnicities of fellow citizens. In this chapter we argue that contrary to this view as articulated by Joppke (2008: 535) 'neutrality' must not be mistaken for contentlessness as pure universalism is impossible, so equality in citizenship is best pursued as (1) anti-discrimination; (2) recognition of open, mixed and changing ethnicities/identities; (3) multi-logical plurality; and (4) inclusivity and the fostering of a sense of belonging.

Of course, to illustrate this we need to recognise how citizenship requires some notion of a self-governing political community in which individuals have rights and correlative duties enforced by law but are also likely to have a sense of shaping and being shaped by a public space that goes beyond law and politics. Moreover, it is only when we have a conception of citizenship that we can identify who among long-term residents should remain non-citizens, why they should remain so and what rights they should and should not have. As such we need to ask at least three questions of a theory of citizenship (Patten 2001, cited in Gagnon and Iacovino 2007: 125):

1. **Membership**: who is to be granted this status?
2. **Entitlement**: what rights are implied by this status?[5]
3. **Social expectations**: what responsibilities, dispositions and identities are expected of someone who holds this status?

In relation to the first question of membership, there is indeed a trend in some countries to de-ethnicise citizenship, or at least to dilute the link between citizenship and a single ethnicity. This also means breaking the link between mono-nationality and citizenship, which sees several states, such as Germany, moving towards the British and French example of taking a pragmatic view of dual citizenship (Modood and Meer 2009). By the beginning of the twenty-first century, most EU states were awarding citizenship to long-term residents and those born to non-citizens, though some states were struggling with the concept of dual nationality. In relation to the second question of entitlement, the fundamental point is that citizenship is about equal membership. Increasingly, member states and the European Union as a whole have recognised that non-white immigrants and their children and grandchildren do not have effective equality. While some EU states to differing degrees select or deselect by ethnicity those to whom they will grant citizenship, all EU states are now committed to the principle of non-discrimination amongst citizens.

In accordance with the Treaty of Amsterdam (1997), two broad directives were issued to member states to prevent discrimination on the basis of race, ethnicity or religion. The first established a general framework for equal treatment in employment and occupation (the Employment Directive), which would require member states to make discrimination unlawful on grounds of racial or ethnic origin, religion or belief, disability, age or sexual orientation. The second directive implemented the principle of equal treatment irrespective of racial or ethnic origin (the Race Directive). Like the Employment Directive, the Race Directive required member states to make discrimination on grounds of racial or ethnic origin unlawful in employment and training. It went further than the Employment Directive in requiring member states to provide protection against discrimination in non-employment areas, such as education, access to social welfare and the provision of goods and services. While these directives were accompanied by an 'Action Programme' (which was set up by the Commission and allocated a budget of 100 million euros over six years to fund practical action by member states in promoting non-discrimination), what can be distinguished is how countries adopted these directives in terms of anti-discrimination policy action ranging from low to high as follows:

- **Low**: where anti-discrimination laws to promote equality of opportunity are rarely applied in practice, little or no data on ethnicity and race is collected, and no public agency is charged with publicity, coordination and enforcement.
- **High**: where appropriate data is systematically and extensively collected and used, cases are routinely investigated by employers and other institutions, with many reaching the law courts, and are widely publicised by the media and by agencies such as the Belgian or French HALDE (High Authority to Fight Against Discrimination and for Equality) model or the UK EHRC (Equality and Human Rights Commission) that is proactive and responsible for policy development and enforcement and that reports to a government department or minister.

In some respects this issue of non-discrimination is also a question of socio-economic integration and full social citizenship, but it is not merely that. During most of the twentieth century there was a left–right struggle about the extent to which citizenship should or should not entail social welfare and economic rights, as illustrated in Marshall's well-known typology (1950). In the 1980s and early 1990s, there was a shift away from citizenship towards post-national membership (Soysal 1994), since then there has been a focus that put citizenship as identity (Joppke 2008) and citizenship as a common public space for dialogue (Modood 2007; Parekh 2000) at the top of the political agendas. This indeed is the fundamental question in relation to post-immigration diversity: what is the identity of citizenship itself and what does it imply for other identities that citizens may have or want to have?

In an attempt to chart this evolution, we have employed six category ranges examining (1) the promotion of equality of opportunity; (2) the extent of the emphasis on national identity;[6] (3) the recognition of 'difference'; (4) the issue of neutrality; (5) the bearer of rights; (6) the relationship to the state. We use these category ranges as they reflect the most salient or core elements across a variety of normative accounts of citizenship in social and political theory. Equally, each of the three questions about citizenship raised by Patten (2001) above, including the question of civic identity, is not about merely vertical (state to citizen) but also horizontal (citizen to citizen) relationships

(Gagnon and Iacovino 2007: 125). To address the questions of citizenship, especially the third concerning social expectations, is also to ask about how the state and citizens should relate to diversity. Let us examine how some scholars, from both European and North American contexts, have typologised these relationships and what normative and explanatory purchase we can derive from them.

2.3 Normative models of citizenship

Modood (1997) has identified five ideal ways in which the state (and its citizens) can respond to the new cultural diversity that is a consequence of the post-war, large-scale immigration into Europe. Putting aside the straightforward default policy of assimilation, the first of Modood's five ideal types is 'The De-Centred State'. This first type is premised on an understanding that because of factors such as migration and the globalisation of economics, consumption and communications, societies can no longer be constituted by stable collective purposes and identities organised territorially by the nation-state. Thus the state cannot supply and attach a primary identity to individuals because identities are fluid and multiple as individuals identify with like-minded people across borders in terms of lifestyle, cultural consumption, peripatetic careers, diasporas and other forms of transnational networks. We present this and the other ideal types in summary form in Table 2.1 (see Appendix for an explanation of the categories used).

The second of Modood's types is 'The Liberal State', where the state exists to protect the rights of individuals and where the question of recognising new ethnic groups does not arise, for the state does not recognise any such groups. Individuals relate to the state as individual citizens, not as members of the group. The ideal liberal state does not promote one or more national cultures, religions, ways of life, and so on. These matters remain private to individuals in their voluntary associations with each other. Nor does the state promote any syncretic vision of common living or of fellow feeling between the inhabitants of that territory other than the legal entitlements and duties that define civic membership.

The third type, 'The Republic', refers to the ideal republic, which, like the liberal state, does not recognise groups amongst the citizenry but instead relates to each citizen as an individual. Yet, unlike the liberal state, it is amenable to one collective project; more precisely, it is itself a collective project which is not reducible to the protection of the

Table 2.1 Derived from Modood (1997)

Type of State →	Decentred State	Liberal State	Republic	Federation of Communities	Plural State
1. Promotion of Equality of Opportunity	Medium	Low	Low	Medium	High
2. Emphasis on National Identity	Low	Low	High (but prescribed)	Low	High (but remade)
3. Recognition of Difference	Medium	Low	Low	High	High
4. Seeking Neutrality	Not Possible	Yes	No	No	No
5. Bearer of Rights	Individual	Individual	Individual	Group	Individual & Group
6. Relationship to the State	Vertical	Vertical	Vertical	Horizontal	Horizontal & Vertical

rights of individuals or to the maximisation of the choices open to individuals. The republic seeks to enhance the lives of its members by making them a part of a way of living that individuals could not create for themselves; its aim is to make the individuals members of a civic community. This community may be based upon subscription to 'universal' principles such as liberty, equality and fraternity; or to the promotion of a national culture; or, as in the case of France, to both. In a republic, the formation of public ethnicity, by immigration or in other ways, would be discouraged and there would be strong expectation, even pressure, for individuals to assimilate to the national identity. 'The Federation of Communities' is Modood's fourth type of categorisation. In contrast to the first three responses to multicultural diversity, this option is built upon the assumption that the individual is not the unit (or at least not the only unit) to which the state must relate. Rather, individuals belong to and are shaped by communities, which are the primary focus of their loyalty and the regulators of their social existence. Far from being confined to the private sphere, communities are rather the primary agents of the public sphere. Public life, in fact, consists of organised communities relating to each other, and the state is therefore a federation of communities that exists to protect the rights of these communities. The millet system of the Ottoman Empire, in which some state powers were delegated to Christian and Jewish communities that had the power to administer personal law within their communities in accordance with their own legal system, is an example of this model of the multicultural state. The last type of state is 'The Plural State', which can have both strong and weak forms. With it comes a recognition that social existence consists of individuals and groups, and both need to be provided for in the formal and informal distribution of powers, not just in law but in representation in the offices of the state, public committees, consultative exercises, and access to public forums. There may be some rights for all individuals as in the liberal state, but mediating institutions such as trade unions, churches, neighbourhoods, immigrant associations and so on may also be encouraged to be active public players and forums for political discussion, and may even have a formal representative or administrative role to play in the state. The plural state, however, allows for and probably requires an ethical conception of citizenship, and not just an instrumental one as in the the conception of a federation of communities. The understanding that individuals are partly constituted by the lives of families and communities fits well with the recognition that the moral individual is partly shaped by the social

Table 2.2 Derived from CMEB (2000)

Type of State →	Procedural	Nationalist	Liberal	Plural	Separatist
1. Promotion of Equality of Opportunity	Low	Low	Medium	High	Low
2. Emphasis on National Identity	Low	High (but prescribed)	Low	High (but remade)	Low
3. Recognition of Difference	Low	Low	Medium	High	High
4. Seeking Neutrality	Yes	No	Yes	No	No
5. Bearer of Rights	Individual	Individual	Individual	Individual & Group	Group
6. Relationship to the State	Vertical	Vertical	Vertical	Horizontal & Vertical	Horizontal

order constituted by citizenship and the public that amplifies and qualifies, sustains, critiques and reforms citizenship. For the plural state, then, multicultural diversity means reforming national identity and citizenship and offering an emotional identity with the whole, to counterbalance the emotional loyalties to ethnic and religious communities (Modood 2007).

The types mentioned above are simply one typology; it is not contended that all five options are equally suitable and/or feasible in contemporary Europe. Before we consider that point, let us briefly compare this typology with later conceptualisations. The Commission for Multi-Ethnic Britain (CMEB) (2000: 42), chaired by Lord Professor Bhikhu Parekh, provided the following five possible models of cohesion, equality and difference:

1. **Procedural**: the state is culturally neutral, and leaves individuals and communities to negotiate with each other as they wish, providing they observe certain basic procedures (see Table 2.2).
2. **Nationalist**: the state promotes a single national culture and expects all to assimilate to it. People who do not or cannot assimilate are second-class citizens.
3. **Liberal**: there is a single political culture in the public sphere but substantial diversity in the private lives of individuals and communities.
4. **Plural**: there is both unity and diversity in public life; communities and identities overlap, are interdependent and develop common features.
5. **Separatist**: the state permits and expects each community to remain separate from others and to organise and regulate its own affairs, largely confining itself to maintaining order and civility.

Koopmans et al. (2005) take on the same task, but unlike the previous two models, which are based on identifying positions in political theory, they identify two distinct features of citizenship practice and allow them to interact in order to create four possibilities. Thus, using the following two dimensions

1. The formal basis of citizenship: civic-territorial versus ethno-cultural (Patten's Question 1)
2. The cultural obligations tied to citizenship: cultural monism and cultural pluralism (Patten's Question 3).

they produce four conceptions of citizenship:[7]

Table 2.3 Derived from Koopmans et al. (2005)

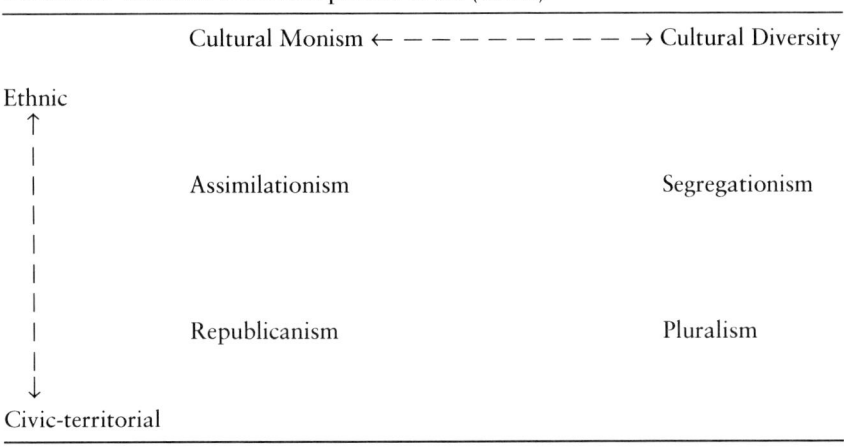

```
                  Cultural Monism ←  — — — — — — — — →  Cultural Diversity
Ethnic
  ↑
  |
  |               Assimilationism                      Segregationism
  |
  |
  |
  |
  |               Republicanism                        Pluralism
  |
  ↓
Civic-territorial
```

(a) Ethnic assimilationism (Germany; Switzerland)
(b) Ethnic segregationism
(c) Civic republicanism (France; and the UK, qualified by d below)
(d) Civic pluralism (Netherlands) (see Table 2.3).

In Koopmans et al. (2005: 73), this model is applied to the position of five countries (as shown above) at three moments in time (1980, 1990 and 2002), and finds that two important movements occurred between 1980 and 2002. The first was a movement towards cultural pluralism in all five countries, though to differing degrees and from quite different starting points, and the second was a movement towards civic conceptions of citizenship.

The North American context is, however, different. Hartmann and Gerteis (2005: 224) produce a two-by-two model but that is not based on dimensions of citizenship but rather on social integration. They produce four ways of responding politically to diversity, according to:

1. the basis for cohesion: substantive moral bonds versus procedural norms
2. the basis for association: individuals in society versus mediating groups.

The four ways are:

EUROPEAN MULTICULTURALISMS

Table 2.4 Derived from Hartman and Gerteis (2005)

	Basis for Cohesion	
Basis for Association	Substantive Moral Bonds	Procedural Norms
Individual in Society	Assimilation	Cosmopolitanism
Mediating Groups	Interactive Pluralism	Fragmented Pluralism

(a) assimilationism (based on social expectations rather than policy)
(b) cosmopolitanism (multiple hybrid identities based on individual choices)
(c) interactive pluralism or multiculturalism (substantive moral bonds mediated through groups as well as individuals, so that there is unity in diversity)
(d) fragmented pluralism (see Table 2.4).

As in the four typologies above, civic or interactive pluralism or multiculturalism emerges as an attractive option, even the favoured one[8]. Let us then look at a typology expressly aimed at showing the limitations of multiculturalism and the attractions of 'interculturalism'. In this respect Alain Gagnon and Raffaele Iacovino (2007) argue that Quebec has developed a distinctive political approach to diversity explicitly in opposition to federal Canadian multiculturalism. Their starting point is that two broad considerations are accepted by a variety of political positions, including liberal nationalist, republican and multiculturalist; indeed by most positions except liberal individualism, which they critique and leave to one side. The first of the two stipulations is that 'full citizenship status requires that all cultural identities be allowed to participate in democratic life equally, without the necessity of reducing conceptions of identity to the level of the individual' (2007: 96). Second, with respect to unity: 'the key element is a sense of common purpose in public matters, a centre which also serves as a marker of identity in the larger society and denotes in itself a pole of allegiance for all citizens' (ibid.).

For Gagnon and Iacovino, however, Canadian multiculturalism has two fatal flaws that make it de facto liberal individualist in practice if not in theory. First, it privileges an individualist approach to culture: as individuals or their choices change, the collective culture must change. In contrast, Quebec's policy states clearly the need to recognise the French language as a collective good that requires protection and encouragement (Rocher et al., cited in Gagnon and Iacovino 2007: 99). Second, Canadian multiculturalism does not locate itself in democratic public culture but rather, 'Public space is based on individual participation via a bill of rights' (2007: 110–11); judges and individual choices, not citizens debating and negotiating with each other become the locus of cultural interaction and public multiculturalism.

Gagnon and Iacovino's positive argument for interculturalism can perhaps be expressed as follows:

1. There should be a public space and identity that is not merely about individual constitutional or legal rights.
2. This public space is an important identity for those who share it and so qualifies and counterbalances other identities that citizens value.
3. This public space is created and shared through participation, interaction, debate and common endeavour.
4. This public space is not culture-less but nor is it merely the 'majority culture'; all can participate in its synthesis and evolution and while it has an inescapable historical character, it is always being remade and ought to be remade to include new groups.
5. Quebec, and not merely Federal Canada, is such a public space and so an object immigrants need to identify with and integrate into; they should therefore seek to maintain Quebec as a nation and not just a federal province. (The same point may apply in other multinational states but there are different degrees and variations of 'multinationalism'.)

2.4 The resilience of a multicultural framework

What is remarkable about these four exercises in typology and the idea of interculturalism, despite differences in nomenclature, is the degree of agreement on what the options in relation to diversity are (see Table 2.5). Moreover, there seems to be virtually no difference between Modood's Plural State, CMEB's Pluralism, Hartmann and Gerteis's Interactive Pluralism and Gagnon and Iacovino's Interculturalism: they all seem to be different ways of stating a preference for a form of multicultural citizenship (Modood 2007). Specifically, there seems to be no difference between Interculturalism and Multiculturalism; Interculturalism is usually stated to be a critical alternative to Multiculturalism, but it seems to be no different from it except for the fact that there is an emphasis

Table 2.5 A synthesis of models of state accommodation of Difference

Type of State →	Plural State (Modood 1997)	Pluralism (CMEB 2000)	Interactive Pluralism (Hartman & Gerteis 2005)	Inter-culturalism (Gagnon & Iacovino 2007)
1. Promotion of Equality of Opportunity	High	High	High	High
2. Emphasis on National Identity	High (but re-made)	High (but re-made)	High (but re-made)	Low (but re-made)
3. Recognition of Difference	High	High	High	High
4. Seeking Neutrality	No	No	No	No
5. Bearer of Rights	Individual & Group	Individual & Group	Individual & Group	Individual & Group
6. Relationship to the State	Horizontal & Vertical	Horizontal & Vertical	Horizontal & Vertical	Horizontal & Vertical
7. Emphasis on Minority Nation Identity	High	High	High	High
8. Emphasis on Interaction between Groups	High	High	High	High

Table 2.6 Contemporary responses to migration-related diversity

Political Orientation →	National Cohesion	Liberal Neutrality	Multiculture	Multicultural Citizenship
1. Promotion of Equality of Opportunity	Medium	Medium	High	High
2. Emphasis on National Identity	High (but prescribed)	Low	Low	High (but remade)
3. Recognition of Difference	Low	Low	Medium	High
4. Seeking Neutrality	No	Yes	No	No
5. Bearer of Rights	Individual	Individual	Individual	Individual & Group
6. Relationship to the State	Vertical	Horizontal & Vertical	–	Horizontal & Vertical
7. Emphasis on Minority Nation Identity	Low	Low	Low	High
8. Emphasis on Interaction between Groups	High	Low	High	High

on multinationalism in the latter, which interestingly is a key feature of Kymlicka's theory of liberal multiculturalism (Kymlicka 1995). This can be seen in Table 2.5, where to emphasise the strengths of interculturalism we have inserted two more categories, one of minority nationalism and another of interaction between groups. Interaction is supposed to be one of the alleged fundamental failings of old-style multiculturalism, of which an explicit emphasis is reflected in the term 'interculturalism'. This, however, is present in the theoretical conceptualisation of multiculturalism we have been considering (for a discussion of interculturalism in relation to multiculturalism, see Meer and Modood forthcoming).

It is clear from the political mood and practical proposals across Europe today that ethno-religious separatism is regarded as the most undesirable outcome, and for many assimilation as a policy is regarded as impractical if not also unjust. Recent events and anxiety about Muslims and whether they are 'integrating', illustrates that the following four political orientations may be the main recommendations for Western Europe. Each takes socio-economic integration (anti-discrimination and countering of social disadvantage) and a certain amount of liberalism (individual rights) as a given:

1. **National cohesion:** the assertion of civic nationhood and placing of social cohesion as a goal above the recognition of group 'difference' (see Table 2.6).
2. **Liberal neutrality:** the state must be neutral between all conceptions of good and should simply administer a uniform set of individual rights and not promote a particular nation, culture or religion.
3. **Multiculture:** an acceptance of the multicultural experience and hybridity at the level of everyday reality (especially in terms of consumption, entertainment and expressive culture) and political emphasis on the local, with scepticism about collective identities, especially the national and the Islamic, but openness to the cosmopolitan.
4. **Multicultural citizenship:** A rebalancing of the politics of accommodation and inclusion focused on ethno-religious groups, with a greater emphasis on hyphenated and plural forms of national citizenship, plural identities and individual rights than some multiculturalists argued for in the 1980s and 1990s.

From the point of view of multiculturalism, these developments can be reduced to the question: can categories 1, 2 or 3 above fully meet the contemporary challenges being experienced in Western

Europe, normatively or in terms of viability, or will a notion of group recognition prove necessary? This is what we explore in Chapter 3 in relation to the empirical developments on the ground in the nine countries studied in the EMILIE project.

Conclusions

The theoretical formulations in this chapter are not offered as pure models to fit any contemporary country on a one-to-one basis, but rather as a basis for understanding, tabulating and comparing the different perspectives and initiatives that are discernible both in any one country and amongst countries, though in varying combinations and to different degrees. As such, we argued that a normative conception of multiculturalism remains a resilient means of explicating empirical developments in fields of contemporary nation-state citizenship. We have shown how it is striking that, in interpreting and evaluating a new emphasis on national identities, some authors ignore how some degree of particularity is both pragmatically necessary and justifiable within a variety of ideational and empirical political orientations. That is to say that where we are currently witnessing various political projects of remaking and updating national identities that are not being departicularised, an opposing trend would not have to empty out the historical-cultural character of nationality but instead include minority ethnicities. The latter, therefore, need not be about being blind to minority ethnic groupness but, on the contrary, seeks to pluralise, and not empty, cultural content. We maintain that for the dominant ethnicity to demonopolise the state and the citizenship by not making cultural assimilation a condition of full citizenship, of full social acceptance, is to respect, not blank out the varied ethnicities of fellow citizens. We have argued that contrary to this view and as articulated by Joppke (2008), 'neutrality' must not be mistaken for contentlessness because pure universalism is impossible. So, equality in citizenship is best pursued as (1) anti-discrimination; (2) recognition of open, mixed and changing ethnicities/identities; (3) multi-logical plurality; and (4) inclusivity and the fostering of a sense of belonging. As such we have detailed a variety of models and shown how these remain valid in traversing the issue of addressing neutrality in contemporary liberal citizenship regimes while advancing a solution from normative accounts of multicultural citizenship.

Appendix I

CRITERIA FOR TABLES

1. Promotion of equality of opportunity

- **Low:** where anti-discrimination laws to promote equality of opportunity are rarely applied in practice, and little or no data on ethnicity and race is collected, and no public agency (such as the Belgian or French HALDE model or the UK EHRC) is charged with publicity, coordination and enforcement.
- **High:** where appropriate data is systematically and extensively collected and used, cases are routinely investigated by employers and other institutions, with many reaching the law courts, and are widely publicised by the media and by agencies responsible for policy development and enforcement and that are answerable to a government department or minister.

2. Emphasis on national identity*

- **Low:** where accounts of nationhood do not feature prominently in characterisations of collective identity and/or are de-emphasised in arenas of public policy and public discourse in favour of local, regional or other scales of identification or competing notions of collective identity. So the state does not seek to promote a vision of common living, of fellow feeling between the inhabitants of that territory, other than the legal entitlements and duties that define civic membership.
- **High:** where political and popular discourse promulgates the idea of a collective nationhood through concrete and symbolic means, for instance, educational policy pertaining to the school curricula, particularly with respect to history, naturalisation and civic orientation and requirements that have a strong and clear sense of nationhood, as well as public discourse characterising the collective identity in national terms.

*National identities can be a variety of prescribed or remade categories. The former would be more exclusive in the way of a benign or active *Leitkultur*, while the latter would be more dialogical or incorporating of 'difference'.

3. Recognition of 'difference'

- **Low**: where minorities are expected or even required to privatise their cultural differences in the course of taking part in a pre-organised public space. This implies that the state will not take into account more than minimal involuntary identities (such as those pertaining to disability) in the construction of the public space, such that policies and practices pertaining to education, discrimination and representation, amongst others, will treat minority difference as invisible and not as a source of legitimate contestation.
- **High**: where minority cultural differences and particularities are incorporated into and help fashion the public space so that there is both unity and diversity in public life, and communities and identities overlap, are interdependent and develop common features. Examples can include the adoption of headscarves, turbans and yarmulkes as part of school or work uniforms, or targeted socio-economic policies that are oriented to the specific obstacles or challenges disproportionately experienced by some minorities.

4. Seeking neutrality – yes/no (and possible or not possible)

- Where the state does not promote one or more national cultures, religions, ways of life, and so on. Such things would remain private to individuals in their voluntary associations with each other. There is a single political culture in the public sphere.

5. Bearer of rights

- **Private**: where although there may be substantial diversity in the private lives of individuals and communities, the state exists to protect the rights of individuals and the question of recognising new minority groups does not arise, for the state does not publicly recognise or enfranchise any groups to represent citizens. Individuals therefore relate to the state as individual citizens, not as members of the group.
- **Public**: there may be some rights for all individuals but mediating institutions such as immigrant associations or the *Conseil Français du Culte Musulman* are also encouraged to be active public players and forums for political discussion and may even have a formal representative or administrative role to play in the state. Thus, the state recognises that individuals are partly

constituted by the lives of families and communities as well as shaped by the social order constituted by citizenship and the public that amplifies and qualifies, sustains, critiques and reforms citizenship.

6. Relationship to the state

- **Horizontal:** where the state engages and formulates public policy on the understanding that individuals belong to and are shaped by communities which are the primary agents of the public sphere. One outcome is that public life can consist of organised communities relating to each other (which overlaps with the minority nations in Spain and Belgium and with the historical minorities in Greece and Poland). Another outcome is that minority communities would remain intact but outside the public sphere (as in the case of pre-2000 German federal policies oriented towards the return of migrant communities).
- **Vertical:** where the state–citizenship relationship is not mediated by groups, communities or third parties, and more directly seeks the protection of the rights of individuals or the maximisation of the choices open to individuals. Danish social citizenship in the access to highly universal and non-means-tested social welfare provisions is a good illustration of this.

7. Emphasis on minority nation identity

- **Low:** where the very fact of minority or historically autonomous regions does not invite or seek the political capacity to instil or represent its identity in educational and migration policy, and civic or other integrationist measures, such as devolution and regional assemblies in the UK.
- **High:** where federal bodies devolve power, including integration policy, to historically autonomous regions and furnish them with the capacity to promote and sustain minority nation identities through such means as regional languages. Thus in some regions, linguistic departments may be established to enforce laws that give the regional language an equal status to a national language, not least in compulsory education, such as in the Catalan and Basque provinces in Spain.

8. Emphasis on interaction between groups*

- **Low:** where the state does not pursue strategies to engender 'social mixing' either nationally or locally; this may be because it leaves civil society to serve this function or perhaps does not deem it a policy priority.
- **High:** where notions of 'segregation' or other issues of social division are deemed to require concerted efforts and emphases upon social interaction at a variety of levels, and particularly locally. Ideas and emphases upon community cohesion are often illustrative of these sorts of concern, as is the more popular complaint that some minorities 'self-segregate'.

*An inquiry into the emphasis on 'interaction' needs to take into consideration the starting points; for example, in some states there will be little formal emphasis on interaction because civil society performs this function.

Notes

1. The Commission on Multi-Ethnic Britain was chaired by Bhikhu Parekh and included, among others, Stuart Hall, Tariq Modood, Yasmin Alibhai-Brown and Trevor Phillips.
2. See European Council press release, 19 November 2004 (http://ue.eu.int/ueDocs/cms_Data/docs/pressData/en/jha/82745.pdf). Other relevant documents on the issue are the Commission's first response to the Basic Common Principles of the Council (COM/2005/0389 final), the Second Annual Report on Migration and Integration (SEC/2006/892) and the European Parliament Resolution on Integration of Immigrants (P6_TA(2006)0318).
3. Justice and Home Affairs, 2618th Meeting (Council of the EU, 14615/04, 2004, pp. 17–18).
4. See Orgad (2009: 15) for interesting counter examples, showing how even if ECHR verdicts are favourable they are not easily operationalised at national level.
5. To Patten's formulation we should perhaps also add obligations and duties to entitlements.
6. National identities can be more or less open to change and remaking. The less open would be more exclusive in the way of a benign or active *Leitkultur*, while the more open would be characterised by internal differentiation and dialogically woven together through difference.
7. We have adapted their vocabulary.
8. Koopmans et al. (2005) do not express a preference between the alternatives that they track.

References

Archibugi, M. K., D. Held and M. Köhler (1998), *Re-imagining Political Community: Studies in Cosmopolitan Democracy*, Stanford, CT: Stanford University Press.

Archibugi, M. K., D. Held and M. Zuran (2005), *Global Governance and Public Accountability*, Hoboken, NJ: Wiley Blackwell.

Barry, B. (2001), *Culture and Equality: An Egalitarian Critique of Equality*, London: Polity Press.

Bauböck, R., E. Ersbøll, C. A. Groenendijk and H. Waldrauch (eds) (2006), *Acquisition and Loss of Nationality. Policies and Trends in 15 European Countries. Vol. 1: Comparative Analyses*, Amsterdam: Amsterdam University Press.

Brubaker, R. (2001), 'The return of assimilation? Changing perspectives on immigration and its sequels in France, Germany, and the United States', *Ethnic and Racial Studies*, 24(4), pp. 531–48.

Caldwell, C. (2009), *Reflections on the Revolution in Europe: Immigration, Islam and the West*, London: Penguin.

Cameron, D. (2011), 'PM's speech at Munich Security Conference', 5 February. Available at www.number10.gov.uk/news/speeches-and-transcripts/2011/02/pms-speech-at-munich-security-conference-60293, accessed on 29 May 2011.

Commission on the Future of Multi-Ethnic Britain (CMEB) (2000), *The Future of Multi-Ethnic Britain*, London: Profile Books.

Entzinger, H. (2003), 'The rise and fall of multiculturalism: The case of the Netherlands', in C. Joppke and E. Morawska (eds), *Toward Assimilation and Citizenship*, Basingstoke: Palgrave Macmillan, pp. 59–86.

Entzinger, H. (2007), 'The parallel decline of multiculturalism and the welfare state in the Netherlands', in K. Banting and W. Kymlicka (eds), *Multiculturalism and the Welfare State*, Oxford: Oxford University Press, pp. 177–202.

Gagnon, A. G. and R. Iacovino (2007), *Federalism, Citizenship and Quebec: Debating Multinationalism*, Toronto: University of Toronto Press.

Gilroy, P. (1987), *There Ain't No Black in the Union Jack: The Cultural Politics of Race and Nation*, London: Routledge.

Gove, M. (2006), *Celsius 7/7: How the West's Policy of Appeasement Has Provoked Yet More Fundamentalist Terror – And What Has to be Done About it*, London: Weidenfeld and Nicolson.

Hansen, R. (2006), 'The Danish cartoon controversy: A defense of liberal freedom', *International Migration*, 44(5), pp. 7–16.

Hartmann, D. and Gerteis, J. (2005), 'Dealing with diversity: Mapping multiculturalism in sociological terms', *Sociological Theory*, 23(2), pp. 218–40.

Home Office (2004), *Life in the United Kingdom: A Journey to Citizenship*, London: HMSO.

Jacobs, D. and A. Rea (2007), 'The end of national models? Integration courses and citizenship trajectories in Europe', *International Journal on Multicultural Societies*, 9(2), pp. 264–83.

Joppke, C. (2004), 'The retreat of multiculturalism in the liberal state: Theory and policy', *British Journal of Sociology*, 55(2), pp. 237–57.

Joppke, C. (2008), 'Immigration and the identity of citizenship: The paradox of universalism', *Citizenship Studies*, 12(6), pp. 533–46.

Joppke, C. (2009), 'Limits of integration policy: Britain and her Muslims', *Journal of Ethnic and Migration Studies*, 35(3), pp. 453–72.

Kiwan, D. (2008), 'Citizenship education at the cross-roads: Four models of citizenship and their implications for ethnic and religious diversity', *Oxford Review of Education*, 34(1), pp. 39–58.

Koopmans, R., P. Statham, M. Giugni and F. Passy (2005), *Contested Citizenship: Immigration and Cultural Diversity in Europe*, Minneapolis, MN: University of Minesota Press.

Kymlicka, W. (1995), *Multicultural Citizenship*, Oxford: Oxford University Press.

Leonard, M. (1997), *Britain™: Renewing Our Identity*, London: Demos.

Malik, K. (2007), 'Thinking outside the box', *CRE: Catalyst*, January–February. Available at www.kenanmalik.com/essays/catalyst_box.html, accessed on 19 June 2008.

Mandaville, P. (2009), 'Muslim transnational identity and state responses in Europe and the UK after 9/11', *Journal of Ethnic and Migration Studies*, 35(3), 491–506.

Marshall, T. H. (1950), *Citizenship and Social Class and other Essays*, Cambridge: Cambridge University Press.

McGhee, D. (2008), *The End of Multiculturalism? Terrorism, Integration and Human Rights*, Milton Keynes: Open University Press and McGraw-Hill Education.

Meer, N. and T. Modood (2009), 'The multicultural state we are in: Muslims, "multiculture" and the "civic re-balancing" of British multiculturalism', *Political Studies*, 57(3), October 2009, pp. 473–97.

Meer, N. and T. Modood (forthcoming), 'How does interculturalism contrast with multiculturalism?', *Journal of Intercultural Studies*.

Meer, N. and P. Mouritsen (2009), 'Political cultures compared: The Muhammad cartoons in the Danish and British press', *Ethnicities*, 9(3), pp. 334–60.

Modood, T. (1992), *Not Easy Being British: Colour, Culture and Citizenship*, London: Runnymede Trust/Trentham Books.

Modood, T. (1997), 'Introduction: The politics of multiculturalism in the new Europe', in T. Modood and P. Werbner (eds), *The Politics of Multiculturalism in the New Europe*, London: Zed Books.

Modood, T. (2007), *Multiculturalism*, London: Blackwell.
Modood, T. and N. Meer (2009), 'Multicultural citizenship in Europe: The states we are in', paper for the EMILIE Conference, 24 September, 'Migration and Diversity Challenges in Europe: Theoretical and Policy Responses'.
Mouritsen, P. (2008), 'Political responses to cultural conflict: Reflections on the ambiguities of the civic turn', in P. Mouritsen and K. E. Jørgensen (eds), *Constituting Communities. Political Solutions to Cultural Conflict*, London: Palgrave, pp. 1–30.
Mouritsen, P. (2009), 'Citizenship versus Islam? Civic integration in Germany, Great Britain and Denmark', draft paper.
Müller, J. W. (2007), 'Is Europe converging on constitutional patriotism? (And if so, is it justified)', *Critical Review of International Social and Political Philosophy*, 10(3), pp. 377–8.
Orgad, L. (2009), '"Cultural defense" of nations: Cultural citizenship in France, Germany and the Netherlands', *European Law Journal*, 15(6), pp. 719–37.
Parekh, B. (2000), *Rethinking Multiculturalism: Cultural Diversity and Political Theory*, London: Palgrave.
Phillips, M. (2006), *Londonistan: How Britain Created a Terror State Within*, London: Gibson Square Books.
Policy Exchange (2007), *Living Apart Together: British Muslims and the Paradox of Multiculturalism*, London: Policy Exchange.
Prins, G. and Robert Salisbury (2008), 'Risk, threat and security – the case of the United Kingdom', *RUSI Journal*, 153(2), pp. 22–7.
Schönwälder, K. (2001), *Einwanderung und ethnische Pluralität. Politische Entscheidungen und öffentliche Debatten in Großbritannien und der Bundesrepublik von den 1950er bis zu den 1970er Jahren*, Essen: Klartext Verlag.
Soysal, Y. (1994), *Limits of Citizenship: Migrants and Postnational Membership in Europe*, Chicago, IL: Chicago University Press.
Uberoi, V. (2008), 'Do policies of multiculturalism change national identities?', *The Political Quarterly*, 79(3), pp. 404–17.
Uberoi, V. and T. Modood (2009), 'Who doesn't feel British? Divisions over Muslims', *Parliamentary Affairs*, 63(2), pp. 1–19.
Van De Vijver, F., S. Schalk-Soekar, J. Arends-Tóth and S. Breugelmans (2006), '"Cracks in the wall of multiculturalism?" A review of attitudinal studies in the Netherlands', *IJMS International Journal on Multicultural Societies*, 8(1), pp. 102–18.
Weaver, M. (2010), 'Angela Merkel: Multiculturalism has "utterly failed"', 10 October. Available at www.guardian.co.uk/world/2010/oct/17/angela-merkel-german-multiculturalism-failed, accessed on 28 March 2011.

3

The Multicultural States We're In[1]

Nasar Meer and Tariq Modood

Introduction

This chapter directly follows on from the last by applying the theoretical formulations proposed in Chapter 2 to explore the possible ways citizenship conventions concerned with membership, entitlements and social expectations are incorporating minority identities within five north-western European countries and two southern European countries. What emerges from our discussion is that clusters of policy developments in each national context display some similarity but rarely any symmetry, thus suggesting that national models remain an important means of conceptualising developments in political orientations toward migration-related diversity.

3.1 France: embracing anti-discrimination

Within north-western Europe, France is a good illustration of – though not necessarily the closest fit to – a political orientation geared toward national cohesion as set out in Table 2.6 in the previous chapter. It is so because of its assertion of civic nationhood and the placing of social cohesion as a goal above the recognition of group 'difference'. Nationality and citizenship in France remain formally inseparable in a manner that precludes non-French nationals from political and civic participation. This is because the acquisition of French citizenship remains synonymous with a relatively prescriptive political and territorial national identity underlying the state's expectations that migration-related minorities must integrate into an established social and political order. For example, the national school curriculum refuses to incorporate, acknowledge or 'recognise' migration-related experiences, for fear of detracting from the inculcation of a primary republican national and citizenship identity, even while this perpetuates an ethnocentric and exclusive account of French identity.

Alongside a mono-cultural school curriculum is of course the 2004 ban on ostentatious religious dress in state schools, which dramatically illustrated the steadfast capacity of the French republican model to resist the recognition of migration-related ethno-religious diversity. As Table 3.1 illustrates, France places a high emphasis upon national identity that bears little incorporation of minority 'difference', which is privatised with rights squarely restricted to the individual in a concomitant vertical relationship with the state.

This tendency continues to owe much to the defeat of the *ancien régime* during the Revolution of 1789. Before the Revolution, during the monarchy, birth and the belonging to a specific 'group' allocated status within a hierarchy, the social position of a citizen in the subsequent Republic would, theoretically at least, reflect a non-hereditary standing. This established and perpetuated the public policy that various incarnations of the Republic should not recognise among its citizens any form of group belonging on the basis of birth or 'origin'. This is evident in the Constitution of the Fifth Republic (1958), whereby it was reasserted that France 'shall ensure the equality of all citizens before the law without distinction of origin, race or religion'. Formally, therefore, a recurring feature of French citizenship is its non-distinction among citizens. As such France is simultaneously illustrative of Modood's (1997) characterisation of a republic, Parekh's (2000) description of a (civic) nationalist state and Hartmann and Gerteis's (2005) outline of an assimilationism forged by the promotion of substantive moral bonds as a basis for cohesion according to an individual basis for association. It also confirms France's response to migration-related diversity in the 'civic-monist' corner of Koopmans et al.'s (2005) grid; the authors also noted some tendencies towards cultural pluralism (though to a differing degree and from a different starting point in their citizenship regimes) that are present in our analysis.

One implication of the formally linear relationship between citizenship, nationality and integration is that France presently boasts a relatively porous rate of naturalisation that allows for a rather sizeable admission of non-nationals. Interestingly, France, like the UK but unlike Germany, Denmark and Belgium, has not made civic integration measures (such as language proficiency) a precondition for the naturalisation of non-EU citizens seeking national citizenship. One should ask, then, what the significance is of consultation bodies which coopt non-citizens into the political processes of decision-making that France has created? The practice of political consultations at the local level – illustrated by the creation of a Parisian consultation body for third country nationals (TCNs) is an example. This undoubtedly suggests that there is some regional innovation exemplified by how the city council of Paris allows for group-based claims, though these remain confined to a consultation body that affords little power to those taking part in it. Upon further inspection, the creation of consultation bodies potentially entrenches a double standard in that non-EU migrants' interests are expected to be channelled through these kinds of relatively powerless institutions. Such institutions continue to marginalise or neutralise the potency of their minority group claims. The creation of the *Conseil Français du Culte Musulman* at the highest level of the state is perhaps another illustration of limited movement, for while the creation of this Muslim council has been symbolic, its success has been piecemeal because of internal division and external obstacles.

Perhaps most significant is that over the last decade matters of ethnic and racial discrimination in public policy have received greater attention, with connections being made between an educational system that disproportionately channels ethnic minority children into the least prestigious education, and a job market that discriminates against them. The lack of ethnic monitoring does not allow for precise data and analysis, which exemplifies one of the ways in which national models still matter because different national models generate different data or non-data (cf. Joppke 2007). Indices of parental nationality (which of course ignore third or more generations) along a range of indicators establish a pattern of systemic discrimination against people of North African descent (Meurs et al. 2006).

Consistent with a national cohesion framework that is substantively concerned with formally enabling citizenship, France appears to be taking active steps to encourage equal treatment – effectively to implement the republican promise – and the role of the EU is proving to be crucial in this regard. For example, in 2004 the HALDE (High Authority to Fight Against Discrimination and for Equality) was created to comply with EU directives. Inspired in part by its Belgian counterpart, the HALDE constitutes a significant institutional development in France's approach to anti-discrimination, for it wields extended powers of an almost judicial form and is capable of issuing recommendations that although do not have legally binding powers do have some influence over the public and private sectors and materially support litigation in challenging discrimination.

A related development to anti-discrimination is that in the private sector major French companies have now implemented a wide variety of diversity training programmes which are often accompanied by the establishment of a specific diversity post in their human resources unit. The diversity unit as a whole often brings together various grounds of discrimination such as disability, age, gender, sexual orientation and 'diversity of origins'. The tensions therein between diversity and anti-discrimination are exemplified by the name of the diversity unit in one of the leading employment agencies: 'Combat Discrimination'. This unit seeks to eschew the complex issue of diversity and only addresses the issue of discrimination. In other companies, however, diversity is conceived as a positive means of talking about anti-discrimination (in a manner that is proactive and does not seek to apportion blame), so for some non-governmental organisations (NGOs) with diversity consulting remits, diversity goes further than anti-discrimination or the guarantee of equal treatment. What is crucial to note is how such approaches have been criticised by HALDE, which maintains that they have no legal basis and that in the promotion of diversity, human resources managers and diversity consultants are going beyond what the law requires.

What this suggests is that while HALDE and its development is a cornerstone of the institutional anti-discrimination landscape in France, it is still very much embedded in the principle of a colour-blind egalitarianism. As a result, HALDE has no interest in measures such as ethnic monitoring or the promotion of positive action that are more discernibly orientated towards multicultural citizenship. The prospect of such measures was, in fact, rejected upon the creation of HALDE in favour instead of a Republican National Cohesion framework in which operative notions of ethnic or racial/ethno-cultural/ethno-religious minorities are minimised and specific policies for such minorities remain absent (reflected in Table 3.1).

As such the present French response contains little that resembles either liberal neutrality or multicultural citizenship, even though there appears to be some 'multiculture' in conceiving contemporary colour consciousness as a vehicle for anti-discrimination, but one that is overwhelmingly orientated towards a national cohesion political response.

3.2 The UK: developing civicness and intersectionality

In contrast to France, the present political orientation of the UK is closer to multicultural citizenship than national cohesion, even while matters of national unity assume a greater prominence than they have previously, and where a discernable securitisation of ethnic relations has emerged over fears of Muslim extremism. At the same time categories of ethnic, racial and religious minorities are being employed and further entrenched by the state. Minorities are allowed to maintain and develop their cultural specificities, with host institutions sensitive to this cultural diversity and – to the extent that this is feasible – encouraged to modify their procedures and practices accordingly. This means that the UK continues to bear some resemblance to Modood's (1997) and the Commission on the Future of Multi-Ethnic Britain's (CMEB) (2000) 'plural state', and rests somewhere in the ethnic-diversity quadrant of Koopmans et al.'s (2005) grid – though perhaps more towards a liberal universalism.

This does not mean that it lacks an impetus for national cohesion since the emphasis on a national identity is presently high, though moderated by the rise of countervailing sub-nationalisms within the UK. This represents something like Hartmann and Gerteis's (2005) 'interactive pluralism' in that, like France, the UK has recently been promoting substantive moral bonds as the basis of cohesion but, unlike France, conceives the basis for cohesion as both individual and group-orientated. Hence, ethnic minority groups are stimulated to organise themselves on an ethnic basis – amongst other things for interest in representation. More specifically, migrant communities and post-migrant British-born generations have been recognised as ethnic and racial minorities requiring state support and differential treatment. This includes how, under the remit of several Race Relations Acts, the state has sought to integrate minorities into the labour market and other key arenas of British society through an approach that promotes equal access as an example of equality of opportunity.

Indeed, it is over thirty-five years since the introduction of a third Race Relations Act (1976) cemented a state sponsorship of race equality by consolidating earlier, weaker legislative instruments (RRA 1965 and 1968). Alongside its broad remit spanning public and private institutions, recognition of indirect discrimination and the 2000 and 2003 imposition of statutory public duties to promote good 'race relations', it also created the Commission for Racial Equality (CRE) to assist individual complainants and monitor the implementation of the Act (see Dhami et al. 2006: 19–25). This approach is an example, according to Joppke (1999: 642), of a citizenship that has amounted to a 'precarious balance between citizenship universalism and racial group particularism [that] stops short of giving special group rights to immigrants'.[2]

The original legal approach to anti-discrimination was the statutory tort of unlawful discrimination created by the Sex Discrimination Act 1975 and the Race Relations Act 1976. This technique grafted an important collective value of non-discrimination on the grounds of sex and race onto the existing private law structure. Although private law and individual rights were chosen as the preferred paradigm, there was also recognition that a discrimination law serves important collective interests. This means that British anti-discrimination frameworks have tried to address the rights of distinct groups as well as their modes of interaction, and thus are not merely concerned with the rights of individuals.

Subsequent developments, especially European developments, have meant that this 'public function' of discrimination law has become more explicit. Most importantly, UK discrimination law has to accommodate the provisions of the Equality and Human Rights Commission (EHRC), for example the equality provision in Article 14 or the right to privacy in Article 8. This requirement has created a body of constitutional discrimination law which is now incorporated into domestic law through the Human Rights Act (HRA) (1998).

These developments have led to what is sometimes described as the 'constitutionalising' of discrimination law (Malik 2008). In other words, the incorporation of the EHRC through the HRA has proven to be a catalyst in shaping recent changes to anti-discrimination measures. This is perhaps most evident in the decision to name the new commission entrusted with the task of monitoring the implementation and practice of all previous anti-discrimination legislation, as well as the two EU directives, the Equality and Human Rights Commission, which is further seen in the introduction of the Single Equality Act (see Meer 2010).

Therefore, we currently have a new focus upon both 'inter-sectionality', or multiple discrimination, and a commitment to mainstreaming a variety of non-discrimination 'strands' to simultaneously address gender and racial discrimination, or disability and age-based discrimination. To this end, the government consultation document *Towards Equality and Diversity* (2002) stated that a single statutory equality commission would offer integrated guidance and support to individuals and businesses and help ensure a coherent approach to equality issues across the board. It insisted, moreover, that a single point of contact for individuals would provide information, advice and guidance across the full breadth of their equality rights, reflecting their real-life experience. It also insisted that this commission would act as a single point of advice to employers and service providers covering all grounds for discrimination and discrimination on multiple grounds, as well as support partnerships with other organisations providing advice.

This recognition of complex discrimination is, like France, but unlike Denmark, Germany and Belgium, coupled to a new emphasis on a 'journey' into citizenship in which the acquisition of citizenship marks neither the beginning nor the end of the processes of integration. A good illustration is *Secure Borders, Safe Haven: Integration with Diversity in Modern Britain* (2002), which sought the transformation of processes of naturalisation into 'an act of commitment to Britain [as] an important step in the process of achieving integration into our society' (p. 32). Hence, it promoted the acquisition of English language competencies and knowledge of life in the UK as a means of successful integration for new migrants. It also characterised civic engagement as a means of 'active citizenship' in a way that was horizontally tied to measures such as citizenship education and other civic integrationist matters. These in turn have formed the points-based managed migration system introduced in the *Controlling Our Borders* White Paper of 2005, and the earned citizenship proposals made in the *Paths to Citizenship* Green Paper in February 2008. Despite some interpretations of these developments (Joppke 2004), the concern with unity through community cohesion, citizenship, common values and Britishness cannot at present accurately be called a 'retreat' from multiculturalism. For indeed, it was none other than the 'communitarian' CMEB (2000) that advocated the promotion of a renewed British identity through a 'rethinking' of the national story (as the commission's title implies). Rather, the emergent multiculturalism of the 1990s that was attempting to accommodate Muslim communities has been simultaneously subjected to a variety of critiques of which the concern with unity is but one.

3.3 Germany: from ius sanguinis to integration

Muslims indeed feature prominently in the two further cases of Germany and Denmark, both of which register a political

Table 3.1 Five countries in north-western Europe

National Contexts → Political Orientation ↓	France	Germany	UK	Belgium	Denmark
1. Promotion of Equality of Opportunity	Medium	Low	High	Medium	Low
2. Emphasis on National Identity	High	Medium (federalism)	Medium (multi-nationalism)	Low (multinational federalism)	High
3. Recognition of Difference	Low	Low	High	Medium (North/South differences)	Low
4. Seeking Neutrality	No	No	No	No	No
5. Bearer of Rights	Individual	Individual	Individual & Group	Individual & Group	Individual
6. Relationship to the State	Vertical	Horizontal & Vertical	Horizontal & Vertical	Horizontal & Vertical	Horizontal & Vertical
7. Emphasis on Minority Nation Identity	Low	Low	Medium	Strong	–
8. Emphasis on Interaction between Groups	Medium	Medium	High	High	High

orientation much closer to national cohesion than either the UK or France.

Following decades of pursuing an ethno-national citizenship,[3] Germany has since the late 1990s undergone significant changes in the management of immigration, integration and its concept of citizenship. This comprises some movement diagonally downwards and across in Koopmans et al.'s (2005) model (see Table 2.3 in Chapter 2), from the ethnic-diversity and segregationist quadrant, toward the monist column; though it is unclear how much is civic or ethnic in orientation. Federal policies had previously focused almost entirely on the control and return of migrants (Schönwälder 2001), until the Red–Green coalition government recast Germany as a country of 'immigration' and amended the Citizenship Law (2000) to introduce the principle of *ius soli*. This led to a slew of new legislation such as the Immigration Law (2005), which is geared toward integration strategies, and the invitation to migrants and civil society actors to take part in a National Integration Summit (2006). Each of these is said to comprise 'milestones' in that they speak with migrant minorities and not solely about them. This is evident in the Federal Commissioner for Integration Maria Böhmer's (CDU) statement in which she corrected earlier accounts by saying, 'Germany is not an immigration country, but an integration country'.

To this end formal citizenship can be acquired through a process of naturalisation after eight years of legal residence, provided the applicant has sufficient German language skills and other civic competencies. The amendment to the Citizenship Law (2000) means that the children of 'foreigners' now automatically acquire German citizenship if one parent has been legally residing in Germany for at least eight years with a 'right to abode' permit. These children can retain dual nationality until the age of twenty-three, after which they have to choose between German citizenship and the citizenship of their parents.

One outcome of this policy is that when thousands of Turkish migrants applied for the reissuing of their Turkish passports in 2001 after having been naturalised, German authorities responded by withdrawing their German nationality and residence permits. The fact that the right to vote on the municipal level is only valid for EU nationals and that there is no parliamentary will to afford the franchise to TCNs disproportionately affects German Turkish nationals.

So while the German developments have marked important shifts, they have not overcome the issue of dual nationality nor entirely decoupled citizenship from an ethnic project. There is little neutrality in a liberal political orientation towards migration-related diversity in Modood (1997) or Parekh's (2000) models for, in Hartmann and Gerteis's (2005) terms, the basis of cohesion amounts to substantive moral bonds while the location of rights remains with the individual. This is not to say that strict assimilation strategies are followed but rather that the accommodation of cultural, lingual and religious diversity is minimised in a way that is reminiscent of republican approaches. This is visible in the education system and the National Integration Plan, which both insist on a 'mono-lingual habitus' (Gogolin et al. 2003). A suspicion this raises is that in the present climate, 'integration' means the de facto prioritisation of German language and dominant culture. This view is shared by Gerdes and Faist (2006), who outline two simultaneous versions of republicanism in German public debates. These comprise a liberal equal rights perspective and a communitarian conception of citizenship. The latter, however, is not so much plural since it contains a resurgent ethno-national sentiment. An illustration of this could be when Jürgen Rüttgers, a very senior figure in the Christian Democratic Union (CDU), promoted the slogan *Kinder statt Inder* ('Children instead of Indians') in response to the planned recruitment of specialised skilled labour. The slogan and sentiment occurred in a context of the emergence of the idea of a German *Leitkultur* (leading or core culture) conceived as the context for integration (Manz 2004). Further symbolic progress, which may be indicative of diversity-friendly political orientations, was witnessed in July 2006 when German Chancellor Angela Merkel (of the CDU) invited migrant organisations, as well as representatives of other relevant social groups, to take part in the first National Integration Summit (NIS). This was the first governmental initiative in German immigration history that explicitly acknowledged the reality of immigration and conceived post-migrant minorities as social partners. After the second Summit, in July 2007, the results of the working groups were presented to the federal *Länder* and local authorities, associations of migrants and numerous other non-government actors, with the government adopting more than 400 measures and voluntary commitments relating to integration. Again in November 2008, Chancellor Merkel presented the progress of the implementation of the NIS. In the run-up to the second National Integration Summit in July 2007, the legislature passed an amendment to the Immigration Law which included the requirement for new immigrants of non-EU countries to have basic German language skills as well as the introduction of a minimum age of eighteen for immigrating family members. These restrictions mainly affect migrants from Turkey and indeed were implicitly characterised as a means of reducing forced marriages for young women from Turkey. As with the securitisation in other countries, the impact of terrorism has featured prominently in the German discourse and several stipulations in the citizenship law and citizenship test reflect an associated anxiety toward Muslims in general, including an emphasis on the desirability of a 'deeper' integration in general.

As the Federal Minister of the Interior insisted, the 'observing of [legal] rules alone does not lead to successful integration . . . if we want to feel belonging to a community [*Gemeinwesen*] then there must be something which interconnects us on a more profound human level'.[4] Such sentiments have perhaps most infamously been illustrated by the citizenship test of Baden-Wuerttemberg, especially in its first version created in January 2006. The citizenship test quite explicitly suspected Muslim applicants of not sharing the norms and values of German society through questions such as: 'Do you think that it is adequate to keep one's daughter at home, in order to avoid her breaking the rules of honour?' or 'Imagine your son declares he is homosexual and wants to live with another man – how would you react?' The notion of Islam as a threat to the core values of German society is therefore a recurring theme within German integration debates.

The previous chapter identified anti-discrimination legislation as an important vector of varying political orientations and we have already traced development in this area in France and the UK. German civil society, however, seems to contain less in the way of the promotion of anti-discrimination measures or its institutional or structural implications in particular. For instance, positive action of the kind envisaged by the EHRC, and to a lesser extent HALDE, to be proactive in preventing discrimination is presently being resisted. The *Antidiskriminierungsstelle des Bundes* (Federal Anti-Discrimination Authority) does, however, argue that there is a business case for diversity management, in a manner not dissimilar to the French. So there are in fact some forms of recognition of migration-related cultural diversity, even if this recognition is fairly limited. For instance, the NIS includes commitments by the state and federal states to 'inter-culturally open up' by increasing the number of employees with a migration-related background. Education policies are in particular trying to respond to migration and cultural diversity challenges. Hence, since its recommendations from 1996, the Conference of the Ministers of Education and Cultural Affairs of the *Länder* has formulated relatively significant intercultural and multilingual principles, although the structural features of discrimination were only minimally considered. This means that, on the one hand, the *Länder* Ministries of Education and Cultural Affairs along with several individual schools are working on school reforms with new curricula and teaching methods for either principled or often pragmatic reasons. But on the other hand, a general and systematic implementation of intercultural principles and equal opportunities is far from being achieved. At this stage, therefore, recent German developments appear tentative in their move away from *ius sanguis* towards a national cohesion political orientation that has the hallmarks of an ethnically inscribed republicanism. It seems to be distant from both liberal neutrality and multicultural citizenship; in this manner Germany shares something with Denmark.

3.4 Denmark: a restrictive civicness

While Denmark is regarded as performing better than some European Union countries in terms of its acceptance of refugees and emphasis on equal rights, reported discrimination and the incidence of racist violence, the content and 'tone' of popular discourse, particularly around cultural diversity and Islam, arguably sets Denmark apart (Meer and Mouritsen 2009). The country's traditional lack of any legal, institutional or policy-level accommodations towards cultural diversity is matched by official and widespread popular hostility to any hint of a political orientation towards multicultural citizenship. Moreover, Denmark very clearly conceives citizenship as a prize and not, as in the UK or France, as a means of fostering integration. Citizenship has become an extension of the politics of immigration management in a manner that appears to be inscribed with nationalism, identity and anti-Muslim sentiment.

Generally speaking, most of the components of the politics of integration in Denmark display scepticism of cultural diversity that is linked to a nation-building project premised upon a high degree of cultural homogeneity. Arguably, therefore, Danish political culture has always reflected a tendency toward uniformity (Østergård 1992). Two controversies that have been especially pertinent concern the policies of the language teaching provision, including the dismantling of mother tongue teaching and the increased regulation of the faith schooling provision. The first case demonstrates a particularity of the national education system, which is tailored to recognise one form of diversity in mainstream state schools. Although religious and ethnic diversity are politicised as problems, immigrant children are institutionally categorised as bilingual. Yet bilingualism is treated as an interim state, as a means of acquiring a 'normal' standard of Danish language proficiency along with cultural norms and knowledge, in order to facilitate educational success and market functionality. That is to say that being bilingual is never either a social asset or a legitimate aspect of a multicultural identity. The second controversy surrounds Muslim faith schools, which have been criticised for poor academic performance (in a few instances justifiably), but also for two further elements. The first is that schools did not promote appropriate liberal values, and were believed to encourage fundamentalism or even terrorism. As a result these schools saw a significant tightening of controls and changes in their statutory framework. The second element concerns the way such schools are characterised as a form of cultural separatism. Even though research indicates that students in these schools perform well, and certainly better than students of equally de facto segregated state schools in minority neighbourhoods, it appears that this type of diversity breaches the limits of what is regarded as legitimate pluralism in Danish education institutions (despite the autonomy of schools being a hallmark of the Danish educational system).

The Danish take on anti-discrimination testifies in a different way to the hold of Danish egalitarianism that is conceived as cultural sameness. At the most general level, Denmark stands in marked contrast to a Belgian, British or emerging German tradition of acknowledging migration-related diversity. In Denmark such recognition has been more recent, and the initial political response to it has seen an emphasis on integration, and even assimilation. This has been true in particular of visible religious diversities (headscarves, prayer practices, and so on) such that support for anti-discrimination on these matters has been conspicuous by its absence. Aligned to this is a deep-seated public conviction that Danish egalitarianism and universalism by definition renders discrimination a marginal phenomenon. Thus treating individuals equally by treating them uniformly has blinkered public policy makers to the extent that in the debate over implementation of the EU directives, it was generally assumed that compliance in a minimal way was necessary to honour treaty obligations, but that the relevant components in the directive were already covered. What this suggests is that the legal basis of anti-discrimination is relatively recent and, in some areas, very weak. A general law against labour market discrimination was not introduced until 1996 – before then this area had been delegated to civil society actors and social partners who largely ignored it. The law emphasises violations against the formal equality of persons but puts no emphasis on equality of opportunity and has weak concepts of direct and indirect discrimination. As a result, it has been difficult to prove in order for complainants to secure redress. Anti-discrimination therefore remains a grey area, where most minority members are unaware of their rights and of complaints procedures and supporting institutions; thus, the vast majority of violations appear to go unreported. These developments, or non-developments, occur in a context in which Danish citizenship culture has become increasingly identity-related in ways that make it appropriate to speak of a culturalised civic nationalism (Mouritsen 2006; 2009). While traditional cultural assimilationistic nationalism is increasingly relegated to a right-wing fringe, national identity has not gone away. On the contrary, Danish politics and public life has become strongly characterised by no less chauvinistic ideas of a national liberal democratic superiority, in the sense that universal values are more realised in Denmark than elsewhere (that the Danish version and institutionalisation of such values is superior), or even that acquiring such citizenship qualities is a function of a long historical heritage (which excludes those born off the Northern shores of democracy). One also finds in Denmark a type of liberal communitarianism (Walzer 1994: 99ff.) where the majority culture is assumed to have a right to dominate the national public space and institutions such as state schools. Here, strong social equality does not translate into a cultural or religious equality captured by political orientations of multicultural citizenship, and so instead Denmark leans more toward the political orientations of national cohesion.

3.5 Belgium: permanent tensions and pragmatic solutions

In contrast to the four north-western European countries surveyed thus far, Belgium is a complex multinational and federal country characterised by deep and far-reaching linguistic community divisions. In order to grasp its recent evolution in the face of migration-related challenges, it is important to be familiar with the fact there have long been at least two divergent approaches within the same country; two sub-state nationalisms characterised by political–linguistic cleavages (Bousetta and Jacobs 2006). These comprise the Dutch speakers, mostly Flemish, and the French speakers, mostly Walloons (plus a small group of German-speakers). Belgium's two largest regions are the Dutch-speaking Flanders in the north and the French-speaking southern region of Wallonia. Countervailing pressures assume a profound role in Belgian political orientations to citizenship, not least the mainstream presence of an organised political racism in the form of the Vlaams Belang (a party which boasts a quarter of the popular vote) (Jacobs 2004). The pressure this places in terms of its impact on actual policy is ambiguous. For example, in some instances a crude assimilationist approach that goes well beyond political orientations towards national cohesion might be pursued, while on other occasions ethnic diversity is accommodated in an orientation towards multicultural citizenship. Migration-related differences can therefore be both ignored and accommodated depending on the issues at stake and the actors involved. That is to say that on the ground, policy may be de facto multicultural in nature while all involved will deny it has anything to do with the idea of multiculturalism. Or, conversely, while a strict assimilationist policy scheme may be announced it may not in the end be implemented on the ground.

While Belgium has long been an immigration country, with historians charting migration to before the creation of the Belgian State in 1830 (Morelli 1992), political discourses on contemporary migration-related diversity began to evolve from 1974 onwards with the Belgian authorities' decision to cap the entrance of new migrants. Thereafter, the 'returnist' approach was overcome when it became accepted that migrants would settle permanently and that family reunification would ensue. The first notion of integration that emerged therein and proved durable was promoted by the *Commissariat Royal à la Politique des Immigrés* (CRPI) which itself was created after the 1988 elections and the breakthrough of the extreme right in Antwerp. At this stage integration was conceived as supporting migrant participation in mainstream Belgian society and promoted in opposition circles to either a purely assimilationist or multiculturalist orientation. It was therefore an earlier incarnation of more contemporary integrationist measures in that it insisted upon 'fitting in' with the principles that supported the culture of the host country (embracing values of 'modernity', 'emancipation' and 'true pluralism'). This was allied to an unambiguous respect for cultural diversity as a means of providing mutual enrichment. Following the constitutional reforms that enforced institutional changes, the different linguistic communities took responsibility for integration politics. As a result, the Flemish and French-speaking governments have distinctively emphasised one dimension or another of this definition, such that their approaches to dealing with integration issues are consequently quite different. Jacobs (2008: 30) has argued that one of the reasons for this is that 'through structural homology, the Flemish elite no longer wished to impose on their ethnic minorities what they themselves endured as a former minority group'. More precisely, the Flemish community framework is based on the recognition of ethno-cultural minority groups and supports active participation through self-organisation of migrants. It adopted a model of integration that is more in line with a political orientation of multicultural citizenship. For example, the Flemish government, inspired by an earlier Dutch approach, has had a clear preference for supporting the organisations of migrants which are willing to cooperate in federations and be coordinated by quasi-autonomous non-governmental organisations. It has financially supported local initiatives aimed at urban renewal and adopted an overarching policy framework clearly based on the recognition of ethno-cultural groups of (settled and legal) migrants, refugees and travelling communities. Yet running parallel to this approach, it has equally developed policy measures that are said to be aimed at the assimilation of newcomers (Jacobs 2004). Since the end of the 1990s, the Flemish have been preparing and experimenting with civic integrationist measures (*inburgeringstrajecten*) which stress the requirement of Dutch language competencies and a familiarity with the norms of Flemish/Belgian society, with the overall aim of actively promoting a certain degree of language and cultural assimilation. This scheme, once again appropriated from the Netherlands, has become compulsory for most non-EU newcomers in Flanders from April 2004 onwards and is optional in Brussels.

On the French-speaking side, ethnic minorities are defined as immigrants or as people of foreign origin who, in a manner more orientated towards national cohesion, comprise individuals to be inserted into Belgian society, rather than members of groups. For example, the Francophone and Flemish governments have not been willing to recognise the participation of immigrants in society as specific ethno-cultural groups. In practice, however, the dominant policy category used is 'people of foreign origin', which is often primarily directed towards ethnic groups. Other policy initiatives may target immigrants primarily but may not be termed immigrant policies. The same can be said of several measures taken by the Brussels-capital region. The large numbers of foreign residents and the de facto residential concentration of ethnic minorities have nevertheless forced officials in Brussels to recognise the fact of migration-related diversity. Yet in contrast to the Flemish situation, the proactive measures for newcomers on the Francophone side are quite limited and mainly focused on learning the French language.

The linguistic cleavage has therefore cultivated diverging approaches to the settlement and integration of immigrants in the different parts of the country (Bousetta 2000). What has nevertheless emerged as a profound development across the divide is the public significance of Muslims and Islam. In this respect, 1998 constituted a turning point when Muslims in Belgium were canvassed to elect key spokespersons capable of representing collective interests to the state. Nonetheless, the institutional recognition of Islam remains in many aspects a long way off, which is unfortunate, given that one of the consequences of 9/11 is that multiculturalism and the position of Islam within Belgian society have become central issues in public debate (Bousetta and Jacobs 2006).

One means through which this public debate has taken place was the Intercultural Dialogue Commission. Set up by the federal government, it issued in 2005 a report marking a transition in the federal level emphasis from integration to cultural diversity. It did so by identifying several historical tendencies, concerning (1) a political pluralism that facilitated working-class emancipation and wider political consultation; (2) philosophical pluralism that incrementally led to the official recognition of various public religions (Catholic, Protestant, Jewish, Islamic and Anglican) and non-religion; and (3) community pluralism as stemming from Flemish and Walloon movements that created the current Federal State of Belgium. Importantly, the Commissioners underscored a further form of pluralism as the next step: (4) cultural pluralism. More precisely they insisted that integration issues should take into account relevant cultural dimensions and that it no longer made sense to qualify the descendants of migrants as *'migrant'* (migrant in French) or *'allochtone'* (immigrant in Flemish); instead 'cultural minorities' would be a much more relevant definition. The report, on the whole, focused its conclusions on the lack of cultural recognition in a manner that invited the criticism that the Commission had been highly influenced by communitarian theories instead of 'trying to develop civic responsibility and common citizenship rather than thinking about an increasing space for cultural communities' (*La Libre* 6 June 2005). What this example and wider discussion reveals is that the Belgian case is mixed in its simultaneous political orientation to national cohesion and multicultural citizenship, though with important caveats including a horizontal relationship to the state, particularly for autonomous regions.

3.6 Southern Europe

Our two cases from southern Europe remain at an early stage compared to the level of orientation toward multicultural citizenship surveyed in Chapter 2 and found in the Belgian case above. This early stage is primarily due to the resilience of *ius sanguine* conceptions of nationhood. While the prioritisation of national identity in southern Europe goes unquestioned, the recognition of minority difference remains low and the location of minority identity remains restricted to the private sphere (with the exception of historically established minorities or autonomous regions). Thus, Greece maintains a strongly ethnic understanding of the core of the nation as 'the Greeks of Greece', allowing only for the partial integration of 'other' Greeks, notably co-ethnic returnees from the various places where Greek diasporas were established in earlier centuries (although there has been movement in this regard, as discussed below). This is paralleled by keeping immigrants of non-Greek descent strictly outside the polity but inside the economy, and the underground economy in particular (Triandafyllidou and Veikou 2002). So while difference is perceived as part of Greek society, it is external to conceptions of the nation. Spanish national identity, meanwhile, is promoted in the design and implementation of policy according to the twin vectors of a majority religion and language. This favours Spanish-speaking migrants over others and resurrects the Franquist prescription '*habla cristiano*' (speak Christian), serving as a clear illustration of how previous regimes have embedded the interaction between language and religion into the notion that Spain is 'without diversity'. This locates our cases from southern Europe squarely in the national cohesion political orientation set out in Table 2.6 (see Chapter 2) though with important caveats. First, an often horizontal relationship to the state is noted, particularly for autonomous regions, and second, developments in 'interculturalism'[5] are noted particularly with respect to matters of education.

3.7 Greece: developing agendas

The first thing to note about Greece is that it has undoubtedly developed as a host society. Debates on the accommodation of cultural and religious differences are slowly evolving even while the challenge of migration-related diversity is yet to be fully addressed. The following four issues are integral to conceptualising contemporary political orientations:

1. The EU's symbolic characterisation of Greece's belonging to 'core' Europe has overcome to a certain extent the idea of an ethno-religiously defined unitary national identity that is closed to difference. The Greek government has introduced a new law on naturalisation that has begun to alter the landscape for children of migrants. They can now naturalise at birth upon a 'declaration' from their parents, provided they have been legally present in the country for at least five years. Children who came to Greece before the age of eighteen and who have completed six years in Greek schools can also naturalise. Simultaneously, migrants can apply for citizenship after seven years of legal residence, and provided they have already obtained long-term resident status at the EU level (which is conferred after five years of legal residence).
2. EU enlargement policy towards Turkey and the Balkans has opened yet another question of identity and geopolitics.
3. The large number of immigrants that currently account for approximately 10 per cent of the total resident population have slowly required state institutions and public opinion to recognise that Greece has become de facto 'multicultural'.
4. Regional legal and institutional frameworks that have promoted the recognition and protection of minorities across Europe are influencing the debates and policies on the position and rights of minorities in Greece.

The main policies enacted by the Greek state to respond to this increasing diversity are orientated towards the special language and educational needs of non-Greek mother tongue students. These include a tiny set of so-called intercultural schools (twenty-six in total, accounting for less than 1 per cent of the total schools in Greece). They also include programmes that train teachers in the promotion of special activities for cultural dialogue and integration within schools and reaching out to local communities. Finally, they comprise reception classes for up to two years for newly arriving children with limited or no knowledge of the Greek language. These policies have had some success but also have shortcomings, including the failure to transpose a notion of intercultural or multicultural education onto the mainstream educational system. In particular, cultural diversity has been seen as a problem of 'foreign pupils' rather than a broader challenge. The policy and discourse adopted so far with regard to the integration of non-Greek mother tongue pupils has therefore been one of implicit assimilation which is often termed 'integration' but which does not recognise the reciprocal nature of the integration process. Present interpretations are therefore some way from Gagnon and Iacovino's (2007) characterisation of interculturalism as comprising a public space and identity that is created and shared through participation, interaction, debate and common endeavour. While not culture-less, this would not merely be the 'majority culture', so that all could participate in its synthesis and evolution. So even while it has an inescapable historical character, this public culture is always being reworked and ought to include new groups in its next incarnation.

The conception of non-discrimination is also at an early stage, surrounded by widespread confusion among policy actors, civil society bodies and the migrant workers themselves as to what constitutes exploitation and discrimination in the labour market. That is to say, while immigrants face widespread inequality in terms of their employment and conditions of employment, it remains unclear whether such inequality is the result of opportunistic discrimination or simply a question of unscrupulous employers who know that it is unlikely that they will be monitored, and so take advantage of minority socio-economic vulnerability. For example, employers may take advantage of the weak position of the migrant because they are either undocumented or have a short-stay permit which requires welfare contributions to prove they are employed as a prerequisite to permit renewal. Thus, the employer pays less money to the migrant and/or may not pay full welfare contributions or overtime. This is a dilemma which also arises in the discussion of Spain (Zapata-Barrero 2008) and other southern European countries. It is a dilemma because they have formally fully transposed the EU directives discussed in the previous chapter yet experience a significant gap in the manner in which they are implemented (reflecting a lack of awareness among policy and civil society actors as to the rights and duties in the field of equality and anti-discrimination). Given the pervasive understand-

Table 3.2 Two countries in southern Europe

National Contexts → Political Orientation ↓	Greece	Spain
1. Promotion of Equality of Opportunity	*Low*	*Low*
2. Emphasis on National Identity	*High*	*High (multi-nationalism)*
3. Recognition of Difference	*Low (for new minorities) & High (for old minorities)*	*Low (for new minorities) & High (for old minorities)*
4. Seeking Neutrality	*No*	*No*
5. Bearer of Rights	*Individual (for new minorities) & Group (for old minorities)*	*Individual (for new minorities) & Group (for old minorities)*
6. Relationship to the State	*Vertical & Horizontal*	*Vertical & Horizontal*
7. Emphasis on Minority Nation Identity	*Low–Medium*	*High*
8. Emphasis on Interaction between Groups	*Medium*	*Medium*

ing of national identity as the 'cultural property' of the Greek people, defined on the basis of their ethnic descent rather than their civic and socio-economic participation in the community, discrimination is implicitly considered legitimate. 'Greece belongs to the Greeks' is a widespread sentiment and much of the immigration debate echoes this view.

Greece has a history of reactive and delayed responses in the field of migration policy. This can be explained in part by the fact that it is a more recent immigration country with migrants only relatively recently being acknowledged as a permanent reality in Greek society and labour markets. These attitudes prevalent in public administration, among civil servants, and wider public opinion and employers, have yet to catch up with the reality of immigration to Greece. The obligation and responsibility to apply equally non-discriminatory principles to third country nationals in the workplace has only recently started to become a common practice. There is also the traditional weakness of Greek civil society, which has not yet been able to raise awareness on anti-discrimination issues, nor to pressurise the various public and private authorities to respect, implement and adhere to the new legislative framework.

3.8 Spain: selective treatment

Greece is by no means unique in southern Europe regarding its attitude and policies towards immigrants, for in Spain the words 'multiculturalism' and 'inter-culturality' were absent from public policy discourse until 2004. What instead occupied such discourse was the level of immigration to historically autonomous regions, particularly Catalonia, where immigration is perceived as a potential challenge to Catalan culture and identity, especially with regard to the future of the Catalan language. As a consequence, an immersion in Catalan language is a core integration objective. These levels of autonomy over citizenship-making processes far exceed some multinational settlements in north-western Europe, such as devolution in the UK, but are not radically dissimilar to the kinds of federalism found in Belgium or Canada in relation to Quebec. Indeed, there is some invocation here of Gagnon and Iacovino's (2007) characterisation of interculturalism as demanding that a region (in their case Quebec), and not merely the federal state, is a public space and thus an object immigrants need to identify with and integrate into (in order to maintain it as a nation and not just a federal province). In the case of Spain, in those autonomous regions where a second official language is promoted (such as Catalonia, the Basque country and Galicia), immigration is deemed to present a particular challenge of how to manage bilingualism and now multilingualism in schools. In each region, linguistic departments have been established to enforce laws that give the regional language an equal status to Spanish, not least in compulsory education. So there is a kind of Federation of Communities and Separatism for established minorities, with mediating groups as the basis for cohesion that are bound by exclusive substantive moral bonds of a prescriptive language and religion. This is why a condition for the acquisition of voting rights for immigrants is the completion of naturalisation courses and citizenship exams. The Spanish example is opposite of the French and British examples given previously, but interestingly consistent with the Danish and Walloonian approaches – to incorporate integration into the receiving society. For Spain, an alleged crisis of integration in north-western Europe illustrates that naturalisation rights will not guarantee immigrant integration. In this regard, the legal framework plays an important role in the management of diversity, mainly because of the 'Foreigner's Law' (*Ley de Extranjeria*) in the Spanish Constitution (1978). This law created a legal framework of democratic principles and made equal treatment and non-discrimination (alongside liberty, justice and political pluralism) basic pillars of the non-confessional state. It simultaneously, however, precluded non-nationals from voting and from being elected except in those cases where it is established by treaty or when the law attends to the principle of reciprocity. With the 'Foreigner's Law' the Constitution has therefore created a framework of institutional discrimination or ethnicisation since preferential nationalities are granted full political rights. As such, in the public sector EU citizens and third country nationals are discriminated against in their access to employment considered to be the object of state and public security. The nationality law in Spain in this context also results in indirect discrimination. Since for certain national groups, it is far easier to obtain Spanish nationality than for others (typically migrants bearing historical ties from a select group of countries are favoured, such as from Latin American countries and Equatorial Guinea).

The case remains that there is a clear ethnic selection and nationality preferences procedure. For example, Article 22.1 of the Spanish Civil Code establishes that while legal residence in Spain of ten years is required to be granted citizenship, two years is sufficient for those nationals coming from Ibero-American countries (Andorra, the Philippines, Equatorial Guinea, Portugal), or those who are of Sephardic origin. This clearly repeats the tradition of the *Hispanidad* of selection by origin (Zapata-Barrero 2004: 55). In other words, the Spanish Civil Code establishes a framework of institutional discrimination (ibid.), which has a direct impact upon political rights whereby preferential nationalities have more rights than other nationalities.

There are parallels with Greece also, in that while the Spanish approach to education is based on human rights beyond other legal considerations, it is also concerned with intercultural education. Policy makers in Spain too have different views about the meaning of this approach, viewing it as located somewhere between assimilation and multiculturalism.

Broadly speaking, intercultural education in Spain is conceived as an approach to inculcating values such as tolerance and respect, in order to *vivir en convivencia* (coexist peacefully). Since immigrants are considered to be *homo economicus* it is difficult to enter into a more nuanced discussion in which immigrants are integrated not only into the labour market but also into social, cultural and political spheres. Thus the discrimination of immigrant workers primarily refers to those working in the underground economy, facing harsh working conditions without basic rights and protection. The fragmentary anti-discrimination legislation and lack of civil society awareness confines the legal fight against discrimination to combating the exploitation of irregular workers. The ethnicisation of the Civil Code (or the discrimination by origin in relation to naturalisation) is illustrative of a context that restrains proactive policies. This is because Spain is immersed in a history and a structure that impedes innovation and change, and reacts against the accommodation of migration-related diversity in its conceptions of nationhood.

Conclusions

This chapter has detailed permutations in movement, to differing degrees and from different starting points, in conceptions of nationhood as *ius soli*, the valorisation of national identities and the enactment of anti-discrimination legislation, amongst other criteria, across northwestern and southern Europe. Following the theoretical developments set out in Chapter 2, the present chapter has shown that while France provides a good illustration of a political orientation geared towards national cohesion, specifically in the assertion of civic nationhood and the placing of social cohesion as a goal above the recognition of group 'difference', Denmark is presently moving along this trajectory in a much more restrictive manner, a manner that contains a negative tone of popular discourse surrounding cultural diversity in general and Islam in particular. Indeed, both Denmark and Germany display national identities long out of kilter with the diversity of their respective citizenry. This is not to detract from the progress Germany has made, for after decades of pursuing an ethno-national citizenship, there have been significant changes in the management of immigration, integration and its very conception of citizenship with the introduction of *ius soli*. This has been followed by further amendments geared towards integration strategies, as well as the invitation to migrants and civil society actors to take part in National Integration Summits. In other countries the developments are different again. The UK is closer to multicultural citizenship than national cohesion, even while matters of national unity assume a greater prominence than they have previously, and where a securitisation of ethnic relations has emerged over fears of Muslim extremism. The situation of our two cases from southern Europe, meanwhile, is related to the resilience of ethnic conceptions of nationhood, which means that the recognition of minority difference remains low and the location of minority identity remains restricted to the private sphere, with the exception of historically established minorities or autonomous regions.

Notes

1. This chapter draws upon the culmination of working papers authored by the EMILIE consortium and so reflects input from team members Laure-Anne Bernes, Hassan Bousetta, Nynke de Witte, Angéline Escafré-Dublet, Ruby Gropas, Eléonore Lépinard, Sine Lex, Lasse Lindekilde, Nasar Meer, Frauke Miera, Tariq Modood, Per Mouritsen, Valerie Sala Pala, Patrick Simon, Anna Tryandafillidou, Jason Zaragoza Cristiani and Ricard Zapata-Barrero. Full national reports are available at http://emilie.eliamep.gr/
2. The *Reichs- und Staatsangehörigkeitsgesetz*, implemented in 1913, defines citizenship exclusively upon descent (*ius sanguinis*).
3. Schäuble, Wolfgang: 'Einwanderung und Integration. Muslime in Deutschland', *Frankfurter Allgemeine Zeitung*, 27 September 2006. Available at www.faz.net/s/RubC4DEC11C008142959199A04A6FD8EC44/Doc~E268337CD8D8940F19D87988EB8071591~ATpl~Ecommon~Scontent.html, accessed on 20 November 2010.
4. We use the term 'interculturalism' as it is locally understood, not as it is understood in our taxonomy in Chapter 2, which refers primarily to a political idea developed in Quebec and not to an educational policy.

References

Bousetta, H. (2000), 'Institutional theories of immigrant ethnic mobilisation: Relevance and limitation', *Journal of Ethnic and Migration Research*, 25, pp. 229–45.
Bousetta, H. and D. Jacobs (2006), 'Multiculturalism, citizenship and Islam in problematic encounters in Belgium', in T. Modood, A. Triandafyllidou and R. Zapata-Barrero (eds), *Multiculturalism, Muslims and Citizenship, A European Approach*, London: Routledge, pp. 23–36.
Commission on the Future of Multi-Ethnic Britain (CMEB) (2000), *The Future of Multi-Ethnic Britain*, London: Profile Books.
Dhami, R. S., J. Squires and T. Modood (2006), *Developing Positive Action*

Policies: Learning from the Experiences of Europe and North America, Department for Work and Pensions Research Report no. 406.

Gagnon, A. G. and R. Iacovino (2007), *Federalism, Citizenship and Quebec: Debating Multinationalism*, Toronto: University of Toronto Press.

Gerdes, J. and T. Faist (2006), 'Von ethnischer zu republikanischer Integration. Der Diskurs um die Reform des deutschen Staatsangehörigkeitsrechts', *Berliner Journal für Soziologie*, 16(3), pp. 313–35.

Gogolin, I., U. Neumann and H. J. Roth (2003), *Förderung von Kindern und Jugendlichen mit Migrationshintergrund. Gutachten*, Bonn: Bund-Länder-Kommission für Bildungsplanung und Forschungsförderung. Available at www.bmbf.de/pub/studie_foerderung_migration.pdf, accessed on 20 November 2010.

Hartmann, D. and Gerteis, J. (2005), 'Dealing with diversity: Mapping multiculturalism in sociological terms', *Sociological Theory*, 23(2), pp. 218–40.

Jacobs, D. (2004), 'Pacifying national majorities in the Brussels Capital Region: What about the immigrant minority groups?', in E. Lantschner and A. Morawa (eds), *European Yearbook of Minority Issues*, vol. 2 (2002/3), Leiden: Martinus Nijhoff Publishers, pp. 309–29.

Joppke, C. (1999), 'How immigration is changing citizenship: A comparative view', *Ethnic and Racial Studies*, 22(4), pp. 629–52.

Joppke, C. (2004), 'The retreat of multiculturalism in the liberal state: Theory and policy', *British Journal of Sociology*, 55(2), pp. 237–57.

Joppke, C. (2007), 'Beyond national models: Civic integration policies for immigrants in Western Europe', *West European Politics*, 30 1), pp. 1–22.

Koopmans, R., P. Statham, M. Giugni and F. Passy (2005), *Contested Citizenship: Immigration and Cultural Diversity in Europe*, Minneapolis, MN: University of Minnesota Press.

Malik, M. (2008), 'Modernising discrimination law: proposals for a Single Equality Act for Britian', *International Journal of Discrimination and the Law*, 9 (2), pp. 73–94.

Meer, N. (2010), 'The impact of European equality directives on British anti-discrimination legislation', *Policy & Politics*, 38(2), pp. 197–215.

Meer, N. and P. Mouritsen (2009), 'Political cultures compared: The Muhammad cartoons in the Danish and British press', *Ethnicities*, 9(3), pp. 334–60.

Meurs, D., A. Pailhé and P. Simon (2006), 'The persistence of intergenerational inequalities linked to immigration: Labour market outcomes for immigrants and their descendants in France', *Population-E*, 61(5–6), pp. 645–82.

Modood, T. (1997), 'Introduction: The politics of multiculturalism in the new Europe', in T. Modood and P. Werbner (eds), *The Politics of Multiculturalism in the New Europe*, London: Zed Books.

Morelli, A. (1992), *Histoire des étrangers et de l'immigration en Belgique. De la préhistoire à nos jours*, Brussels: Éditions Vie Ouvrière.

Mouritsen, P. (2009), 'The culture of citizenship. A reflection on civic integration in Europe', in R. Zapata-Barrero (ed.), *Citizenship Policies in the Age of Diversity. Europe at the Crossroads*, Barcelona: Cidob, pp. 23–35. Available at www.cidob.org/en/publications/books/monographs/citizenship_policies_in_the_age_of_diversity_europe_at_the_crossroads, accessed on 29 May 2011.

Østergård, U. (1992), 'Peasants and Danes: The Danish national identity and political culture', *Comparative Studies in Society and History*, 34, pp. 3–27.

Parekh, B. (2000), *Rethinking Multiculturalism: Cultural Diversity and Political Theory*, London: Palgrave.

Triandafyllidou, A. and M. Veikou (2002), 'The hierarchy of Greekness. Ethnic and national identity considerations in Greek immigration policy', *Ethnicities*, 2(2), pp. 189–208.

Walzer, M. (1994), *Thick and Thin*, Notre Dame, IN: University of Notre Dame Press.

Zapata-Barrero, R. (2004), *Multiculturalidad e inmigración*, Barcelona: Editorial Síntesis.

Zapata-Barrero, R. (2008), 'Perceptions and realities of Morocco immigration flows and Spanish policies', *Journal of Immigration and Refugee Studies*, 6(3), pp. 382–96.

4

Beyond Post-national Citizenship: Access, Consequence, Conditionality

Per Mouritsen

Introduction

With the political crisis of multiculturalism as a progressive idiom, a shift towards citizenship discourse has taken place in many countries, including those that had previously never appropriated multiculturalism in legal and policy terms (Mouritsen 2008, 2009a). This shift is particularly visible at the entry gate and immediately thereafter, that is, in the fields of asylum and work immigration, residence and naturalisation policy. The 1980s and early 1990s allegedly saw a decreasing salience and material importance of the status of citizenship, for immigrants and receiving countries alike, particularly in the context of a north-western European experience with guest workers (Soysal 1994). This chapter argues that this trend is now the opposite and that broadly similar reasons exist for this throughout the region. In Germany, the UK and Denmark, the countries covered in this chapter, the new importance of citizenship is caused by governmental preoccupation with cohesion, the growth of allegedly illiberal parallel societies and the integration of Muslim immigrants. Since the mid- to late 1990s, each country has been concerned with educational and labour market integration[1] and social unrest in 'ethnic' neighbourhoods (more so in the UK and Denmark than in Germany). Above all there has been a growing perception since 2001 and 9/11 that Muslim communities contain alienated segments, hostile to 'Western' liberal and democratic values.[2]

In each country the emphasis on citizenship combines concern about social cohesion and illiberalism with a critique of cultural pluralism and 'multiculturalism'. The solutions on offer share the broad characteristics of civic integration, that is strategies to shape and mould citizens' outlooks and abilities (Mouritsen 2009a, 2009b; Joppke 2007a, 2007b). Commenting on an emerging EU consensus, Joppke claims that 'distinct national models of dealing with immigrants are giving way to convergent policies of civic integration and anti-discrimination' (Joppke 2007b: 243). The latter element represents an impetus – in most countries driven by EU directives – to realise, protect and police the right to difference in society and the workplace, although, crucially, this protection is in terms of individual rather than positive group rights. The former element of civic integration, also sanctioned by the EU, is about conformity to a civic culture whose elements and realms are steadily expanding. It is a moving force of Europeanisation in the sense that states, as they respond to common European challenges, including some that emanate from the EU system as either legal norms, policy goals or elite policy networks, seek to strengthen national sovereignty in the process. The paradoxical European renationalisation of citizenship, which is now visible, represents attempts to control and monitor what is increasingly seen as a strategic resource of globally competing nation-states, that is the quality of the citizenry.[3]

But how should these ambitions of European nation-states be interpreted? Some authors emphasise a normatively progressive, inclusive potential: the conditioning of good citizenship in integration programmes or naturalisation policy may be exclusive, but unlike forced assimilation it involves the voluntary participation of immigrants (Brubaker 2001). It suggests a liberal contract, which couples rights with duties (Joppke 2008a: 35). The emphasis on universal, liberal-democratic values as the core of a suitable civic allegiance vindicates a Habermas-style constitutional patriotism (cf. Mouritsen 2009b). To Christian Joppke, although de facto restrictive, the new politics of citizenship acquisition and civic integration is still 'embedded within an overall liberal, sometimes even liberalizing framework' (Joppke 2008a: 1). This 'liberalising' impetus assumes a Rousseauian (or Foucauldian) character of enforced mind-control of what Joppke terms 'repressive liberalism'; he states, 'instead of being nationalist . . . the exclusionary impulse is often couched in the language of liberalism, in terms of the notion that the liberal state is for liberal people only' (Joppke 2007c: 45).

In the latter part of this chapter, this diagnosis, with its emphasis on ideological liberalism, is challenged. I argue that emerging migration state governance (Hollifield 2004) takes place at the interface of several sometimes conflicting forces. These forces certainly do include liberal resistance to Islam (conceptualised as a threat to liberal societies) and emphasise the economic necessities of labour force management. But they also include, on the one hand, functionalist ideas about value cohesion and cultural integration of minorities as a key means to maintain or increase the competitive edge of national societies, and, on the other hand, the continuing hold, in some quarters, of more traditional nationalist ideologies of cultural assimilation.

The main concern in this chapter is empirical, as it investigates the new political significance of the status and practice of citizenship, such as the aspects of membership and 'good' citizenship, and of how the second element is being conceptualised as a condition of the former. Civic membership increasingly must be earned and is reserved for those who prove themselves to be worthy and competent. The background for this investigation is based on Yasemin Soysal's often-cited thesis from the early 1990s of post-nationalism and broader claims about an apparent 'banalisation' of citizenship. The second section of this chapter briefly rehearses these ideas. The third section looks at the increasing significance or consequentiality of citizenship, while the fourth examines the development of citizenship acquisition policies. The chapter concludes by examining the conditionality of citizenship, that is the policies and broader discourse governing the normative content of required citizenship virtues, or what it takes for individuals to be integrated to citizenship.

4.1 From post-national to renationalised citizenship

Yasemin Soysal's thesis about post-national membership ran against the grain of a post-war concept of citizenship as the very 'right to have rights' (Warren 1958), this fragile and precious protection against the mere 'abstract nakedness of being human' (Arendt 1951: 299). There are two related ideas inherent in the notion of post-national citizenship. One is that nationality is no longer a precondition for the enjoyment of (important) rights and material membership, and so is seen as less important by individual immigrants. The other is that identification as loyalty may be replaced by a merely functional relationship, and that attempts by states to integrate, let alone assimilate newcomers may be regarded as illegitimate, impossible or, at any rate, unnecessary.

Differently put, post-nationalisation may also be seen as a 'banalisation' of the status of citizenship, that is of its value, seriousness and meaning, from the points of view of states and individuals alike. Viewed thus, 'banalisation' of citizenship may be associated with two further distinct developments. One, visible through the 1980s and 1990s (Weil 2001), was the relatively steady liberalisation of citizenship acquisition, with shifts towards conditional *ius soli*, dual nationality, shorter waiting periods and less administrative discretion. This trend deepens Soysal's post-nationalism not only in the sense that residents within countries arguably enjoy most of the rights and advantages of citizens worth having, but also that they could easily move between the rights-regimes of different countries (easy residence access and family reunifications, for example). States increasingly matched this ease with a recognition that citizenship itself should be more accessible and less tied to ethno-national membership or loyalty.

The other development represents the 'banalisation' of the material content and consequentiality of membership, whether as full citizenship or as permanent residence. According to Soysal it made little difference to the guest workers of the 1980s whether they were residents or full citizens, as both groups by and large enjoyed similar social rights. The point about the increasing similarity of the two statuses may still be made, only nowadays more negatively. With the rolling back of welfare states, there is relatively little to enjoy in the first place in terms of transfers or services. In essence, the post-national ease of access, lack of difference between permanent residence and naturalisation, and lack of *pathos* from states and individuals alike all comes down to the fact that the only remaining prize of 'thin' neo-liberal membership is the right to access national labour markets (Joppke 2009a: 38).

The new citizenship recognition discourse and policy may be seen as a way of denying, resisting or reversing this post-national 'banalisation'. Citizenship as the status of full membership is increasingly recaptured and repoliticised by nation-states. First of all, the consequentiality or material significance and value of citizenship, already underestimated by the post-nationalism thesis, in fact remains considerable and is increasing. This increase is illustrated by states attempting to differentiate more between the value of citizenship and mere residence, and in some countries between permanent and temporary residence, where, as in Denmark, permanent residence is being turned into a kind of 'citizenship right'. The devaluation of social citizenship is much exaggerated in the first place, and attempts are increasingly made to make it an insider's status. As a consequence, several states have considerably tightened access to citizenship and to permanent residence. Where, as in Germany, important liberalisation of a naturalisation regime has taken place, or where access is still relatively liberal, as in the UK, increasingly tough conditions and restrictions have been introduced. Formal liberalisation does not mean relaxing the status of citizenship, as assumed by post-nationalism literature. These conditions increasingly link the politics of integration and the politics of citizenship acquisition, suggesting that citizenship is not trivial after all and that access to it should be restricted. Contrary to the predictions of the post-nationalism thesis, states increasingly wish to maintain that citizenship comes at a price, both in the sense of expected gratitude or allegiance, and in the sense of ambitions to 'make citizens' or posit explicit civic competences and values. Such ambitions lie behind state attempts to govern and steer integration more broadly (and reflect beliefs that steering is possible as well as legitimate) from the perspective of the host country. From the point of view of immigrants the present state-projected ideals of citizenship are likely to be seen as more important than was previously the case. Positively, the new policies may produce a civic cultural status, which is worth affirming and striving for. Negatively, they may be experienced as screening devices to detect the civic unworthy which replaces previous benign neglect or indifference.

4.2 Consequentiality: the new significance of citizenship

It has been argued that the recent revival of citizenship discourse constitutes 'desperate, ultimately futile, rearguard actions against the inevitable lightening of citizenship in the West', both in the sense that the difference between citizenship and legal residence is small, and in the sense that the material and symbolic consequentiality for individuals of either is waning – over and above access to territory. It is certainly the case that the discussion of a blurred distinction between permanent residence ('denizenship') and full citizenship is an insider's controversy, which ignores the fact that a much more formidable barrier separates members of both these groups from the vast majority of individuals in the world who are permanently excluded from ever living within what Joppke calls the 'comfort zone'. From the perspective of those on the outside the green card, not the passport, is the main prize (Joppke 2009a: 39).

Even so, the current repoliticisation of citizenship is more than a symbolic gesture to newcomers or a strategy to pacify hostile electorates. The material and subjective value difference between citizenship and denizenship – permanent residence – in fact remains considerable and may be increasing (Hansen 2009: 12–14). The importance of political citizenship, which was always underestimated by the post-national thesis, increases from a collective group perspective with the length of stay and accumulated stakeholding. Indeed the significance of changes in naturalisation law from a 'minority vote' perspective is considerable in both Germany and Denmark; and the impact of citizenship on British immigrant mobilisation, representation and political influence is well established (Meer and Modood 2009). It seems obvious then that large parties would be far less prone to ignore the interests of migrant groups – or even belittle the contributions of such groups – if votes were at stake. In fact some noises may be heard about curtailing such rights that do exist for permanent residents. For instance, local voting rights for non-EU citizens in Germany have expressly been deemed unconstitutional, the waiting period for such rights in Denmark has recently gone up from three to four years[4] and conservative opinion in the UK wishes to restrict the historical rights of commonwealth citizens to vote in general elections.

Non-citizens cannot hold public sector jobs, particularly in Germany. Should you not have a 'good' European passport, your ease of movement[5] and access to mobility within the EU (read education and labour markets) is diminished. While mobility of non-EU work migrants without citizenship has clearly decreased since Soysal published her book, it is important to note that many entrants are political refugees, who are especially vulnerable as they often lose their original citizenship and passport in the process and are thus rendered stateless.

Arguably, however, security of residence remains the most basic element of citizenship, which even permanent residence does not entirely guarantee. Although European conventions increase protection levels with length of residence and intensity of family ties, states increasingly resort to deportation in the case of graver crimes. This is probably one reason that immigrant and post-migrant group interest in citizenship has grown considerably. Their fear is that poorly integrated and alienated young men who have joined street gangs may end up committing such crimes whereby they could risk expulsion (serious drug offences, trafficking, membership or support of terrorist organisations).[6] The risk of deportation is of course much more immediate for those refugees and others who do not meet the requirements of permanent residence and whose status depends on developments in their country of origin, changes in their personal circumstances (employment, health, marital status) or unpredictable changes in legislation. Even for the ostensibly post-national *Gastarbeiter* (and their descendants without citizenship), citizenship would have secured them the basic right to return. As noted by Hansen, after the immigration halt in the 1970s many guest workers in fact faced this very dilemma. If they went back to Turkey and Morocco, they could not after some years return to Germany or Denmark (Hansen 2009: 14).

Concerning social citizenship, the neo-liberal onslaught on the welfare state has been exaggerated. Good schools, subsidised care for infants and the elderly, and largely free hospitals remain very real attractions for immigrants. So does the transfer aspect of social citizenship (such as unemployment benefits), although it is increasingly circumscribed and tied to work and availability obligations. However, with some significant local exceptions (Howard 2009: 6), on the transfer side of social citizenship the main boundary of rights-access lies between those who are 'permanents' (whether or not they are full citizens) and those who merely have temporary residence status.

Still, several points bear noting concerning the social rights of newcomers. First, there are signs of an emerging two-tier social citizenship system. Systems such as the Danish *Starthelp*, a significantly reduced social benefit for unemployed immigrants who have been in the country for less than seven out of the last eight years, may be the shape of things to come in universalist, Beveridgean welfare states. Many north European politicians fear 'welfare magnet' dynamics and, more seriously, declining social solidarity in the general population (Jurado and Bruzzone 2008).[7] The distinguishing criterion is the period of residence and of assumed productive employment – this is the universal welfare state's version of the labour market-based social insurance contributions on the continental model. Incidentally, in Denmark the residence period/employment criterion also limits access to social rights for those who become naturalised, as well as for Danish nationals returning from outside the EU. In this regard, we may say that social citizenship in order to retain some of its material value is rendered more exclusive – irrespective of nationality. Second, while social citizenship is neither materially thin nor unserious either in the case of services or transfers, one key difference for non-citizens is that these rights are based at the national level. They cannot be enjoyed at leisure just anywhere in the European Union, but remain tied to the country of permanent residence. Third, the enjoyment of such transfers is only, in a very real sense, 'safe' for citizens. One of many new restrictions on citizenship acquisition in most countries, including Denmark, Germany and the UK, is the requirement of employment. Whoever has ambitions to become a citizen must avoid burdening public transfer schemes, or either forfeit or delay the chance to be naturalised.

Of course, the 'danger' of receiving benefits dramatically increases for temporary residents. In Denmark permanent residence, among other things, is conditional on self-support and employment. There is a deeper point here: the argument for post-national membership assumes not only that the difference between permanent residence and citizenship is insignificant (not only in terms of social rights), but also that access to the former is relatively easy – as was indeed the case for the European guest workers and their families. But this, as we shall see in the next section, is increasingly no longer the case in comprehensive welfare states. The value and the exclusivity, in terms of integration requirements and conditions, of permanent residence has rendered it a form of second-class citizenship, which is still much better than no citizenship at all. Permanent residence, in the eyes of immigrants and receiving states alike, is already a highly consequential civic antechamber with its own conditionality and civic requirements, valuable and difficult to obtain. Hence, more important than the 'lightening' of national citizenship (Joppke 2009a), is the renationalised governance also of rights to safe residence and work (not only the right to vote and be mobile). We see the emergence of not one but two types or levels of memberships that are jealously guarded by states.

Arguably one of the most significant elements in the value of citizenship – that is, full, first-class citizenship – remains more immaterial. Where citizenship is increasingly difficult to get and also politically presented as worth having, the social stigma and self-doubt involved in not having it is bound to increase. In Germany *ius sanguinis*, long waits and resistance to dual citizenship previously made not being citizens a quasi-natural default option for most immigrant guest workers. Denmark, while historically slightly more liberal, belongs in the same category. By contrast, in the UK the tradition of commonwealth membership rendered citizenship more or less a non-issue to immigrants. Crudely put, citizenship was either inaccessible (Germany until recently, and Denmark increasingly) or overly accessible (UK). In all three countries, the introduction and public controversy about language requirements, knowledge tests and screening for self-support, clean criminal records and non-radical leanings, now specifies what constitutes 'good' citizenship. This specification of civic worthiness is linked to the formal status and the passport. If only good citizens can become citizens, then non-citizens are almost inevitably regarded as less worthy. This is even more so the case where the requirements of citizenship are made very difficult to meet, as in Denmark and Germany. The exclusivity and political *pathos* makes it valuable to have – or associated with a sense of misrecognition not to have.

The fact that many immigrants do not consistently seek citizenship does not mean it is trivial, but that it remains quite difficult to obtain, that it may involve great costs (such as where dual citizenship is not an option) or that the barriers introduced are frustrating, even alienating, in either a social, a political or a more personal sense. Whatever reasons immigrants may have, eschewing citizenship is a serious normative problem. It produces inequality of life chances, denies a democratic voice to underprivileged groups, blocks long-term full integration and testifies to a continuing deficit of civic belonging, even alienation.

Receiving states for their part increasingly recognise the importance of citizenship, which reflects the competitive success of national welfare state institutions and economies. Citizenship is increasingly regarded as a club to be protected, in environments of fiscal strain and potentially hostile electorates, from abuse and 'thinning' by unproductive and non-contributing, politically alien or culturally inadaptable outsiders. In this view, citizenship must be relatively exclusive, properly signalling incentive structures to steer and mould prospective members.

4.3 Access: selecting and dividing the demos

Until quite recently a consensus was emerging that citizenship acquisition policies in Europe were becoming more open, because of liberal legal norms at the supranational level, pressure from growing immigrant populations and consolidated nationhood (Weil 2001). This general liberal trend towards openness was more important than the remaining differences, stressed by some sociologists, between more republican French-style regimes and the ethno-cultural Germanic model. With the present more restrictive turn, at least in some countries[8] authors have looked at why an apparent elite-driven default tendency towards liberalisation is only furthered in some places (more likely in centre-left regimes where there has been no popular mobilisation and xenophobia parties).

Moreover, there is an issue as to what liberalisation of the access regime means. According to Christian Joppke, governments wish 'to tie citizenship more firmly to shared identities, civic competences, and public order concerns' (Joppke 2008a: 7). This tendency, however, which accounts for the formalisation and toughening of all the new integration requirements, from language and cultural knowledge to clean criminal records and self-support, is treated rather subjectively. Hence, as noted by Joppke, the reason that a comparative citizenship scholar found only trends towards liberalisation and no new restrictions (but certainly 'restrictive continuity') (Howard 2009: 31) is that his 'citizenship policy index' only includes measures linked to *ius soli* legislation, length of residence and dual citizenship. Howard omits new civic integration requirements in all their legal and administrative detail. This omission, however, is defended by Joppke, because 'the restrictive trends occurred within an overall liberal, in some cases even liberalizing framework' (Joppke 2008a: 33). The argument here is that citizenship may be seen as a contract voluntarily entered into, which involves obligations as well as rights. Whereas citizenship acquisition has recently become more tilted towards the 'obligation pole' in the liberal contract, 'the new requirements are all individual-level requirements; they can in principle be met by all individuals irrespective of ascriptive origin traits' (Joppke 2008a: 35).

When looking at the three countries inspected in this chapter, however, although Germany has clearly liberalised access on the legal front, the more immediate observation is that all have given up the 'automatic' character of their access system, whether open-liberal or closed ethno-cultural. Whatever the voluntarism 'principle' the sheer difficulty of the naturalisation requirements – particularly in Denmark – suggests other predicates than 'liberal' – perhaps 'selective' or 'de facto exclusive'. Moreover, inasmuch as the individualist and achievement-orientated nature of integration conditions may be interpreted as a contractual relationship, not all of the content of the obligations – the competences and virtues required – is obviously liberal.

In Germany, the picture is mixed. On the one hand, liberalisation of the dated *ius sanguinis* system, while reflecting the normalisation of a very specific West German predicament after the Second World War, has dramatically increased long-term access to citizenship of 'non-ethnics' and irrevocably cemented a more republican conception of membership. On the other hand, Germany's residence requirements remain strict, and a clash continued through the 1990s between conservatives (the CSU and CDU) and the SPD, FDP and

Greens. An important step was taken in 1990 when immigrants 'as a general rule' could naturalise after fifteen years (second generation after eight); the fee was lowered and dual citizenship was permitted and could not be revoked. Soon thereafter, 1992 saw the introduction of 'the right to naturalisation' and removal of any deadline for applications, which had excluded many first-generation immigrants. Finally, after political stasis and a 'children's citizenship' compromise, a settlement was reached in 1999, following unexpected popular mobilisation by the CDU against the dual citizenship plan of the SPD–Green government. The compromise still did not introduce dual citizenship (although it is becoming a de facto reality through the growing numbers of those exempted from giving up their previous citizenship) but put in place a ten-year-residence regular *ius soli* system (residents must choose at the age of twenty-three), representing a crucial shift in German naturalisation tradition.

However, the 1999 stand-off also demonstrated a deep public conviction that German citizenship – now that it had become open – was special, required loyalty and ought not be given too quickly or easily. The road towards civic integration began as a result, with the introduction of a loyalty oath, language test and raised fees. Since 2005, the *Zuwanderungsgesetz*, while lowering residence to eight years, requires attending a comprehensive language course (300–600 hours) and a general knowledge course (Germany's modern history of overcoming Nazism and national division, constitution, legal system, political institutions, relations to Europe), just for temporary residence – and a passing score in exams for permanent residence. Non-adherence to such formal requirements makes immigrants in principle subject to fines, benefit cuts or even refusal of renewal of permits. Since 2008 a knowledge test for naturalisation has also been operative. At the moment, naturalisation is subject to the ability to support oneself and one's family, an absence of serious convictions, taking a loyalty oath, having an 'adequate' knowledge of German, having a knowledge of '*Rechts- und Gesellschaftsordnung sowie die Lebensverhältnisse in Deutschland*' and – very importantly – no history of suspected activities that are hostile to the Constitution.[9]

Denmark, by contrast, has seen tightening on all fronts. Since taking office in 2001, the Liberal–Conservative minority government has been pressured into increasingly restrictive policies by the Danish People's Party, whose leading politician in the field believes the practice of granting citizenship has been a 'catastrophe and betrayal of Denmark as a nation inhabited by a people' (Krarup 2005). Unlike contemporary Germany, citizenship is granted discretionarily, with applicants' names being placed on a bill to be discussed and voted on in parliament. Naturalisation access and rules have been tightened and become increasingly detailed as an integral part of restrictions at all gates including temporary and permanent residence, and citizenship.

A distinct EU hardliner, Denmark increased (in 2002) the residence requirement from seven to nine years (eight for refugees and stateless people), upheld its resistance to dual citizenship and – through the insistence of the Danish People's Party – made previously automatic (declarational) *ius soli* citizenship access of second-generation descendants dependent on a clean criminal record and the same conditions (including language requirement) which immigrants have to meet. The 2005 'Agreement on Citizenship', which shifted requirements in a more 'civic' (rather than neo-liberal employment/self-support) direction, stepped up the language requirement to a prohibitive 'level 3', which in essence bars most non-Europeans from ever getting citizenship.[10] It removed exemption on grounds of post-traumatic stress disorder diagnoses, and introduced a citizenship test (including questions on 'history' and 'Danish culture', which are much more controversial and difficult than the German ones).[11] Most recently, test questions are no longer published in advance and more correct answers must be given in a shorter period of time, strangely responding to the Danish People's Party's concern that not enough failed the test. Even the language requirement has been further tightened, with a required minimal mark (Adamo 2008), along with conditions of self-support (4½ out of 5 years without social benefits) and waiting periods, or they must forfeit the right of naturalisation in case of criminal convictions. Denmark is also tough on family reunification, with its notorious twenty-four-year rule and stiff requirements of suitable living space for the family and a proof of substantial bank deposits for their support.

The UK, regardless of imposing tighter restrictions, is still less restrictive on citizenship compared to Germany, let alone Denmark. However, the continuing openness of UK citizenship (six years' residence, recently increased from five; conditional *ius soli*; acceptance of dual citizenship; easy access for spouses of citizens) is coupled with an increasingly tough asylum system and Australian-style points-based immigration process. The latter is designed on the one hand to discourage low-skilled migrants and on the other to encourage those who hold permanent residence permits to naturalise.

The Nationality, Immigration and Asylum Act of 2002 introduced a citizenship test (implemented in 2005), whereby applicants should show a 'sufficient' knowledge of one of the three British languages as well as pass a test about life in the UK (which can be retaken). The requirements introduced, including self-support and absence of convictions (as in the German and Danish cases), are not meant to be too difficult. They test a minimum language and practical knowledge facility, very far from their Danish counterpart, and signal the desired direction of integration with the new status of 'probationary citizenship', which may be speeded up if active participation in defined civil society activities is documented.

Whereas the common denominator of all three countries is an increasingly complex battery of requirements, including language proficiency and knowledge tests, there are important differences in the details. Regardless of the fact that about a third of applicants in the UK fail the citizenship test,[12] what comes across is a system that still sees citizenship as the natural status of those who remain in the country on a permanent basis. It is linked to a broader agenda of civic integration incentives, which is also targeted towards those who have resided for a long time in the country and who are urged to become citizens. Germany's move to *ius soli* goes hand in hand with stricter integration requirements and *Verfassungsschutz* screening (Schiffauer 2006: 97–8), signalling profound unease about a too quick extension of membership. Naturalisation numbers have been falling since the reforms; in fact, in 2008 they reached their lowest level since 1990. That level was 16 per cent lower than in 2007, meaning that only one in forty-five eligible foreigners successfully applied for a German passport (Hailbronner 2010: 23). While security screening, difficult tests and language requirements may well account for some of this, new research indicates the significance of the fact that the decision to naturalise is very often taken in families (Street 2010) and not as a 'contractual' choice by individuals. Denmark's severe language test and old-school high cultural knowledge questions on art and history are very much out of sync with the illusion of the liberal incentive-and-contract ideal. The strictness of this apparently ethno-cultural regime has caused a steady decline in naturalisations from 10,037 in 2005 to 6,960 in 2006 and fewer than 4,000 in 2009.

The development in requirements for permanent residence is also noteworthy. In all three countries access to this status now depends on substantial periods of employment, not receiving social benefits, paying social insurance contributions (Germany) and having no criminal record. Germany and Denmark add further requirements, including integration programmes (in Denmark a three-year programme has been in place since 1999), language courses and tests (in Denmark at the quite demanding primary school level '2'), and courses and tests in society, culture and history. The latter was introduced in Denmark as recently as March 2010, where the target group was broadened to include green card immigrants and students. At the other end of the scale, the UK has also required permanent residents to take the citizenship test since 2007. In Denmark a declaration of integration and active citizenship, listing values and virtues, must be signed. Arguably, the place where the 'nation-state strikes back' (Hansen 2009: 14) the most and its impact is most severely felt by immigrants and refugees is at the second gate of permanent residence. Countries increasingly reserve safe and permanent residence, with all its attendant benefits, to those who earn their keep and indicate a capacity for integration. The countries differ, however; the UK makes much less distinction between permanent residence and citizenship, and encourages those who have made it this far to take the next step. Citizenship, despite recent civic integration rhetoric, remains somewhat unimportant. Not so in Germany, whose new 'republican' citizenship is heavily securitised – and certainly not in Denmark. Recent developments in Denmark are illuminating. The Danish March 2010 law, while further tightening residence requirements, also introduced a points system, whereby employment, language learning and test scores, with additional points given for volunteering in schools, local associations and sports clubs, can now earn the applicant permanent residence after only four years instead of the previous seven. Here emerges a two-tier membership construction, where the willing, able and culturally adaptive integrators are allowed quicker access to a nationally bounded 'societal citizenship', but where full citizenship, the right to vote and to move freely across borders, remains the privilege of an even more select inner circle.

To sum up, all three countries have significantly increased the conditionality of both citizenship and permanent residence. The move is one from automatism (of inclusion or exclusion) towards selecting and shaping the requirements of citizenship and permanent residence. If the UK model, with its relatively easy and uncontroversial *Life in the United Kingdom* test, may be seen to signify a liberal contract the much tougher requirements and civic screening attitudes and practices in Denmark and Germany are better described as a 'republican' practice of shaping their citizenry. The additional emphasis in Denmark on complete language fluency, high culture and 'old' history still testifies to the existence of assimilatory ambitions and ethno-nationalism.

4.4 Conditionality: creating virtuous citizens

In each of the three countries citizenship is closely linked to discourses of integration such that European nation-states seek to make citizens not out of regional peasants, but rather out of immigrants. The following section examines the semantics of this civic conditionality in each country, placing it in the slightly broader context of public discourses of good citizenship.[13]

The German development has been described (Faist 2008) as a move towards French-style republicanism, away from the ethno-cultural conception of nationhood dominating the country's previous *ius sanguinis* conception of citizenship. Too much has probably been made of Germany's blood-and-soil history in relation to the old Wilhelminian naturalisation legislation, which was maintained as a functional means to fulfil the constitutional mission of an 'incomplete nation state' to eventually deliver Eastern brethren from communism (Joppke 1999: 201). Even so, the new 1999 law, noted above, represented a landmark symbol that citizenship is not strictly natural; and also – following the Mölln and Solingen fire bombings and growing recognition of the untenable situation of large disenfranchised groups of *Gastarbeiter* and their descendants – that the status of citizenship should be accessible to newcomers. In this sense, Faist (2008) has noted that the main dispute in Germany has not been between die-hard ethno-nationalists and civic integrationalists, but between two concepts of 'republicanism' on a left–right scale of politics, where liberals and social democrats want citizenship to be a positive incentive (and hence relatively easy), while conservatives or statist-communitarians see it as a prize at the end of the road (and hence that it should be demanding).

This dichotomy, important as it is, easily overshadows how the normative content of citizenship has become a highly politicised issue after the cessation of the more automatic descent-based system. Citizenship, whether as an incentive or as a prize, raises the old German question of membership in a new way. The conceptual meaning of citizenship in Germany clearly remains tied to the meaning and delineation of belonging – of answering the question 'who can be German?' This question is still answered with reference to a history of insecure, divided and late statehood, conceptualised as requiring the maintenance of a unified community of culture and language. What is new is that this community and its governing common culture have been self-consciously transformed in a political-liberal direction.

The 'culture' in 'ethno-cultural' lives on in terms of German *Einbürgerung* in several ways, above all in debates over the new citizenship test and the 2005 *Zuwanderungsgesetz*, which coincided with a rerun of the German *Leitkultur* discussion. Whereas the original CDU-driven use of Bassam Tibi's term had taken the notion in the direction of religious-Christian and national meanings, the thrust of the debate and its reflection in public policy was liberal-universalist and European. The common culture that Germany needed, reflecting a tradition of national self-criticism particular to the country's history, at least superficially looked a lot like Habermasian constitutional patriotism. *Leitkultur*, however, unlike Habermas's concept, is typically employed to re-invent rather than criticise and deconstruct the idea of the German nation. Its political context is one of national self-defence against illiberal Islam, rather than – as in Habermas's case – debates over European unity (Mouritsen 2009a). The required civic (leading) culture remains a very German concept in its proponents' emphasis on basic and constitutional values and their insistence that a consensus on values must be a deeply embedded, almost spiritually shared identity that transcends mere adherence to the rules. The notion that such an identity is a fragile accomplishment, delicate to cultivate in a country with Germany's past but of utmost importance to transmit to new citizens who have not gone through the German post-war school of democracy is also a part of the civic culture.

In comparison, Denmark in some ways appears much more like the stereotypical 'German' ethno-cultural model. The strong and exclusionary emphasis on language proficiency is even more conspicuous in Denmark, as are the elements of cultural integration proper, such as the onus on knowledge of ancient Danish history and high culture (Mouritsen and Olsen forthcoming). Each aspect of the Danish case reflects the continuing influence of the Danish People's Party. Although language and culture can be learned, the very point of the integration to citizenship exercise, for this party, is that some immigrants will not, and should not, pass the threshold. Indeed, members of the party, including the prominent priest-turned-politician Søren Krarup, actively resist the notion that 'good behaviour' or the acquisition of a set of competences should earn immigrants a right to citizenship:

> Is Denmark a nation, inhabited by a people, or is Denmark merely an inhabited area characterised by certain rules of conduct? ... The Danish People's Party insists on the former. Therefore we have something called citizenship [indfødsret] and therefore it shall only be granted to those who belong to the Danish people. (Krarup 2005)

This idea of citizenship as a birthright associates it with a deep and comprehensive sharing of culture (including Lutheranism), whose roots grow with the passage of time and imply a strong and ongoing psychological investment of *dansk-sindethed* – affection and partiality towards what is Danish. While this version is particular to the Danish People's Party, the broader idea that citizenship must be seen as a special and emotional commitment is widely shared.

Unlike Germany, Danish nationalism has never been subject to self-critical ambivalence and reconstruction. Conceptions of loyalty and belonging often transcend the parameters of constitutional allegiance and liberal trustworthiness, connoting emotional attachment, *Heimat* and love in a way which has been discredited by Denmark's southern neighbour. Further, the country's version of a *Leitkultur* debate – the so-called '*kulturkamp*' over Danish common values – was rather less self-reflective and more complacent than in Germany. As in other countries (Joppke 2008b), the 'Danish' values projected were civic and liberal in content (with the Danish People's Party a partial exception) – freedom of speech, gender equality and democracy being prominent among them. Yet apart from tendencies to present them as essentialised, unchanging and not-to-be-discussed,[14] the universality and givenness of these values are also often, paradoxically, seen as specifically Danish accomplishments. As such they are associated with particular features of Danish institutions, culture and history – including, by some politicians and commentators, with Lutheran Christianity – which makes them less accessible to recent inhabitants of the country. Above all, the 'thicker' stuff of ethno-culture comes back as connected to an influential form of instrumental liberal nationalism which identifies traditional Danish cultural homogeneity as a precondition of trust, social cohesion and the welfare state (see Mouritsen 2006).

In the UK, the recent emphasis on civic integration conditions for citizenship has been characterised as a 'civic re-balancing' (Meer and Modood 2009). What has been re-balanced is a multiculturalism that, to some observers, had failed to adequately stress national unity and civic engagement, but whose basic elements should still be retained, particularly the British legal tradition of strong anti-discrimination and the public affirmation of diversity. Moreover, the use of 'good' citizenship as an integration concept reflects in the UK more than in Denmark a recognised historical citizenship deficit, and a series of modern attempts to alleviate it, which to some degree preceded concerns about immigrants, and Muslims in particular.[15] The most obvious sign of this was the origin of citizenship concerns in the field of national education (QCA 1998), where it was part of a reaction to reports of civic apathy and political illiteracy among young people in general. Only later did these concerns move into the field of naturalisation (Home Office 2003), following ethnic unrest in predominantly Muslim areas in Oldham, Burnley and Bradford (Cantle 2001).

This 'weak' sense of citizenship (Mouritsen forthcoming) reflects deep historical continuities, including Britain's relative lack of state-centred civic orientation (apart from monarchical allegiance), in terms of either weak national identity (there was always more than one nation) or the absence of a 'republican' democratic equality of a citizens' body (because of British gradualism and indirect/elitist democracy). There was also the relative weakness – compared to continental northern Europe – of state regulative ambition and the concomitant liberal emphasis on leaving individuals and groups alone in civil society and family as well as the relatively weaker material content of (social) citizenship. Compared to both Germany and Denmark the most striking difference relative to the politics of citizenship acquisition is that British musings over the meaning of citizenship, reflecting the legacy of the commonwealth and early monarchical and multinational statehood, have been much less about identity boundaries and culture. They have largely taken for granted who could and should be citizens (Harris 2004: 74) and attached relatively little significance to the *Leitkultur* nexus of citizenship, state and nation. There are neither 'natural' citizens nor a strong sense of the need to create and mould them.[16] Despite increasingly restricted access to British territory, and even given recent tightening, it is still comparatively undemanding – particularly in terms of deep belonging and liberal-democratic credentials so strongly politicised elsewhere – to be naturalised.

The status of citizenship as an incentive, rather than a prize at the end of a long road, contrasts with Denmark's two-tier citizenship.

Whoever meets the requirements for permanent residence – meaning they must be productive, working citizens who contribute to their community, obey the law and master functional English – should not just be allowed to stay but also be positively encouraged to naturalise and become full members of the polity. Compared to Denmark, the labour-market–welfare-state functionality is a straightforward question of 'paying your way'. Official publications such as the 'Life in the United Kingdom' citizenship test booklet (Home Office 2007) illustrate the generally fact-based knowledge about health, work contracts, childcare, education, law and public order, and racial tolerance, equal rights and anti-discrimination that citizens must master. The political-liberal aspect is simply 'to obey and respect the law', 'to treat others with fairness and respect' and 'to treat all races equally' (ibid.: 108). The very concept of citizenship in Britain, since the 2001 Cantle report on the northern disturbances, has been closely tied to community cohesion, denoting a local, moralised practice of being a good neighbour and sustaining a larger sense of (eventually national) community by helping others, volunteering and in doing so bridging groups and communities. In the words of the citizenship booklet, 'in addition to obeying the law, people want to get on well with their neighbours and contribute to the wellbeing of all' (ibid.: 107).

4.5 *The nation-state is moving – but where to?*

Around the new millennium, each of the three countries addressed in this chapter at different times participated in the broader northwestern European trend towards civic integration with structured programmes, explicit conditions and tests, and accompanying politicisation and changes of naturalisation policy. The direction of these changes is not quite the same in all three countries examined. Germany's rules have been liberalised, although at a level that remains fairly restrictive. British citizenship is still more open and less conditional than in each of the other countries. In all three, however, citizenship is increasingly treated as something profound, not only in its value and material content, but also in terms of conditionality of access, incentive structures, and screening procedures. While the value of citizenship – in terms of political rights, mobility, security and status – was underestimated by Soysal and others, the tightening of migration controls has added further substance to it. Although the most important difference remains that between the permanent (whether residents or citizens) and the temporary, the key point is not that citizenship is thereby rendered banal or unimportant, but that there are now – in Germany and Denmark at least – two classes of citizenship, both consequential and sought, and both are attached to tough integration requirements. Such developments must be seen as the attempts by states to jealously guard this important aspect of sovereignty in order to maintain and secure the 'quality' of their citizenry as a central concern of governance. Far from indifferent, states again regard it as necessary, feasible and normatively legitimate to select and mould their new inhabitants.

When Soysal's book came out in the early 1990s, its thesis of the declining importance of national citizenship went against the grain of normative discourses of citizenship. These discourses in turn reflected different debates, which tapped different theoretical dimensions of this multi-faceted concept. During the Thatcher years in Britain, citizenship became a rallying call for long overdue constitutional rights. In Germany Habermas's notion of constitutional patriotism was about reinventing a reflective loyalty to a *Rechtstaat,* in a way that was untainted by nationalism. In the 1980s, citizenship was primarily associated with participation in social movements and civil society mobilisation (particularly in Eastern Europe). Finally, debates about Western European welfare state crises reinvigorated T. H. Marshall's idea of equal social citizenship. Each of these diverse citizenship discourses – about constitutional rights, loyalty, participation and social membership – were conducted 'inwards' and isolated from the new post-national scenario of immigrants and globalisation. They were also 'progressive' ideas, used to criticise and mobilise *against* the state (the trespassing security state, the nationalistic state, the centralised and democratically unaccountable state, and the socially segregating, neo-liberal state respectively).

This chapter demonstrates that as state elites themselves have begun to reinvest citizenship with meaning and pathos, each of these critical citizenship discourses have become utilised to politicise, and to question immigrants', and particularly Muslims', right to membership. What were not long ago seen as fragile accomplishments or even visions of an ideal future, used by social actors to criticise states, are now being complacently presented by these states as 'our way of life', which newcomers must learn to navigate. This is the case whether citizenship means respecting rights, practising a civic-constitutional form of allegiance, fitting into democratic-participatory traditions or conforming to the microculture of egalitarian welfare state citizenship. Equally notable, there is a concomitant shift in each case from emphasis on rights and empowerment to obligations and virtues, and from inclusion to potential exclusion.

But how should we interpret the re-emergence of European nation-states in the field of citizenship? In light of the considerations above, one recent interpretation by Francis Fukuyama appears to be somewhat off the mark. Fukuyama has argued that problems with Muslim integration in Europe, particularly in terms of the alienation of young Muslims who have lost touch with their parents' national cultures and customs, is due to the absence of American-style citizenship. This refers to incorporation that includes a civic culture of patriotic allegiance, based on an espousal of fundamental liberal democratic values, the rites of passage associated with citizenship acquisition and naturalisation ceremonies, and the chance to redeem one's dignity through contributions to the community, including productive work and voluntary association. Problems of Muslim incorporation are not inherent in Islamic religion, but they arise from the manner in which host societies meet their newcomers, particularly those of the second generation (Fukuyama 2006: 9–14).

Europe, he argues, fails to meet its immigrants as America does. In Europe, 'old national identities continue to hang around like unwanted ghosts'. These national identities, 'compared to those in the Americas, remain far more blood-and-soil based, accessible only to those ethnic groups who initially populated the country' (ibid.: 14). This analysis, however, has struck one European observer as 'an obvious non-starter'. In a recent book, Christian Joppke, whose work has already been cited extensively, rhetorically asks, 'Where is the blood. Where is the soil?' (Joppke 2009b: 107). He again insists that the problem with integration of Muslim immigrants lies not in European nationalism, but inherently in European Islam (ibid.: 111), and that this is reflected in the increasingly liberal citizenship integration regimes of northern European countries.

The question of what in fact causes the alienation and radicalisation of Muslim youth is well beyond the scope of this chapter. However, the preceding analysis suggests that the truth about European responses to Muslim immigration, at least in terms of citizenship acquisition and integration policy, lies somewhere in between the two authors' claims, as well as beyond both. On the one hand, these European countries are well on their way, from different starting points, towards discourses and legal and political practices of political and citizenship-orientated integration. These discourses and practices drink from the same theoretical wells as Fukuyama's

American tradition of civic religion. In the words of J. W. Müller, a German academic working in the US, Europe may be converging on constitutional patriotism whereby 'social strategies to civic integration and immigration ... are oriented towards liberal-democratic norms and their affirmation by citizens and aspiring citizens' (Müller 2007: 379). Moreover, these strategies are clearly a response – although much more critical in Germany and Denmark than in the UK – to multiculturalism as an ideal or a reality of culturally isolated parallel societies. They are indeed integration strategies and even, in an American sense of this contested word, assimilation strategies.

However, the assumption of scholars such as Müller and Joppke that European states are converging on political liberalism as a symbolic boundary marker and yardstick of integration is itself problematic, for several reasons. First, many different versions of the liberal citizen exist, ranging from the spiritual *pathos* of constitutional allegiance in Germany to the institutionally culturalised, one-size-fits-all welfare state autonomy of Denmark, to Britain's residual respect for law. What meets newcomers is not clear 'liberal principles' but historically institutionalised national liberal cultures, which come in quite different shapes. Second, the pendulum, in Christian Joppke's terms, noted in the introduction to this chapter, is no doubt swinging away from the soft liberalism of diversity tolerance and equal treatment towards the more austere liberalism of creating autonomous people. The very semantics of liberalism, however, may be queried. Joppke himself recognises that some of the latter is a paradoxically 'repressive liberalism'. The requirement that conformity to liberal values must go beyond practice and rule adherence to constitute a form of inner spiritual conversion, and that such *Gesinnung* must be monitored by the state, may well be seen as anti-liberal. It is also arguable, at least in the Danish case, that integration measures aimed to create 'liberal people' overstep conventional boundaries of privacy and so drastically limit the field of socially legitimate lifestyle choices – for example, in the field of religious and traditional cultural practices – that we hardly speak of liberal autonomy at all. More broadly, the very interpretation of European responses to problems of integration as an ostensibly liberal backlash and reasonable self-defence may be criticised. The construction of Muslim minorities in particular (in contrast to many 'mainstream' youth and urban subcultures) as inherently unliberal often reflects a culturally biased interpretation of specific practices as signs of heteronomy, inequality, radicalism or dangerous separatism.

On the other hand, the same countries are clearly also concerned with national identity, again in rather different ways, with the UK as the much more benign case of the three. Although Fukuyama's 'blood and soil' is increasingly an idea of the past, Denmark belongs to a diminishing class of Western states – along with countries such as Austria and Switzerland – where a combination of xenophobic parties' electoral influence and unreconstructed histories of national identity continues to shape citizenship and integration policies. Here, high culture (often types of knowledge no longer shared by old nationals nor taught in schools), strong and undivided loyalty or linguistic perfection becomes a condition of full national membership. Besides such die-hard, old-school nationalism, clearly there is another, more modern but not necessarily less exclusionary version, at least at a symbolic and psychological level. In all three countries, although more in Denmark and Britain than in Germany, civic and quite general liberal principles become presented as particular national values, often connected to rosy narratives of national history. The most essentialist and chauvinistic versions of this tendency are again seen in Denmark. The fact that such values are often indistinguishable at the level of political discourse, so that a politician in Britain sounds much like another in Denmark or the Netherlands, is not terribly significant. Modern European nationalism does not depend, as the nationalist doctrines of old (nineteenth-century nationalism was often remarkably similar in semantic and symbolic content), on particularistic representations of self vis-à-vis other nations. It only depends on the representation of self as a liberal nation, vis-à-vis that increasingly common European Other, which is Islam (Mouritsen 2009a).

Both the constitutional patriotism and the new nationalism interpretations represent the policy reaction of states as exclusively identitarian and principle-driven. Politicians certainly instrumentalise both vocabularies to produce ongoing interpretations of national selfhood relative to a Muslim Other 'within' their societies. This instrumentalisation of identity is only a part of the story and partially developed in this chapter. In both varieties they coexist, and at times are subsumed under a more economic-functional set of considerations, within emerging strategies of state governance of migration (Hollifield 2004). These strategies are Europeanised reactions, where state elites face largely similar economic, demographic and electoral challenges in the face of immigration, some level of which is fiscally necessary but extremely politically unpopular. The point is not that cultural identity and conformity to liberal values is becoming obsolete in the face of structural 'necessities'. Each is, however, increasingly articulated as sociological parameters of civic integration, connected to state economic performance and institutional competitiveness.

Citizenship, here, constitutes a vocabulary of state level 'human-relations management', packaged in two versions. One of these corresponds to the fiscal-economic functionalism of labour markets and welfare states, which concerns not just employability and self-support but also the need for increasing productivity and flexibility. These goals are furthered through successful and targeted education, female participation in the workforce and, above all, tax contribution. An increasingly important second version concerns social cohesion (in the UK *community cohesion*; in Germany *Integration*; in Denmark *sammenhængskraft*) which, unlike traditional nationalism, is valued instrumentally as forging a path towards strong societies. Strong societies have active citizens, cultural homogeneity (Denmark), shared European-constitutional values (Germany) or a common civic identification (UK). Such societies, with volunteering, culturally interacting citizens, are more trustful, more flexible and adaptive, and safer and nicer places to live. They have a competitive edge in the global struggle of states to exploit niches, attract investment and foster innovative businesses. This is increasingly the established policy wisdom in ministries and government think tanks, whose effects are visible in the new European politics of citizenship access, consequence and conditionality.

Notes

1. Denmark, in fact, has seen remarkable improvement in both areas over the last decades.
2. This chapter derives from a part of a paper presented at the closing conference (*A European Approach to Multicultural Citizenship. Legal, Political and Educational Challenges*) in Berlin, 24–5 September 2009, of the EMILIE project funded by the European Commission Research DG, 6th Framework Programme (2006–9). It also relates to a smaller comparative project, CiviTurn, Citizenship Integration in North Western Europe, financed by the Aarhus University Social Science Faculty programme on 'Globalisation' and the Sportgoodsfonden Foundation, whose support is hereby acknowledged. The treatment of the British case owes much to the insights of Dr Nasar Meer, EMILIE colleague and collaborator in CiviTurn.
3. As a species of Europeanisation it may also be paradoxical, although

the question of convergence of national models is not at issue here, in the sense that states after all respond to a common challenge differently, 'colouring' their citizenship politics in ways that reflect very old cultural and institutional continuities (Mouritsen forthcoming).
4. This is also the new minimum waiting period for permanent residence.
5. And security of not forfeiting one's residence requirement.
6. Or even on grounds of suspicion by intelligence offices of terrorist activity or affiliation, as was the case with two Tunisian citizens suspected of plotting against the Muhammad cartoon artist Kurt Westergaard in 2008 in Denmark.
7. In the Netherlands, the VVD liberal party recently pledged to introduce legislation barring immigrants from receiving any social transfers for the first ten years of residence in the country. See www.lfpress.com/comment/columnists/rory_leishman/2010/06/18/14442141.html, accessed on 15 May 2011.
8. This trend is by no means universal. While some countries (such as Switzerland, Greece and Italy) have not changed their (quite restrictive) rules, and some who have tightened their rules (Ireland, France, the UK) have done so from a very liberal level, countries like Portugal, Spain, Belgium and – in terms of the retreat from *ius sanguinis* – Germany have liberalised. For comparative analysis and discussion, also on the various measures and political causes of liberalsation and restriction, see Bauböck et al. (2006), Joppke (2008a) and Meer and Modood (this volume).
9. www.bundesregierung.de/Content/DE/Publikation/IB/Anlagen/2008-07-02-wege-zur-einbuergerung,property=publicationFile.pdf, accessed on 15 May 2011.
10. Numbers dropped significantly with the introduction of the language test at level '3'. Rough estimates from a variety of NGOs are that as few as 30 per cent of potential applicants with a non-Western background, refugees chief among them, will ever be able to become citizens.
11. For example, 'About when and by whom Christianity was introduced?'; 'When was the word "Denmark" first used?'; 'What is the text on the Jellinge Rune Stone?'; 'Give names of Danish painters and scientists throughout history', and so on.
12. http://news.bbc.co.uk/2/hi/uk_news/politics/8707152.stm, accessed on 15 May 2011.
13. The section draws upon Mouritsen (forthcoming).
14. 'Freedom of speech can never be made a matter of degree. It cannot be negotiated' (Rasmussen 2006).
15. Muslims are in fact latecomers rather than pioneers of present anxieties over civic participation in Britain, a point explained to me by Nasar Meer.
16. This remains the case, I believe, even given the trend, since 2001, of

British 'nation-building' with the discourse of Britishness and British values. It is a characteristic of this discourse, first, that it continues to emphasise very civic, procedural and liberal values; to tie these to a need for a new national unity and solidarity as well as to local community cohesion (rather than the exclusion of Muslims as an out-group); and to emphasise respect, or even celebration of diversity, as an integral part (Mouritsen forthcoming).

References

Adamo, S. (2008), 'Northern exposure: The new Danish model of citizenship test', *International Journal on Multicultural Societies*, 10(1), pp. 10–28.

Arendt, H. (1951), *The Origins of Totalitarianism*, New York: Harcourt, Brace Jovanovich.

Bauböck, R., E. Ersbøll, C. A. Groenendijk and H. Waldrauch (eds) (2006), *Acquisition and Loss of Nationality. Policies and Trends in 15 European Countries. Vol. 1: Comparative Analyses*, Amsterdam: Amsterdam University Press.

Brubaker, R. (2001), 'The return of assimilation? Changing perspectives on immigration and its sequels in France, Germany, and the United States', *Ethnic and Racial Studies*, 24(4), pp. 531–48.

Cantle, T. (2001), *Community Cohesion: A Report of the Independent Review Team*, London: HMSO.

Faist, T. (2008), 'We are all "republican" now: Changes in, prospects for, and limits of citizenship in Germany', in O. Schmidtke and S. Ozcurumez (eds), *Of States, Rights, and Social Closure: Governing Migration and Citizenship*, Basingstoke: Palgrave Macmillan, pp. 113–34.

Fukuyama, F. (2006), 'Identity, immigration and liberal democracy', *Journal of Democracy*, 17(2), pp. 5–20.

Hailbronner, K. (2010), 'Country report: Germany', EUDO Citizenship Observatory, The Robert Schuman Centre for Advanced Studies, European University Institute, Florence.

Hansen, R. (2009), 'The poverty of postnationalism: Citizenship, immigration, and the new Europe', *Theory and Society*, 38(1), pp. 1–24.

Harris, J. (2004), 'Nationality, rights and virtue: Some approaches to citizenship in Great Britain', in R. Bellamy, D. Castiglione and E. Santoro (eds), *Lineages of European Citizenship*, London: Palgrave, pp. 73–91.

Hollifield, J. F. (2004), 'The emerging migration state', *International Migration Review*, 38(3), pp. 885–912.

Home Office (2003), *The New and the Old: The Report of the 'Life in the United Kingdom' Advisory Group*, London: Home Office Communication Directorate (2nd Crick Report).

Home Office (2007), *Life in the United Kingdom. A Journey to Citizenship*, London: TSO.
Howard, M. M. (2009), *The Politics of Citizenship in Europe*, Cambridge: Cambridge University Press.
Joppke, C. (2007a), 'Beyond national models: Civic integration policies for immigrants in Western Europe', *West European Politics*, 30(1), pp. 1–22.
Joppke, C. (2007b), 'Transformation of immigrant integration: Civic integration and antidiscrimination in the Netherlands, France, and Germany', *World Politics*, 59, pp. 243–73.
Joppke, C. (2007c), 'Tranformation of citizenship: Status, rights, identity', *Citizenship Studies*, 11(1), pp. 37–48.
Joppke, C. (2008a), 'Comparative citizenship: A restrictive turn in Europe?', *Law and Ethics of Human Rights*, 2(1), pp. 1–41.
Joppke, C. (2008b), 'Immigration and the identity of citizenship: The paradox of universalism', *Citizenship Studies*, 12(6), pp. 533–46.
Joppke, C. (2009a), 'The inevitable lightening of citizenship', in R. Zapata-Barrero (ed.), *Citizenship Policies in the Age of Diversity. Europe at the Crossroads*, Barcelona: Cidob, pp. 37–51.
Joppke, C. (2009b), *Veil. Mirror of Identity*, Cambridge: Polity Press.
Jurado, E. and A. Bruzzone (2008), *Rethinking Migration. Work and Welfare in a Mobile Economy*, Policy Network Paper, London: The Policy Network at www.policy-network.net.
Krarup, S. (2005), 'Striden om indfødsret' [Battle over citizenship], *Jyllands-Posten*, 23 November 2005, Debate, p. 4.
Meer, N. and T. Modood (2009), 'The multicultural state we are in: Muslims, "multiculture" and the "civic re-balancing" of British multiculturalism', *Political Studies*, 57(3), pp. 473–97.
Mouritsen, P. (2006), 'The particular universalism of a Nordic civic nation', in T. Modood, A. Triandafyllidou and R. Zapata-Barrero (eds), *Multiculturalism, Muslims and Citizenship: A European Approach*, London: Routledge, pp. 70–93.
Mouritsen, P. (2008), 'Political responses to cultural conflict: Reflections on the ambiguities of the civic turn', in P. Mouritsen and K. E. Jørgensen (eds), *Constituting Communities. Political Solutions to Cultural Conflict*, London: Palgrave, pp. 1–30.
Mouritsen, P. (2009a), 'The culture of citizenship. A reflection on civic integration in Europe', in R. Zapata-Barrero (ed.), *Citizenship Policies in the Age of Diversity. Europe at the Crossroads*, Barcelona: Cidob, pp. 23–35.
Mouritsen, P. (2009b), 'On the liberal plateau: The meaning of the civic integrationist turn', paper presented to the conference 'Belonging, Britishness and Alienation', organised by COMPAS, Bristol University and the Leverhulme Foundation, St Anne's College, Oxford, 18–19 June 2009.

Mouritsen, P. (forthcoming), 'The resilience of citizenship traditions: Civic integration in Germany, Great Britain and Denmark', *Ethnicities*, forthcoming.

Mouritsen, P. and T. V. Olsen (forthcoming), 'Denmark between liberalism and nationalism', *Ethnic and Racial Studies*, forthcoming.

Müller, J. W. (2007), 'Is Europe converging on constitutional patriotism? (And if so, is it justified)', *Critical Review of International Social and Political Philosophy*, 10(3), pp. 377–8.

Qualifications and Curriculum Authority [QCA] (1998), *Education for Citizenship and the Teaching of Democracy in Schools*, Report of the Advisory Group on Citizenship, London: QCA (1st Crick Report).

Rasmussen, A. F. (2006), New Year's speech, 31 January 2005. Available at www.stm.dk/Index/dokumenter.asp?o=2&n=0&d=2467&s=1, accessed on 15 May 2011.

Schiffauer, W. (2006), 'Enemies within the gates: The debate about the citizenship of Muslims in Germany', in T. Modood, R. Zapata-Barrero and A. Triandafyllidou (eds), *Multiculturalism, Muslims and Citizenship*, London: Routledge.

Soysal, Y. N. (1994), *Limits of Citizenship: Migrants and Post-national Membership in Europe*, Chicago, IL: Chicago University Press.

Street, A. (2010), 'Mum, Dad, and the Fatherland', paper presented to the Council of European Studies Annual Meeting, Montreal, 15–17 April, 2010.

Warren, E. (1958), Chief Justice Earl Warren's Supreme Court Dissenting Opinion in *Perez v. Brownell*, 31 March 1958.

Weil, P. (2001), 'Access to citizenship: A comparison of twenty-five nationality laws', in A. Aleinikoff and D. Klusmeyer (eds), *Citizenship Today: Global Perspectives and Practices*, Washington, DC: Carnegie Endowment for International Peace, pp. 17–35.

5

Islamic Difference and the Return of Feminist Universalism

Nilüfer Göle and Julie Billaud

Introduction

The principles of 'equality' and 'difference', two seemingly opposite principles, have been influential in shaping our modern social imaginations. On the one hand, modern nation-states homogenise and unify different ethnicities, cultures and languages, while on the other recognition and representation of differences becomes a test for democratic mediation. How can states strive for equality among citizens without imposing uniformity? How can equality be enhanced without stigmatising the differences among peoples? Can we live together, being equal and yet different (Touraine 1999)? These questions are not only addressed within the philosophical and political realm, but have also been raised by cultural and social movements that have been shaping the social make-up of European societies since the post-1968 period. The counter-cultural movements of the 1970s have brought issues of gender, race and ethnicity to the public realm, elaborated on the theme of difference and created a politics of identity against a politics of homogenisation and assimilation. The motto 'black is beautiful' inspired many social movements, including post-1968 feminism, whose proponents struggled against assimilation with masculine values and 'humanist' universalism. Protagonists of multiculturalism followed these ideas and tried to provide a political framework that recognised and included minority rights, cultural differences and ethnic claims within European democracies. In different ways, both feminism and multiculturalism have addressed a criticism of the politics of assimilation and cultural homogeneity and have changed our 'universalist' conceptions of gender, race and ethnicity. During the last three decades, however, the public controversies that took place around Muslim difference have raised new questions and put to the test established frames of thought. To what extent do multiculturalism and feminism fall short of providing an inclusive scheme and to what extent do they have the potential to make us re-examine religious and cultural differences?

The present-day claims of Muslim actors bring to the fore of the European public agenda issues crystallised around gender, religion and sexuality. Women's covering (veiling) that makes Islamic difference visible especially disturbs and challenges the established norms of European feminism. Secular feminism and some trends of multiculturalism not only resent Muslim difference and fail to include Muslims in their agenda, but also seek confrontation with Islam. Some protagonists of multiculturalism and feminism are confrontational with Islamic mores, which in turn secures them greater visibility and audibility, not to mention popularity amongst the European public. In this struggle with Islam, universalism gains ground against cultural relativism and gives rise to new tensions between feminists and multiculturalists.

Feminists such as Moller Okin (Moller Okin 1998), have criticised liberal mutliculturalist thinkers for essentialising the notion of 'culture' and silencing other identity markers, such as gender, from where competing claims for recognition can be made. In spite of attempts at reconciling liberal feminism with multiculturalism (Phillips 2007; Young 1990), by underlining the multi-layered identities of members of oppressed minority groups, the dispute continues. Secular feminist voices have become prominent in European public discourses, making more complex interpretations of the relationships between gender and religion inaudible. These tensions reached their climax after 9/11, when Europe started to question its pluralist tradition and the benefits of multiculturalism altogether. The terrorist attacks that occurred in London and Spain as well as the financial crisis starting in the late 2000s have reinforced these concerns and have awakened nationalist feelings, with Muslims becoming the centre of political attention. Within these dynamics, feminist discourse has been used as a marker of an irreconcilable difference between 'us' ('native white Europeans') and 'them' (Muslims). In recent years, feminism and sexual liberalism have become discursive fields, on the basis of which Muslims – now identified in public discourses as Europe's 'others' – can be excluded while multiculturalism has lost its impact even in countries where it used to be vibrant.

This chapter seeks to underline the shortcomings of multiculturalism and feminism as models that originally aimed at avoiding the marginalisation of minorities. We highlight the liberal roots of these two political paradigms, even though critiques from within these traditions have also emerged. For defenders of multiculturalism in Europe, immigrants have also been the subject of attention as minority groups. Tariq Modood, for instance, has introduced the notion of 'cultural racism' for describing and transforming the perception of the status of Muslim minorities in the case of the UK. Such attempts, however, have dealt mainly with conditions of immigration and not with religious claims and gender issues. This chapter underlines how both Western multiculturalist and feminist theories have been derailed by the appearance of religious actors whose ways of experiencing the world fall outside traditional liberal categories.

We mostly focus in this chapter on the French case, although multiculturalism has never gained ground there as in the UK or the Netherlands (Wieviorka 2001: 110). The debates on *laïcité* (the 'orthodox' French version of secularism) in the past twenty years, however, have been particularly prominent in France and French feminism has been repeatedly mobilised in debates on the headscarf ban in schools, and more recently in the 'burqa/niqab' debate. If at one point the French case was unique in Europe, nowadays this uniqueness that characterised the French approach to *laïcité* is spreading throughout Europe. The public debates that have emerged on the construction of minarets in Switzerland, the hijab in the Danish parliament, the construction of mosques in Italy and the accommodation of sharia practices in the UK all have this in common: the visibility of difference in public places is more and more perceived and debated as a threat to European identity.

The French universalist republican model has often been opposed to the liberal Anglo-Saxon one. By universalism, we mean a set of ideas and principles about human progress and justice rooted in the Enlightenment and destined to spread around the world. The comparison between French universalism and Anglo-Saxon liberalism has mostly led to sweeping generalisations, depicting the UK and the US as open and inclusive multicultural societies where difference has been celebrated. France, on the other hand, is perceived as an assimilationist, closed-off society in which difference has been considered as a threat to national cohesion. This binary way of describing the two models has fallen short in underlining the limits of liberal reasoning for a true politics of recognition inclusive of Muslims living in Western societies, not only as a religious minority, but also as a cultural one. The difference between French exceptionalism and Anglo-Saxon pluralism is therefore more blurred than it would seem at first sight.

This chapter is an attempt to discuss the reasons for the failure of the feminist movement and the limits of multiculturalism in producing appropriate frameworks for thinking through Islamic difference. One of the reasons that can be advanced are the secular and universalist assumptions that underpin the European traditions of feminism and multiculturalism, especially under their liberal versions. Within the liberal frame of mind, modernity is coupled with secularism and the critiques of modernity can only emerge from within. Islam appears as a relic from the past, deemed to disappear with progress. This teleological version of history describes Islam as an anachronism and denies Muslim actors' capacity to exercise agency and be part of modernity (Göle 2005).

Other multiculturalists have underlined the limitations of such an approach to understand difference (Modood 2007; Parekh 2002; Taylor and Gutmann 1994). They have shown how contemporary liberal philosophies (Kymlicka 1995; Rawls 1999, among others) tend to perceive 'irrationality' in actors whose way of inhabiting the world is not guided by liberal ethics but by moral values inspired by religion. As such this chapter mostly focuses on the liberal and exclusionary tendencies of some trends of multiculturalism. It does not aim to reject multiculturalism as a whole, but rather it seeks to identify some elements of its foundations that have contributed to the erosion of its inclusive potential.

5.1 Feminism revisited in light of Islamic debates

What are the distinctive traits of feminism that can help us to rethink gender, religion and Islam from a woman's perspective? How is it possible to recapitulate the constitutive principles of feminism of the 1970s?

The early French feminists of the 1970s advocated a feminism of difference based on identity. This movement positioned itself against the egalitarian feminism[2] initiated by the suffragettes' movement that had struggled for women to obtain the same rights of citizenship as men by promoting women's access to public life as a necessary condition of emancipation. In contrast, this trend of feminism based on the recognition of women's differences (*féminisme identitaire*) brought forth the consciousness that women would never be like men and would always remain 'under man'. For 'identitarian feminists' who criticised the masculine bias in Freudian theory, 'the woman was not a (hu)Man like another'(Mossuz-Lavau and Kervasdoué

1997). Starting with the motto 'the personal is political', the locus of women's oppression was not the public realm but the personal, the self conception-deprecation of women, and the arenas where taboos were kept secret: sexual harassment, sexuality, abortion. Consciousness-raising groups became a mode of subjective exploration of these forms of stigmatisation that were common to women's experiences but silenced in public. Feminism brought these issues not only to the attention of women but also to the general public through women speaking out about personal experiences and breaking taboos, as in the case of abortion. For the most radical feminists, emancipation required escaping from the gaze of men and, if possible, renouncing heterosexuality. The notion of sorority was central to the struggle against competition among women and to the rediscovery of relations of solidarity. In that respect, the Eastern way of life gained popularity in the feminist imagery; 'hamams' in European cities were invested as privileged places to enjoy women's sociability and bodily care. The spatial segregation of men and women became the most militant expression of feminism. In the meantime, artistic, creative and scientific fields specific to women were rediscovered. For example, Hélène Cixous researched the possibilities of finding a feminine voice in literature (Cixous 1976) and Teresa de Lauretis theorised feminine film production and analysed its semiotics (Lauretis 1984). The universalist category of 'human' was deconstructed to reintroduce two sexes (Fouque 2004), not only in philosophical and psychoanalytical terminology, but also in the grammar of everyday life practices.

Feminist criticism and praxis gave rise to a flourishing literature on sexuality and politics and opened up a new field of study around gender issues. However, theories of feminism remained distant from the subjectivities and real-life experiences of women involved in the movement. A testimony of a French woman who describes in an interview her aspirations in life, her life trajectory and her rising feminist consciousness in the 1970s provides us with an opportunity not only to 'repersonalise' feminist discourse, but also to adopt a retrospective gaze on the meanings of feminism for a given generation of women. The interview became a play entitled *Suzanne, une femme remarquable* [Suzanne, a remarkable woman].[3] The play is based upon the narration of her life story and the feminist experience of becoming a professor of law. It compiles her life experiences and narrations of being an artist, a playwright, a scientist and a law professor. It depicts the position of women in a legal field as well as in an artistic one. While reflecting on the narrative of the law professor, the playwright realised the commonalities between the experiences of a female actor and a female legal expert. The play is a documentary that attempts to find ways of relating feminism in the distinct life trajectories of two different types of women. It describes the difficulties of a woman who struggles to find a path towards freedom and equality. The prevalent symbolic representations of women – tyrannical mothers, monstrous spouses and fatal seductresses – make it difficult for individual women to find their own path of freedom and singularity. They have to break away from the private realm and the symbolic representations of women and conquer a world that is constructed around masculine norms and values. The norms that are reproduced as 'universal' are common for both men and women and yet impose the category of the masculine as 'human', thereby negating the female difference. Even when women manage to exist in a given professional or artistic field, they are not fully recognised. Women's participation in societal life and the public world are marked by this shared experience of an 'absent-presence', meaning that they are present and absent at the same time since they are not acknowledged and recognised in their singularities. Feminists of the 1970s think of their lives as a personal and social experiment. They find themselves to be marginal, but they advocate their status as exemplary, as a 'minority in the making'. They criticise the universalist logic of equality and make demands for parity that, according to the author of the play, acknowledges difference, singularity and experience.

We shall now turn to the current issues of gender, Islam and feminism and try to comprehend contemporary veiled Muslim women's practices from the perspective of 1970s feminism. The idea that feminism is the consciousness-building of women who experience their lives as a 'minority in the making' can be extended to contemporary Muslim women. Veiled Muslim women constitute a minority in the same way as the law professor describes her minority status, a status that nevertheless is asserted and that does not upset her. On the contrary, this consciousness of marginality leads to new life experiences.

Women who wear the Islamic headscarf are trying to make the best of their situation, like 'Suzanne, the remarkable woman'. They follow their life trajectory in spaces where men are present: in schools and universities, in urban settings and in politics. They are a minority in comparison to traditional Muslim women who do not seek to mingle in the public space that traditionally has been (and to a certain extent still is) a 'man's world'. Modern Muslim women are trying to escape from symbolic stereotypes of being docile, segregated and living among themselves, without permission to conquer public life. But they also find themselves in a minority position vis-à-vis the norms produced by secular feminism (Göle 2010), thus consigning them to a double minority position. They are involved in the public sphere – a sphere traditionally restricted to men only – yet they assert themselves as 'Muslim'. They do not resemble their mothers, who conform to religious and traditional norms and whose lives are confined to female-only spaces. Instead these veiled women seek to conquer the world just as feminists did in the 1970s; however, they do not resemble them in their identification with secular norms of emancipation. They are looking for their own singularity.

The Muslim woman is nowadays in the public realm and struggles to become contemporary with secular women. Muslims who are covered become more visible in the public eye yet are negated in their singularity and in their capacity to be active agents in charge of their own lives. They find themselves in a comparable position of 'absent-presence', like that described by secular feminists. The pious Muslim woman becomes publicly present, but her presence disturbs and is negated by both religious orthodoxy and secular feminism, thus her singularity is banned by two gendered powers. The world she seeks to escape is dominated by the norms and power of an Islamic patriarchy and the world she tries to conquer is closed to her by the norms produced by the secular egalitarian feminism that negates difference and the religious experience of singularity.

A secular universalist trend of feminism gains popularity in counter-distinction with Islam. This could appear ironic given that feminism has initiated a criticism and disrupted frames of universalist definitions of gender. Through deconstructing the commonly held idea that difference between the sexes has been mainly due to biology, feminists have highlighted the structural barriers that prevent women from achieving equality with men. They have shown that the abstract individualism used as the basis for citizenship and equality, especially in France, could not grant their active participation in society as autonomous citizens. On the contrary, they have argued that universalism has excluded women from the political arena, preventing their access to positions of authority.

Joan Wallach Scott (2004), among other scholars, has persuasively documented the history of French universalism. She has shown how the idea of social justice that has guided the democratic construction in France since the Revolution is based on the premise that no representative of the nation, as the expression of people's will, could be a spokesperson for corporate interests. 'The ability of any individual to stand for (to represent) the nation came from the fact that political individuals were understood to be abstracted from their social attributes (wealth, family, occupation, profession, religion)' (Scott 2004: 34). This abstract version of citizenship was understood as the only guarantee for achieving justice and equality and for extracting individuals from the oppressive hierarchies put in place by the Ancien Régime. It is interesting to note that while French universalism is often associated with the secularisation process that followed the 1789 Revolution, in fact the concept of universalism is borrowed from Catholicism (from the Greek *Katholikos*, 'universal') (Schor 2001: 36). France's privileged relationship with the Church made it an essential exponent of the universalist creed. The Revolution, instead of initiating a break-up with the old ethos, ironically inscribed itself in the continuum of the 'civilising mission'. Inside its borders, regional differences were gradually suppressed while outside, France started its colonial enterprise, justified by the necessity to spread 'the rights of man'.

So how – if at all – did feminism manage to challenge the oppressive abstraction of universalism and introduce notions of difference? An interesting example is the law on *parité* that was passed by the French parliament in June 2006 and that could have represented, at first sight, a major concession to the traditional anti-minority position. The legitimacy of such a law prescribing an equal number of male and female representatives in local, regional, senatorial and European electoral lists is no longer much discussed; however, its submission to parliament created intense and heated discussions at the time. Across the political spectrum some commentators, politicians, philosophers and intellectuals feared that the law would open a Pandora's box of minority claims. They warned against the dangers of gender essentialism in creating an absolute difference between the sexes, in a way that would lead France towards a 'puritan, pragmatic and individualist American model', in total opposition to the 'French humanist and universalist tradition'.

Examining the highly rhetorical dimension of the debate, Didier Fassin (2002) and Joan Wallach Scott (2005) have demonstrated that far from initiating a move away from universalism, in order to make their claim heard, French feminists had to anchor their plea in the universalist tradition. Gender difference had to be 'universalised', by this we mean that it was presented as a universal difference, one that transcends other social categories of class, race, age and ethnicity, in order to become a valid public claim. This is not to say that supporters of the law on equality made a radical distinction between notions of difference and universalism, rather they used the ambiguity of the republican rhetoric at their disposal to open a space for asserting their claim to difference. By making 'woman' a universal category, supporters of the law sidestepped the fear of communitarianism (understood in France as the desire of a community to live on its own isolated from the rest of society).

The anchoring of French feminism in the Republican tradition, as a political tool to nationalise identity politics against France's transatlantic neighbours, is not new. Such dynamics have occurred on numerous occasions, especially in the debate regarding the ban on religious symbols in schools. Egalitarian feminism imposed itself as 'universal' and thus became a standard through its identification with the majority. The narrative of 'Suzanne, a remarkable woman' criticises the universal logic behind the defence of equality and advocates for politics of parity. However, egalitarian feminism, which has become predominantly secular, homogenising and exclusionary, is imposing its norm on women's emancipation. In time, the debate on parity disappeared, overshadowed by the debates on Islam and women.

It can be said that those who advocate parity could have seen that the situation of Muslim women had all the conditions for a minority in the making. We can therefore point to an intercultural emancipatory potential in feminism that failed to come to fruition. Secular feminists have failed to see the historical possibility of finding common ground with Muslim women. In the search for their own identity, veiled Muslim women experiment and look for their own voice by reconciling Islam and modernity, thus creating new ways of being female in public. The forms of experimentation they initiate are in many ways similar to those of earlier feminists: creating alternative public spaces, playing with their public appearance, testing the limits of the permissible. Is the encounter with Islam the catalyst that propels egalitarian and universalist feminism onto the front stage, relegating the other feminism of the active minority (Islamic feminism) to the margins?

Feminism was the work of a minority of women who in the 1970s in Europe became aware of their subaltern position and started the struggle for equality of the sexes. Since then, it has become an unavoidable paradigm for all women who seek to conquer the world, assert themselves professionally or in public life, or advocate for equality between the sexes without renouncing feminine difference. Even though feminism was the position of a minority, it gradually gained ground in speaking in the name of all women. Feminist thought incorporated all categories of women, regardless of their educational level, class origin or nationality. Today, the ways in which religious, ethnic and racial differences are discussed in the public domain determine the trends of feminist thought, creating ruptures and divisions between Muslim and non-Muslim women. European feminism is being cut apart and transformed by issues linked to a colonial past, immigration and Islam. This union between women that shaped the feminist movement in the 1970s in Europe and the West is currently being torn apart by the emergence of Islamic feminism. The debate on the veil has become a women's dispute between two femininity regimes: one could be qualified as feminist, the other labelled as Islamist, without the possibility of creating a bridge between the two.

Through its confrontational encounter with Islam, feminism gained a new impulse, a new vitality that reshaped the feminist realm. Secular feminism emerged as the public voice of a combative feminism positioning itself against the Islamic headscarf. From then on, the feminist discourse developed through its dissociation from Islam. Yet women are divided between feminist, uncovered and emancipated and Muslim, covered and submissive. Hence, the major initial claim of feminism 'speaking for all women' is lost. Without the support of secular feminism, laws that prohibit religious symbols and ban veiled girls from attending school (while letting Muslim boys attend schools) would not have acquired legitimacy in the public eye. In the French case, secular feminists gave their total support to the republican legislative power. How then should we characterise the role of laws in the making of society? Are they vehicles for translating changes into societal norms? Can laws become a tool for social transformation or conversely do they represent an obstacle to change? We can argue, in light of the constitutive principles of feminism, that the law that bans veiled girls from attending school annihilates the possibility of social experimentation for a minority in the making. It denies veiled women's agency by seeking to impose a hegemonic universalist model appropriated by secular feminists.

The Stasi Law[4] unwittingly resulted in the legitimisation of veiled girls' exclusion from public spaces. In the years that followed the passing of this law, incidents were regularly reported in the press where veiled women and girls were forbidden access to universities (Inizan 2009), swimming pools (Chrisafis 2009), public transport (TVbruits.org 2009) and other public spaces. This denial of public presence reached a climax during the feminist parade of 8 March 2004 in Paris. Mainstream feminist groups relegated all veiled women to the end of the march, with the other 'unwanted' feminists: the sex workers. The banner of the action group *Une école pour tou-t-es*[5] ('A school for everyone'), which rallied against the Stasi Law, read *Très putes, très voilées* ('Very whorish, very veiled'). This is an ironical nod to the state-sponsored organisation *Ni Putes Ni Soumises* ('Neither Whores Nor Doormats')[6] founded in 2003 to tackle the issue of violence against women in working-class neighbourhoods and Parisian *banlieues*. These two figures – prostitutes and veiled women – were unexpectedly unified, marching next to each other as a symbolic reminder of their absolute marginality. During the march, the veiled women received the same sexist insults as their sisters in exclusion. A young woman heckled the activist carrying the '*Une école pour tout-e-s*' banner: 'I love your banner: you're right! All veiled girls are whores' (Bechoua 2004).

These episodes illustrate the tensions that run through contemporary secular feminism. But if France, because of its long republican tradition, remains a particularly explicit example of the current dynamics of exclusion, debates on the hijab and the burqa have also arisen in other European countries. The appearance of veiled candidates in local and legislative elections has divided the feminist movement in Denmark and Belgium, illustrating that once again the visibility of religious difference in public places has created a dichotomist mode of thinking by presenting veiled candidates as Islamists, incapable of incorporating feminist values.

What do these stories tell us about multiculturalism, which since 2000 has represented the legitimising paradigm of the European Union? Have some trends of multiculturalism ignored the issue of Islamic difference? Are divisive and exclusionary identity politics taking over the European ideal of pluralism? Or has Islam simply become a battlefield that highlights the limits and boundaries of multiculturalism itself? After 9/11, many Western countries embarked on a severe critique of multiculturalism, accusing its supporters of irresponsible and naive tolerance towards minorities. The dominant discourse nowadays is that multicultural politics should be replaced by integration policies, namely the establishment of specific criteria and goals for 'minorities' to gain citizenship rights. If these critiques have been broadly used to reinforce nationalist feelings and exclusionary politics, one should nonetheless try to identify the reasons why the dismantling of the multiculturalist project and the singling out of 'Muslims' were so easily achieved.

5.2 *Culture as a battleground*

Over the past decade, debates surrounding potential tensions between multiculturalism and feminism have been particularly intense. The questions raised are related to the potential conflict of interests between the two political projects: if a state were to promote multiculturalism, would women remain unprotected against 'minority patriarchy'? Or if feminism gained primacy, would pluralism disappear? Criticism of multiculturalism was initiated by Moller Okin in her now famous essay 'Is multiculturalism bad for women?' (Moller Okin 1998). Her work instigated an intense debate among European scholars. Political theorist Chandran Kukathas responded to Moller Okin's assertion by turning the question on its head and asking: 'Is feminism bad for multiculturalism?' (Kukathas 2001).

But let us first define multiculturalism and its ideological framework. The term multiculturalism, both as a description of pluralistic reality in modern societies (cultural diversity) and as a project (the political recognition of cultural diversity), is primarily based on liberal notions of equality rooted in the recognition of difference. Theorists and supporters of multiculturalism, notably Canadian philosopher Will Kymlicka (1996), whose writings became a major reference point in this discussion, have defined a notion of 'culture' as an essential component of any individual's inner sense of well-being and self-respect. For Kymlicka, 'freedom is intimately linked with and dependent on culture' (ibid.: 75), because culture is a 'context of choice' (ibid.: 82); it 'provides options' (ibid.: 89), 'determines the boundaries of the imaginable' and 'provides an anchor for [people's] self-identification and the safety of effortless secure belonging' (ibid.: 89). In this approach, culture is a resource that provides people with a sense of belonging and a context for making choices. This is inspired by liberal theory, especially that of American philosopher John Rawls who in *Political Liberalism* (1993) attempted to reconcile equality with difference, whereby multiculturalists advocate for group rights based on individualist choices, a position often labelled in France as communitarianism (*communautarisme*).

If multiculturalism and feminism have in recent debates been presented as in a state of tension, they nevertheless have some similarities and this is where the universalist tendencies of both projects are most noticeable. Liberal multiculturalists (and this is particularly true for political philosophers like Kymlicka, as Cowan (2006) rightly argues) describe culture as something fixed and stable, which can be defined according to certain criteria. For instance, Kymlicka's definition of 'culture' refers specifically to the ways of life and practices of national minorities. For Kymlicka, 'Culture is that meaningful common life based on shared heritage that defines and establishes boundaries for a group – a group that always already exists, awaiting the state's recognition – and that minority rights and multicultural policies must protect' (Cowan 2008: 12).

Secular feminists' understanding of 'culture', in spite of their disagreement with liberal multiculturalists, retain comparable liberal patterns. While the two parties disagree with what culture means to real people in real life (for example, Okin suggests that 'culture' is a prison while Kymlicka conceives it as enabling individuals to have the choice either to embrace it or to leave it) there is a tendency in these discourses to reify 'culture' as something that can be fully grasped. Both positions assume that cultures exist in essence and that they are not influenced by the specific socio-political contexts in which they are necessarily entangled. In the end, the main response of Kymlicka and other like-minded scholars to feminist critique results in an impasse – that of excluding Islam for its non-liberal approach to individual agency while refusing to acknowledge its cultural and therefore necessarily contradictory dimension.

Indeed, Kymlicka suggests that only liberal cultural groups should be recognised and receive state support while groups imposing restrictions on their individual members, such as that implied by 'patriarchy', should be deprived of that support. In Kymlicka's proposal, as well as in Moller Okin's, the state remains the guarantor of equality, the ultimate decisional institution of delivery of justice. The limit of both proposals is that their primary reliance on the state obstructs the history of oppression and alienation that characterises certain groups (Spinner-Halev 2001), while positioning the state as an impartial, 'a-cultural' political entity. This centrality of the state in mediating relations with minorities is perhaps the main weakness of the multicultural project. Such a top-down approach leaves little room for social experimentation within groups that have endured oppression and for which a certain degree of autonomy is necessary to recapture self-respect and a sense of pride and dignity. As philosopher Jeff Spinner-Halev (2001) rightly argues, the problem of the feminist critique – and, we would add, of the liberal multiculturalists' response to this critique – is that it is grounded in a model of 'secular and liberal citizenship', which is blind to the fact that states have oppressed and still oppress certain groups. Ideals of 'freedom' and 'equality' that represent the cornerstones of liberal thought and of multiculturalism at large cannot be considered as neutral or value-free, for the sole reason that they have served (and continue to serve) imperial projects that have significantly shaped the personal experiences of post-colonial subjects now living in Western societies.

Many Muslims living in Europe carry with them the scars of the post-colonial burden, a sense of political exclusion that can, in some cases, be overcome if, and only if, they assimilate within mainstream society, thereby becoming secular liberal individuals. In this respect, the headscarf ban in France offers an interesting insight into the nature of the secularism the French state is striving to impose. Talal Asad has stated that the pressing argument to defend *laïcité* used by the state implied not only a top-down definition of an external corporeal sign such as the veil but also an interpretation of the psychological (private) motives of the actors under the law's jurisdiction. Asad interprets the banning of the veil as 'an exercise in sovereign power, an attempt to dominate the entirety of public space' (Asad 2005: 3) and to impose an exclusionary version of secularism that in many ways contradicts earlier versions of *laïcité*. Jean Baubérot, a French historian and specialist in *laïcité*, shares a similar point of view and criticises the new turn *laïcité* has taken in the debate on the headscarf in public schools. He was the only member of the Stasi Commission who discussed secularism in France and the conditions under which it could be undermined. Contrary to the dominant view that served as a working hypothesis within the Commission, that 'the veil is a threat to the core values of the Republic' (Bowen 2007: 115), Baubérot tried to relocate the debate within its historical context, showing the multiple interpretations the concept of *laïcité* had undergone through time. He eventually remained the only Commissioner to abstain from voting.

Muslims who express their 'Muslimness' in the European public domain through their clothing, lifestyle or certain demands for rights (halal food, prayer rooms in public administration, Islamic marriage) present an image of 'non-liberal' agency that challenges some of the fundamental values of Western democracies. They are achieving a sense of self-worth by adhering to a certain life discipline that, in addition to its assumed cultural dimension, is part of a broader social movement for self-reform and public recognition. Covered Muslim women, far from being either excluded from or victims of these dynamics, participate through their spatial and corporeal practices in the making of that 'culture' while attempting in sometimes ambivalent ways to preserve a sense of faith and individual agency. These non-liberal forms of cultural experimentation can also be seen as a means of self-empowerment of a 'minority in the making'.

In that sense, the recent debates on the burka/niqab highlight particularly well the limits of liberal multiculturalism and secular feminism. Indeed, niqab-clad women have started to appear in the public domain in Europe and in spite of their extremely limited number, have become the object of intense political attention, dividing both Muslims and non-Muslims alike. The difficulties of naming this all-enveloping robe, interchangeably called 'burka' or 'niqab', or placing it under the umbrella concept of *voile intégral* ('full veil') demonstrates the disruption of meanings that occurs when an object associated with the 'outside' and the 'foreign' appears in a different cultural context. For instance, the word 'burka' appeared in the West after 9/11 when – in an all too well-known contemporary version of 'feminist colonialism' – the liberation of Afghan women was used as an argument to gather support for the invasion of Afghanistan. It was argued that the West, in order to free women from their 'mobile prisons', had the moral duty to launch a military operation in that country. In this moral grammar of war, the 'burka' became the symbol of women's oppression while the war turned into, among other things, a global symbolic instrument for women's emancipation. It is interesting to note that in Afghanistan, the Urdu word *burka* is rarely used, as Afghans prefer to employ the Dari term *chadari* to refer to the full blue veil with a net that covers the eyes. In this region of the world the 'chadari/burka', before being turned into a compulsory religious prescription by the Taliban, was originally a garment used by upper-class women wanting to mark their class distinction by appearing fully covered when venturing outside their homes (Billaud 2009). In the West, the semantic confusion between 'burka' and 'niqab' (the full black veil worn by the women of Saudi Arabia), accentuated by the apparition of hybrid forms of swimwear like the 'burkini',[7] highlights the shifting of meanings that arises when the 'full veil' travels from one cultural area to another (Göle 2005).

While blurring the categories of religion and culture, niqab-wearing women question the liberal norms that regiment interactions between men and women in public. In contrast to the ideal of openness, transparency and availability of women's bodies, they offer to the external gaze closure, darkness and deliberate withdrawal. The confusion becomes even greater when the woman underneath is a native European convert to the Salafi branch of Islam, as is often the case in European countries. In recent debates, both secular feminists and liberal multiculturalists have been caught off guard by this new social phenomenon. Unable to read the intrinsically ambiguous and provocative nature of such a corporeal sign, they proposed a literal reading of this phenomenon based on their own liberal standpoint: the integral veil was necessarily a sign of women's oppression by men. The 'full veil' could only be the patriarchal expression of *mouvements intégristes* (fundamentalist movements).

Both secular feminism and liberal multiculturalism, by suggesting non-contextualised definitions of 'culture', remain deeply rooted in the universalist heritage. Positioning the state as 'a-cultural' and 'a-historical' and therefore an impartial guardian of justice, multiculturalists find themselves entrenched in their old liberal bastion when confronted with the complex phenomenon of the 'full veil' in particular and Islam in general. By failing to acknowledge the inner heterogeneity and the multiplicity of voices that are part of the making of culture, they end up rejecting Islam as a monolith. On the other hand, secular feminists, by placing themselves in the universalist 'ethos' that considers 'religion' and 'culture' as necessarily oppressive to the individual in general and to women in particular, refuse to acknowledge alternative forms of self-assertion that do not follow their own path. By doing so, they may strategically gain some kind of public recognition (parity), but they also lose their initial purpose: speaking for all women regardless of their class, religion and ethnic origin.

In this respect, the emergence of feminist voices of young girls from the migrant suburbs of Paris (*les banlieues*) was an important turning point. The rise of the '*Ni Putes Ni Soumises*' (NPNS) movement in 2003 was an opportunity for '*les filles des quartiers*' (girls from the deprived neighbourhoods) to raise and deal with the issues of sexism and gender violence in their everyday lives. However, the movement was later instrumentalised and appropriated by mainstream politics, propelling the heads of NPNS (Fadela Amara and Mohammed Abdi) into important political positions within the Sarkozy government. This reinforced the stereotypes about the war between the sexes supposedly taking place in *les banlieues*. As sociologist Nacira Guénif-Souilamas argues, instead of proposing pragmatic and self-defined solutions to the multi-layered and complex problems of the suburbs, NPNS has promoted 'statements whereby young Arab men are sexist, violent, anti-Semitic, homophobic and sectarian' (Guénif-Souilamas 2006: 35), all the while showcasing the feminine figures of unveiled and emancipated '*beurettes*' (second-generation girls of North African descent) that fit the republican model as an example of successful integration.

At the centre of these dynamics, we can observe the rise of new spokespersons of universalist secular feminism (a self-proclaimed label) who have achieved a high degree of public recognition by entering into the public debate on Islam. They enter into confrontation not only with protagonists of Islam but also with those they consider to be too tolerant and liberal, namely multiculturalists. In France, the well-known and highly respected philosopher Elisabeth Badinter has been at the forefront of the battle to extend the ban of the headscarf in state schools to the full veil in all public places. In her talk at the Gérin Parliamentary Commission charged with investigating the phenomenon prior to drafting the law, she warned of what she saw as the serious consequences of the appearance of the full veil, which for her indicated 'the disappearance of a common humanity'.[8] Her talk, quoted thirty-seven times in the Commission's final report, was soon to be considered as a major reference for understanding *le voile intégral*. She argued that the full veil was contrary to Western civilisation, which values the 'face' and in which interactions among equal citizens are necessarily 'unveiled'. The visibility of the 'face' was for her the condition sine qua non for the perpetuation of the republican principles of *Liberté, Egalité, Fraternité*. She concluded:

> With this opportunity to be watched without being seen and to look at the other person without their being able to see you, I can perceive a threefold perverted pleasure: the pleasure of one's supremacy over the other person, the pleasure of the exhibitionist and the pleasure of the voyeur . . . I think we are dealing with very sick women'. (Gérin and Raoult 2010: 335)

The feminist relegation of fully covered women to the status of 'insane' and perverted individuals supported the idea that the state had to intervene in order to 'liberate' them from the false consciousness of their distorted psyche. Much like the debate on 'religious signs in public schools', Badinter denied the possibility for women targeted by the law of being active agents capable of choices.

Along the same lines as Badinter, other secular feminists have appeared in French public debates and occupied the public scene. For instance, Caroline Fourrest, who recently gained popularity as a journalist and author in prestigious, left-oriented media, endorses religion-free republicanism, criticises the cultural relativism of the multiculturalists and defends secular feminism against what she perceives as an Islamic 'threat'. Her constant reiteration of stereotypes on Islam, personified in her regular attacks against European Muslim intellectual Tariq Ramadan, who opposed the ban of 'ostentatious religious signs in schools', has allowed her to attract media attention and to be recognised as an 'expert' on Islam and a courageous voice of feminism in the public arena. In spite of her obvious lack of academic rigour, her choice of the 'enemy' and her reiteration of dominant discourses have widened her public horizons and gained her an ever-increasing following.

These discourses were especially welcomed when they were repeated and taken over by voices of Muslim-born, women of Algerian origin. The propulsion of these new public figures in the debate proved, in the eyes of many, the existence of secular Muslims. It also reinforced republican ideals and legitimised state intervention in banning religious signs. In her book *Une femme en colère* ('An Angry Woman'), published in 2009, Wassyla Tamzali accuses 'disabused Europeans' and left-wing intellectuals of 'cultural denial', restricting their universalist ambitions to European countries and failing to support non-Western feminists in their struggle against 'Islamic fundamentalism'.

In line with mainstream public perceptions, now widespread throughout Europe, these new secular feminist figures depict Islam as an intolerant and inherently patriarchal religion trying to gain ground in countries where Muslims live in order to impose their 'archaic' rules. Such voices have gained prominence in public discussions because of their adherence to the discourse of power (republicanism) and their silencing of post-colonial criticism and contextual readings of Islam, which highlight the predicaments of power entangled in Western modernity. It is by means of their polemical confrontation with Islam, their demonisation of a consensual enemy, their adherence to dominant republican discourses and their denial of all kinds of cultural and religious difference that they participate in reframing and perpetuating the political debate. The public recognition they acquire illustrates the reinforcement and the closure of republican secular discourse.

5.3 Sexual liberalism and neo-nationalism

Public resentment of Islamic religious signs and their visibility in European countries is increasingly expressed in defence of Western values and national identities. Consequently, the debate on 'national identity' in France initiated by the Sarkozy-founded Ministry of Immigration and National Identity coincided with the debates for a proposed law against the full veil.[9] The criminalisation of veiled (headscarf and burqa) women and their exclusion from public places is celebrated as a reinforcement of secular feminist norms and republican values of the nation. One can also point to the fact that the political determination to cleanse the public sphere is not limited exclusively to Muslim actors and religious signs. This desire to cleanse has been extended to other groups, namely in the expulsion of clandestine European Roma migrants, and also to sex workers through a new law against 'passive touting'.[10] Such politics indicate a conflation between the assertion of national identity, politics of sexuality and security.

The rise of neo-nationalist politics across Europe is intimately related to Islam. The veiled Muslim woman's body, as the symbolic marker of a specific religion, has become the battlefield upon which categories of 'us' and 'them' can be reinforced. As in earlier colonial encounters, the forced unveiling of women operates not only as a reaffirmation of the norms that distinguish Western women, but also as a reassertion of a 'civilisational project' that promises to emancipate women in spite of themselves.

This movement confirms a transition in European nationalism from discourses of exclusion based on racial grounds towards an identity-based discourse around values, moral universes and lifestyles construed as contrary to European democratic principles. In this framework, liberal notions of sexuality as well as universal notions of gender equality are becoming the benchmarks upon which Muslims' capacity to be incorporated into Europe is being measured.

Judith Butler, in her recent move against what she identifies as 'homo-nationalism', which led her to turn down the Berlin Pride Prize in June 2010,[11] explains that this new form of racism is all the more dangerous in that it constructs conflict over various definitions of 'modernity' and 'progress'. These definitions, according to Butler, are instrumentalised to coerce Muslims and wage cultural assaults against Islam (Butler 2008). Such claims relate to certain ideas regarding sexual freedom, which are presented as unerringly clashing with Islam.

New nationalist actors have emerged everywhere in Europe, instrumentalising LGBT (lesbian, gay, bisexual and transgender) rights and sexual freedom to serve their anti-Islamic agenda. In the Netherlands, Pym Fortuyn, an extreme right-wing and gay politician who was gunned down by a radical environmentalist in 2002, had made the fight against immigrants and Muslims whom he considered as inherently homophobic, the theme of his political campaign. In the same country, Somali refugee and MP Ayaan Hirsi Ali used her personal drama to access the political scene and to wage a cultural war against Islam. At the heart of her argument is the irreconcilable nature of Islam with liberal European societies, because of the abuses it supposedly imprints on women's bodies. Hirsi Ali collaborated with the Islamophobic film director Theo Van Gogh in 2004 to produce a film called *Submission*, which uses the same narrative of women's subjugation within Islam: verses of the Koran on the bare bodies of women in agony, submitting to Allah in spite of their suffering, in a provocative staging of the 'Muslim woman' as a failure of a psycho-cultural development. The appearance of veiled Muslim women on the political scene in Belgium, France and Denmark has provoked moral panic in the media, announcing the end of secularism and flagging the threat of cultural dilution. In all these countries, veiled candidates have had to make an extra effort to convince the public of their allegiance to women's and gay rights, as if their hijab was the symbol of some kind of religious fundamentalism irreconcilable with democracy.

The resulting representations are not only monolithic images of the suppressed Muslim woman and her misogynist oppressor, but also a new form of bio-politics that positions liberal democracies as more 'advanced' and therefore legitimating their definitions of the rules of exclusion and inclusion of minorities. As sociologist Jasbir Puar and philosopher Judith Butler rightly argue, new configurations of sexuality, race, gender, nation, class and ethnicity are realigning in relation to contemporary forces of securitisation and nationalism. In this reconfiguration, sexual freedoms are being instrumentalised to assert Western exceptionalism, to define the preconditions of citizenship and to shape the image of the 'a-historical' 'other' bound to remain untouched by modernity. Even though these critiques have been effective in underlining the sexual dynamics that underpin the re-emergence of nationalist politics in the West, they have tended to privilege the categories of race and ethnicity over that of religion. These analyses have thus been weak at highlighting a new form of political exclusion based on cultural and religious difference – that of 'Islamophobia'. According to sociologist and Islam expert Vincent Geisser (2003), the growing dislike for Muslims and Islam in France cannot be understood without taking into account the bitter colonial history of France in Algeria and in other Muslim countries. This burdensome history that France is reluctant to revisit is kept alive by the million settlers who came to France after the French colonies gained independence and, more recently, by a wider conservative movement that has acquired new force since 9/11.

The post-1968 movements, while proposing new ways of reconciling equality and difference, overlooked the category of religion and cultural difference in which multiple and complex ways of subjectivity and agency can emerge. Both feminism and multiculturalism have fallen short in rethinking non-Western conceptions of modernity and 'civilisational' difference. They have remained mainly Euro-centred and have ended up participating in the establishment of new forms of exclusion based on the very liberal notions that were originally supposed to support diversity. The simultaneous liberal deployment of multiculturalism and feminism and their short-sighted denial of other forms of agency have legitimised politics of exclusion. What is seriously lacking in these concepts is a more subtle understanding of the ways in which individuals who are caught in between post-colonial forces try to make sense of the world and lead meaningful lives. These individuals navigate within a broad range of constraints and opportunities that are the product of often conflicting interactions between secular multiculturalism and feminism. Without the recognition of Islamic difference as a contemporary of European societies, both feminism and secular multiculturalism will remain complacent in perpetuating the supremacy of Western values over those it continues to exclude, in the name of national unity. In order to overcome the continuance of these values and avoid the self-closure of Europe, one needs to acknowledge the critiques addressed by Islamic agencies to the universalist claims of mono-civilisational modernity.

From the perspective of universal secular feminists, contemporary forms of veiling mean a return to the past and a threat to the present. We have argued, however, that another way of approaching feminism, based on the distinctive traits of the 1970s, could have helped to build a bridge instead of creating a schism among the two types of women. To summarise, we have seen how feminist women in the

1970s considered themselves a 'minority' to the extent that they were neither following the ideals of egalitarian feminism nor accepting the masculine norms of public order. They were a minority that forged a new path and experimented with new ways of being a woman and of conquering the world. Veiled Muslim women are also marginal but do not follow the ideals of secular feminism, rather they try to escape patriarchal Islam and seek to invent new ways of being both a Muslim and a modern woman. These women are today's 'minority in the making'. Like the feminists who carried the personal category of gender to the political realm, veiled women manifest religious difference in public and redefine the private–public, secular–sacred distinctions. They find themselves in socially mixed places, in cities, schools and public transport, and yet also claim separation from men, such as in hospitals or in swimming pools. They are experiencing the outside world in experimental ways. European contexts of pluralism and freedom give Muslim women the opportunity to find their own singularity. Feminists have criticised the universal category of 'humankind' because it meant that 'mankind' excluded women and erased their individuality. The appearance of veiled women in Europe questions the norms of liberal emancipation and the Western claim for modernity. Our point is not to establish a similarity between two minority figures of women, secular and religious, but to provide a reading that enhances familiarity and illustrates the parallel logic between two different quests for singularity. Certainly religious faith constrains more than it emancipates; it imposes norms of modesty, self-discipline and control of sexuality. It can, however, also lead to self-reformation and social change, or self-closure and social stagnation. In spite of the complex nature of the exercise, freedom makes room for singularity to be explored, whereas dogma, whether religious or secular, imposes norms and values that maintain uniformity and forbid social experimentation.

Notes

1. For instance, Modood (2007: 8) argues that 'multiculturalism presupposes the matrix of principles that are central to contemporary liberal democracies but multiculturalism is also a challenge to some of these norms, institutions and principles ... Multiculturalism is the child of liberal egalitarianism, but like any child, it is not simply a faithful reproduction of its parents'.
2. The distinction between egalitarian and difference-based feminism is

more accurate than the distinction between 'first-wave' and 'second-wave' feminism, in the French case. Indeed, first- and second-wave feminism mostly refers to developments that took place in the Anglo-Saxon world. What we aim to underline here is a new trend of feminist thought in France that emerged in the late 1960s and advocated for sisterhood, women's consciousness and empowerment through the promotion of a positive image of feminine difference. We have to mention, however, that *The Second Sex*, written by French philosopher Simone de Beauvoir in 1949, remained marginal in the French feminist movement. The book used the argument of the complementary nature of men and women based on biological difference to advocate for equal citizenship rights. See, for instance, the writings of the feminist group Psychology and Politics. Beauvoir's work, on the contrary, was influential to the feminist movements in the US and the UK, where individualist arguments prevailed. The arguments used to interpret difference varied according to the specific social and economic contexts of the countries in which the feminist movement emerged.

3. *Suzanne, une femme remarquable*, a play written by Laurence Fevrier. The text is based on an interview with Francine Demichel conducted in May 2007 by Laurence Fevrier and Brigitte Dujardin. The play was staged at *Le Lucernaire* theatre in Paris from 26 August to 18 October 2009. The script of the play was published by L'Harmattan Publishers in 2009. Nilüfer Göle participated in a discussion on feminism and Islam that was held after the play.

4. The Stasi Commission borrowed its name from Bernard Stasi, an ex-minister who was the president of the Commission. The law passed in 2004 forbids the wearing of all 'ostentatious' religious symbols in public schools. Presented as a measure to protect the French principle of *laïcité*, the law was later remembered as the 'anti-veil law'. Alain Touraine, a sociologist specialising in social movements, Gilles Kepel, a political scientist of Islam, and Patrick Weil, a specialist on immigration laws, were among the members of this Commission and supporters of this law. Each of them found different reasons for its utility and implementation.

5. Christine Delphy (2000) has been one of the very few feminist scholars in France to distance herself from exclusionary feminism and to campaign against the Stasi Law banning headscarves in schools.

6. The organisation has been very much criticised by Muslim organisations for demonising Islam as the main reason for violence against women in deprived neighbourhoods.

7. A burqini (or burkini) swimsuit is a type of women's swimsuit designed by Lebanese- Australian Aheda Zanetti under the company name Ahiida. The suit covers the whole body except the face, hands and feet (enough to preserve Muslim modesty), while remaining light enough to allow the wearer to swim.

8. Talk given by Elisabeth Badinter, 9 September 2009 (Gérin and Raoult 2010: 334).
9. Following the vote in parliament, France's constitutional court approved the law (8 October 2010) that bans the wearing of the Islamic full veil in public.
10. The Law on Internal Security (*Loi sur la Sécurité Intérieure*) was adopted in March 2003. Among other measures taken to tackle delinquency, the law has created a new crime: 'passive touting' (*racolage passif*), which punishes any activity, even in a passive form, that encourages a person to have sex for money. The law targets sex workers and aims to reduce their visibility in public places.
11. In 2010, Judith Butler was awarded the *Zivilcourage* Prize by Berlin Pride, a major network of LGBT activists. Denouncing the marginalisation of people of colour within the movement, she explained that she had to 'distance herself from this complicity with racism, including anti-Muslim racism' and that she could not accept the prize.

References

Asad, T. (2005), 'Reflections on laïcité and the public sphere', *Items and Issues*, 5 (3), pp. 1–5.
Bechoua, D. (2004), 'Et toi, pourquoi tu ne le portes pas le foulard?' *Collectif Les mots sont importants*. Available at http://lmsi.net/spip.php?article228, accessed on 1 May 2011.
Billaud, J. (2009), 'Visible under the veil: Dissimulation, performance and agency in an Islamic public space', *Journal of International Women's Studies*, 11(1), pp. 120–35.
Bowen, J. R. (2007), *Why the French Don't Like Headscarves: Islam, the State, and Public Space*, Princeton, NJ: Princeton University Press.
Butler, J. (2008), 'Sexual politics, torture, and secular time', *British Journal of Sociology*, 59(1), pp. 1–23.
Chrisafis, A., 'French woman threatens legal action over "burkini" ban', *Guardian*, 12 August 2009.
Cixous, H. (1976), 'The laugh of the medusa' (trans. K. Cohen and P. Cohen), *Signs*, 1(4), pp. 875–93.
Cowan, J. K. (2006), 'Culture and rights after *culture and rights*', *American Anthropologist*, 108(1), pp. 9–24.
Delphy, C. (1995), 'The invention of French feminism: An essential move', *Yale French Studies*, 87, pp. 166–97.
Fassin, E. (2002), 'La parité sans théorie : retour sur un débat', *Politix*, 15 (60), pp. 19–32.
Fouque, A. (2004), *Il y a deux sexes: essais de féminologie*, Paris: Gallimard.
Geisser, V. (2003), *La nouvelle islamophobie*, Paris: La Découverte.
Gérin, A. and E. Raoult (2010), *Rapport de la mission d'information sur*

la pratique du port du voile intégral sur le territoire national, Paris: Assemblée Nationale.

Göle, N. (2005), *Interpénétrations: L'Islam et l'Europe*, Paris: Galaade Éditions.

Göle, N. (2010), 'The civilizational, spatial and sexual powers of the secular', in M. Warner, J. Vanatwerper and C. Calhoun (eds), *Varieties of Secularism in a Secular Age*, Cambridge, MA: Harvard University Press, pp. 243–64.

Guénif-Souilamas, N. (2006), 'The other French exception: Virtuous racism and the war of the sexes in postcolonial France', *French Politics, Culture and Society*, 24(3), pp. 23–41.

Inizan, M. (2009), 'Une doctorante licenciée pour port du voile islamique', *Rue89*, 17 April 2009. Available at www.rue89.com/2009/04/17/une-doctorante-licenciee-pour-port-du-voile-islamique, accessed on 1 May 2011.

Kukathas, C. (2001), 'Is feminism bad for multiculturalism?', *Public Affairs Quarterly*, 15(2), pp. 83–98.

Kymlicka, W. (1996), *Multicultural Citizenship: A Liberal Theory of Minority Rights*, Oxford: Oxford University Press.

Lauretis, T. D. (1984), *Alice Doesn't: Feminism, Semiotics, Cinema*, Bloomington, IN: Indiana University Press.

Modood, T. (2007), *Multiculturalism: A Civic Idea*, Cambridge: Polity Press.

Moller Okin, S. (1998), 'Feminism and multiculturalism: Some tensions', *Ethics*, 108(4), pp. 661–84.

Mossuz-Lavau, J. and A. de Kervasdoué (1997), *Les femmes ne sont pas des hommes comme les autres*, Paris: Éditions Odile Jacob.

Parekh, B. C. (2002), *Rethinking Multiculturalism: Cultural Diversity and Political Theory*, Cambridge, MA: Harvard University Press.

Phillips, A. (2007), *Multiculturalism without Culture*, Princeton, NJ: Princeton University Press.

Rawls, J. (1993), *Political Liberalism*, New York: Columbia University Press.

Rawls, J. (1999), *A Theory of Justice*, Cambridge, MA: Harvard University Press.

Schor, N. (2001), 'The crisis of French universalism', *Yale French Studies*, 100, pp. 43–64.

Scott, J. W. (2004), 'French universalism in the nineties', *Differences*, 15 (2), pp. 32–53.

Scott, J. W. (2005), *Parité!: Sexual Equality and the Crisis of French Universalism*, Chicago, IL: University of Chicago Press.

Spinner-Halev, J. (2001), 'Feminism, multiculturalism, oppression, and the state', *Ethics*, 112(1), pp. 84–113.

Taylor, C. and A. Gutmann (eds) (1994), *Multiculturalism: Examining*

the Politics of Recognition, Princeton, NJ: Princeton University Press.
Touraine, A. (1997), *Pourrons-nous vivre ensemble?: égaux et différents*, Paris: Éditions Fayard.
TVbruits.org (2009), 'Quand Tisséo se dévoile', TVbruits.org. Available at http://tvbruits.org/spip.php?article115, accessed on 1 May 2011.
Wieviorka, M. (2001), *La différence*, Paris: Balland.
Young, I. M. (1990), *Justice and the Politics of Difference*, Princeton, NJ: Princeton University Press.

Part II

Cultural Diversity and Policy Responses in the European Union

6

Religious Diversity and Education: Intercultural and Multicultural Concepts and Policies

Ruby Gropas and Anna Triandafyllidou

Introduction

Education is an instrument of social integration and a means through which to construct identity. Access to information and knowledge influences access to employment, socio-economic integration and development. At the same time, education is also a tool through which identity, perceptions and understandings, real or imagined, are developed. The ways in which the dominant cultural majority in any given society frames the educational system and the values that it propagates through schooling (methods of teaching, curricula, and so on) expresses and determines perceptions of its own identity and understandings of the 'other'. Just as it can be inclusive, and a vehicle through which to promote principles of social cohesion, solidarity and equality, it can equally propagate prejudice, stereotypes, perceptions of cultural confrontation, superiority or discrimination. The challenge for plural societies rests in meeting their citizens' expectations for educational policies that are able to respond to the needs of the entire student population, in other words, educational policies that are culturally sensitive and that enhance education, socialisation and personal development opportunities for students of all communities.

During the post-World War II period, and increasingly so during the last two decades, immigration has significantly and irreversibly altered the social, cultural, economic, ethnic, racial and religious characteristics of European societies. Multiculturalism as a description of the diversity in population groups is already a reality across most, if not all, EU societies today. Policy responses to this diversity have, however, lagged behind; although as discussed in Chapter 3, there are, of course, significant variations across European national contexts, and, as shown in Chapter 2, different 'integration philosophies' have been adopted by each country.

In spite of these differences, member states face two common overarching questions: first, how to address the challenges that this diversity poses to the educational system; and second, specifically how to formulate policies that promote unity, frequently characterised as social cohesion, while minimising disparities, social exclusion and polarisation. To a large extent, both questions involve rethinking policies and teaching methods that are already in place as well as devising new strategies. Since educational systems do not exist independently of their social and political contexts, this equally involves reconsidering and even redefining conceptions of citizenship, identity and difference, and reflections on ways of integrating these. In this chapter we seek to answer two main research questions: first, whether there is a common European conception of what education for cultural/religious/ethnic/racial diversity consists of – and whether this is best described as multicultural or intercultural education. The second question we examine is whether state-funded faith schooling is compatible with an approach that valorises cultural/ethnic/religious/racial diversity in education within a secular context or whether, by contrast, it leads to (religious- or ethnically based) segregation and thus to the development of 'parallel societies'. The aim of this chapter is not therefore to repeat significant policy and academic debates on the above two questions but to try and shed some new light, using the new findings from the countries studied in a systematic comparative perspective.

In the next section, we first briefly review the methodology adopted in the nine country case studies: Poland and Latvia in Central Eastern Europe, Greece and Spain in southern Europe, Belgium, France, Germany and the UK in Western Europe, and Denmark in Nordic Europe. In section 6.2 we discuss the difference between intercultural and multicultural education; how these are reflected and/or implemented in education policies; and what kinds of representation of difference or ethnic/cultural diversity they carry with them. In section 6.3 we look at how intercultural or multicultural education can lead to the recognition of minority differences with a view to pluralising national identity. A particular issue addressed here is that of faith-based schooling. To what extent is it or can it be perceived to be in conflict with citizenship education or secular/republican principles? In the current context, modern European societies are perceived as secular; however, religious diversity has been growing and religious matters increasingly occupy the public sphere. Among the numerous political and socio-cultural issues raised, some of the important points that need to be examined are: how can anti-racist principles be rendered compatible with faith-based schooling? How can faith-based schooling not become an expression of separatism?

The concluding section seeks to discuss whether there are some common elements in the values and policies adopted by the countries studied that point to a European approach to education for diversity. We also suggest which education policies can help balance the promotion of social cohesion and common, civic values on the one hand, and the pursuit of implicit or explicit assimilationist approaches on the other.

6.1 *Methodology*

This chapter is based on empirical and theoretical research conducted in the nine aforementioned countries with regard to education policies that respond to the challenges of migration-related diversity. Our chapter is in this respect a meta-study of the analysis and findings produced by each national team on the topic. Although this means that our work is not based on primary data, it has the advantage of building on nine case studies that have followed the same methodology and that were conducted simultaneously in each country by local researchers.

Each study began with a review of the relevant literature both in the national language and in English (or often German or French). Each national research team examined the main normative approaches on how education policies should address cultural/ethnic/religious/racial diversity in schools and the policy instruments developed in their country. Thus, each team reviewed policy documents and the scholarly literature but also complemented the empirical research with approximately fifteen interviews with the main stakeholders in the field of education in each country. Each research team conducted interviews with policy makers in the Ministries of Education, teachers and education specialists, school directors and representatives of immigrant associations. Through these interviews, each research team examined whether there were gaps between policies and their implementation, between needs and measures that have been developed and between formal and informal practices. We also sought to identify success cases and innovative approaches.

While the research design and methodology adopted in each country study was common, the research teams focused on different aspects of educational policy in each of the nine EU member states depending on their relevance. Thus, while in all nine countries we examined the school curricula and recent reforms in the direction of multicultural (or intercultural) education and/or anti-racist education, it was only in Denmark, the UK and Belgium that the question of state-funded, faith-based schooling was investigated. Similarly, minority language education was studied only in the Latvian case, while the Polish team concentrated mainly on provisions for children from asylum-seeking families.

We examined value discourses as well as perceptions of national (majority) identity in order to shed some light on what constitutes 'difference' in each country; the perceived value conflicts in integrating immigrants; and whether, where and how these perceptions are shifting or being redefined. This involved exploring how challenges resulting from migration-related diversity have been addressed in the recent past, as well as how the debates are currently being framed. The reasons for looking at both the recent past (the 1990s) and the current decade are twofold. First, in order to offer a wider picture of how minority cultural differences are understood and accommodated; and second, to explore whether there is a view to pluralising and 'broadening' national and/or European identity.

In all countries, special attention was paid to how religious diversity is accommodated in education policy although the relevance of religious difference (and in particular of Muslim needs and identity-related claims) varied significantly in each case. We investigated the question of teaching religion in schools and of faith-based schooling, particularly with regard to the claims of growing Muslim communities. Given the prominent role these claims have been occupying in the public sphere, and the concerns that have been raised regarding the risk of further separatism (rather than inclusion), this dimension is of particular relevance for policy makers and education specialists across EU member states.

6.2 Education challenges and cultural diversity in Europe today

Each EU member state has its own distinct migration experience. Each country's distinctiveness is the result of its migration history; the demographic characteristics and composition of its population of immigrant origin; the migration pathways through which the immigrant population has come into the country; the relationship between the country of residence and the country of origin; the structure of the economy; and the migration policies that have been applied.

These differences, as well as the existence of historical minorities in the various countries (for instance, the extent to which these may be perceived as posing a threat to national cohesion or territorial integrity) have tended to affect perceptions of 'difference' and consequently the approach that has been adopted towards multicultural education. Moreover, in cases where the first waves of immigrants consisted mainly of repatriates, co-ethnic returnees or immigrants who are culturally 'close', assimilationist directions have defined multicultural educational policies and it appears to be rather difficult to shed ingrained attitudes. Nevertheless, in spite of these differences, the nine countries studied face similar questions and common challenges.

The challenge of educating youth in a culturally diverse society has three core dimensions:

1. Education policies must adequately address the educational needs of very different groups of students: those belonging to the majority, new arrivals, immigrant children who have been living in the receiving country for a number of years, second or even third generations and students who are likely to be short-term or temporary residents, or those whose status is uncertain (for instance in the case of asylum seekers).
2. A core aim of education in democratic societies ought to enable students to be prepared to live in a multicultural society, to counter racism and racist attitudes and ensuing inequalities and discrimination, to build on and develop the strengths of cultural and linguistic diversity, and to respond sensitively to the special needs of minority groups.
3. Last but not least, education is the key to labour market participation. Hence, successful education policies must adequately and innovatively prepare all students for today's increasingly globalised and competitive labour markets.

6.2.1 Intercultural vs multicultural education

In order to situate the conceptual debate and the policy measures that have been adopted in the nine countries under study, it is useful to first identify the core issues that have structured the policy and scholarly debate on education for cultural/ethnic/racial diversity elsewhere.

In North America, the debate grew out of the civil rights movement and the efforts to completely enfranchise African-Americans (and gradually other groups). It has concentrated on the politics of individual and community rights, on the role of liberal education, on principles of social justice and on the recognition and subsequent communication of racial, ethnic, religious or national diversity through 'hyphenism'. Recognition and communication of difference in the pedagogical system has been considered as a way through which to facilitate full, free and deliberative interactions that are necessary to an individual's intellectual growth. It has also been seen as necessary for the development of a pluralistic community, through validating the identities of socially disadvantaged groups and providing them with an empowering education (Martínez Alemán and Salkever 2001).

In Australia, multicultural education developed mainly in response to the massive post- World War II immigration, particularly from non-English speaking countries. Australia's multicultural education has been quite distinct from its indigenous education as the unique identity of the Aboriginal people has made this a highly politicised matter both nationally and internationally (Leeman and Reid 2006). In the Australian context, multicultural education involved curriculum reforms promoting anti-racism and social inclusion principles, as well as teaching English as a Second Language and instruction in languages other than English.

In Europe, multicultural and intercultural education has developed as a way to address the educational needs (linguistic and cultural) of ethnic minority groups (historical autochthonous or national minorities in different countries) and/or to better manage ethnic, racial and cultural diversity resulting principally from post-World War II migration trends. In each European country, the migration experience has been different in terms of:

- history, intensity and length;
- previous relations between the sending and receiving countries (that is, previous colonial relationships);
- demographic characteristics (such as majority from a particular country or region or originating from a number of different countries);
- specific characteristics of the receiving society (that is, its state structure and the degree of its decentralisation, its economy, its approach to secularism and religion, the importance accorded to individual rights and community identity, the context of national

identity construction and the conceptualisation of difference, existence of national minorities, and so on) (see also Gropas and Triandafyllidou 2007).

Nevertheless, the broad objectives of multicultural/intercultural education across Europe are rather similar. Stated in very general terms, they aim at improving relations between any given society's different population groups; raising the educational attainment of ethnic minorities and migrants; providing language support where necessary; and providing the younger generation with the necessary foundations for intercultural competence in culturally diverse societies.

To that effect, both the EU and the Council of Europe have developed extensive initiatives and programmes in the field of educational and cultural policy aimed at increasing tolerance for diversity and awareness of the growing unity between European peoples.[1] Moreover, the economic, social justice and equality dimensions of education are also recognised in very similar terms across Europe. Heightened awareness of the importance of power structures in society and racial, ethnic, religious, socio-economic or gender difference on student development have triggered dialogue on pedagogical methods, on curriculum development, on minority schooling and on education research. However, the theoretical approaches to multicultural/intercultural education, curriculum content, teaching methods and classroom structures have developed in rather distinct ways in each national context (Luciak 2006).

In education policy and theory debates on how to accommodate cultural diversity there is a distinction between intercultural and multicultural approaches. Interestingly, in most of the countries studied here, notably in Belgium, France, Greece and Germany, education-related policy and political debates use the term 'intercultural' and it is only in the UK that the term 'multicultural approach' in education has a mainstream usage.

Conceptually it is indeed useful to distinguish between 'intercultural' and 'multicultural' education. Interculturalism and intercultural education are normative concepts. Both concepts prescribe a desired state of affairs and a prescriptive approach to the goals of education. In contrast, multiculturalism and multicultural societies are seen in some of the countries studied here (for instance, Greece or Spain) as mainly descriptive terms and are often confused with the notion of 'multiculturality'. They refer to a state of affairs, notably the coexistence of different cultures and ethnic or national groups within one society, where society is understood as a state. In this view, multiculturalism is neither a philosophy nor a political ideological approach; it is simply a state of affairs.

Intercultural education is defined in most countries as an ideological perspective that combats any form of discrimination within the educational process where discrimination may refer to gender, race, religion, distinction between good and bad pupils and generally anything that creates closed categories within the educational practice. The intercultural approach is predicated on dialogue and actual engagement with other individuals and other cultures. In this context, the role of the school is twofold; it is both an arena of intercultural practice and an educational institution that prepares children to live in a multicultural society. Students of intercultural schools get to know each other's culture and ways of thinking and exchange views and appreciate each other's specificity. They also learn to live in a society based on mutual communication and understanding of the various groups and communities within it. The objective is to support cultural enrichment, increased understanding and tolerance of the 'other', reject racist discrimination and exclusion, and thereby accept society's multicultural composition.

In our view, the main drawback with the mainstream intercultural perspective in education is that it tends to see cultures as closed units that interact 'en bloc'. Thus, pupils and teachers are seen as carriers of a specific culture who learn to interact and be open to one another in the intercultural education setting. In other words, the normative aspect of the approach (interculturalism) is predicated on the ontological aspect (that multiculturalism means a multitude of cultures but not a pluralised society) which neglects the fluidity of social reality. Moreover, this perspective overlooks the fact that immigrant minorities may demand a stake in the definition of the 'national' culture. They may demand the re-definition of the national culture in ways that incorporate their specificity and the diversity of contemporary multicultural societies (see also Modood 1997). This possibility appears to be overlooked in the intercultural education perspective.

However, a more in-depth analysis of the concept of intercultural education shows that it has developed in three distinct approaches (Govaris 2001: 77–8). The first is based on the theory of 'cultural universalism' and seeks to underline the common ground between cultures. The second approach emphasises 'cultural relativism' and underscores the differences between cultures. The third view is based on the 'ethics of justice' and aims at providing the conditions for equal social participation in a multicultural society. The latter view of intercultural education seems to respond to the request for redefining the national self in ways that recognise its diversity. It can thus be argued that it is closer to the idea of multiculturalism in education as this has been developed and propagated in the UK during the last couple of decades.

It is probably the emphasis on the group level of cultural diversity and how this can be accommodated in education and school life that makes the British approach and terminology distinct from that of other countries. In the British education system, cultural diversity was originally addressed in relation to race. As colour was perceived to be the main dividing line and factor of disadvantage for students in the 1970s, education policy essentially developed as anti-racist policy. Education was premised upon the idea that education should confront and challenge prevailing societal attitudes and practices marked by racial dynamics. It was argued that because racial biases will exist amongst all students, teachers and institutional practices, racism is not just a problem that ethnic minorities should have to address. What this ultimately comprised, then, was a political education that highlighted the processes and effects of racism within society, along with other forms of discrimination, and its implications for all students. As concerns with discrimination rose and the term was broadened to include ethnic and religious forms of discrimination, the related rhetoric and policy approach in education evolved also. Thus, the anti-racist approach was pluralised and partly transformed bottom-up, through the initiative of local education authorities and city councils in the UK to become what is called today a multicultural education approach.

The third variety of interculturalism described above has also been defined as 'reflexive intercultural education' (Miera 2007). In this perspective, 'culture'[2] is perceived not as homogeneous but as variously shaped, not static but dynamic and hybrid. It aims at identifying processes where 'culture' is used to legitimise power or inequality. Reflexive intercultural education therefore questions general pedagogy and asks which norms are applied in education and what is considered 'normal' in school. It enables teachers and pupils to reflect on cultural or social disparities from different viewpoints and on individual perceptions and behaviour in a multicultural context.

In the countries studied, especially those with large Muslim populations, two central questions have dominated the public, political and academic debate. The first question raises the issue of how rent values from different cultures can be integrated in education; the second asks how the rights of groups can be balanced with individual rights in education and other arenas of public policy. As such, both are related to the ongoing global debate on the relationship between 'Islam' and 'Western culture'. Indeed, the German (Miera 2007) and British (Meer and Modood 2007) case studies argue that the discourse on schools and Islam is both an indicator of existing problems in the accommodation of cultural/religious diversity and also the result of codifications of other phenomena, like social or gender disparities, and individual or youth conflicts. Thus, education policy in a culturally diverse society has at least two complex, often conflicting tasks: to accept and accommodate cultural/religious diversity on the one hand, and on the other to try to detect the genuine, often multiple reasons behind certain conflicts and to deconstruct the discourse on migrants, especially on Muslims.

A critical overview of the definitions and discourses of intercultural and multicultural education shows that reflexive intercultural and multicultural education approaches are quite close in their basic understandings of culture, of the school and of the need to recognise, value and accommodate diversity both at the individual and the group level. In this light, countries that have experienced immigration since the 1960s and 1970s (for example, France, Germany or Belgium) initially developed an intercultural education approach that was attentive towards factors of socio-economic disadvantage that usually went hand in hand with cultural and religious diversity. For this reason, territorial holistic interventions were favoured as ways of addressing issues of social disadvantage together with questions of school abandonment or poor school performance of migrant children and their families. Emphasis was given in these countries, as well as in Denmark, to the instrumental role of language (for instance, the host country language) in integrating the child in the school and later into the labour market. Any sophisticated educational approaches developed during this period aimed mainly at improving the linguistic skills of children rather than at integrating them in the national culture, and even less so in pluralising the national culture so that migrant children would feel like active stakeholders. It was only later, in the 1980s and 1990s, as socio-economic disadvantage and poor educational performance persisted, that a critical review of these initial intercultural policies was undertaken.

This initial review led to two main developments. First, there is a raised awareness that it does not suffice to recognise and value minority cultures; they need to also be incorporated into the national identity and culture. This *prise de conscience* has taken place in different ways in each country. In Belgium and France, this was reflected in the need to valorise migration and migration history as part of the national history, whereas in the UK, it has been taking place through a progressive pluralisation of national identity so that minority groups and cultures are also reflected in concepts and symbols of 'Britishness'.

The second development is not only related to issues of education policy; it is also connected with the more widespread concern with what is perceived as a retreat of multiculturalism (Modood 2007). More specifically, this involves the turn to civic education and citizenship courses as a means of emphasising the feeling of belonging to the specific country, and also as a means through which to overcome differences in values and tensions between more or less secular views of public life. In Belgium, the debate has concentrated on the need for all pupils to attend philosophy[3] instead of various religion classes. In Britain, citizenship education has been introduced emphatically in the curriculum. In Germany and Denmark, too, there have been renewed efforts towards educating children towards a civic ideal of citizenship that would help rebuild social cohesion and overcome cultural and religious differences (see Miera 2007; Lex and Mouritsen 2007).

It is worth noting that in several of the countries studied (France, Germany and Denmark) there has been a pressing concern for reforming education policy in view of the continuing poor performance of second-generation migrant children in schools. Thus, apart from the emphasis on citizenship education, there has been an increased stress on integration, which has focused more on the socio-economic integration of the second generation initially in schools and later in society and the labour markets.

Although there is a relatively long tradition and experience of different types of intercultural and multicultural education approaches in 'old' receiving countries, 'newer' hosts like Spain and Greece do not seem to have taken advantage either of the related policy and conceptual debates or of the policies developed in other countries. Both Spain and Greece seem to have entered the policy debate by adopting intercultural education views that pay attention only to individual difference and not to group realities. They emphasise the need to learn the receiving country language as an instrument for integration, and completely neglect the need to reconsider and pluralise the national culture and identity in view of the changing composition of the country's population. To an extent, much of this resembles the respective debates that took place in the older migration countries two or three decades ago, even though the current global context is fundamentally different.

It is perhaps too early to speak of cultural diversity challenges in education in Poland as the number of immigrant and refugee children is still very small, while in Latvia the challenge of bilingual education is pressing but also has a heavy legacy from Soviet times (see Gmaj 2007 and Brands Kehris 2007 respectively). Thus, multicultural education concepts in Latvia are predominantly assimilationist in their perspective since, similarly to Spain and Greece, they are seen to be of concern only to minority children and not to the entire school population. In Latvia, the term 'bilingual', rather than 'intercultural' or 'multicultural' education is most commonly used to refer to cultural diversity challenges in education, given that the entire policy and conceptual debate is organised along the fundamental distinction between ethnic Latvian and Russian speakers.

The overall conceptual and policy approach review in the nine countries studied suggests that the dilemma between terms and approaches coined as 'intercultural' or 'multicultural' may be a partly misleading one. Our analysis suggests that the main division between the two approaches is their respective emphasis on the individual (in 'intercultural' education approaches) vs the group level (in 'multicultural' education approaches). However, in both interculturalism or multiculturalism, we find theoretical and policy approaches that are more or less critical and self-reflexive. Thus, intercultural and multicultural concepts and practices that are critical of power and social inequality relations, and that are reflexive in that they call into question both minority and majority cultures and the role of individuals as 'carriers' of these cultures, can be very similar in their understanding of cultural diversity and how it should be integrated into education policy. As such, reflexive intercultural education as defined by Miera (2007) is very close to the principles and practices of multicultural education as these are theorised, as well as put into practice, in multicultural and anti-racist education in Britain (Meer and Modood 2007). After all, the question posed at the theoretical and policy level in Europe is not choosing between intercultural and multicultural education, but rather is understanding how cultural identities are internally differentiated. They are activated in differently ways in different contexts and experienced at different degrees of intensity by each individual, yet at the same time they are largely subject to material and symbolic structures of power which create cultural and group hierarchies (see also Modood 2007).

6.3 Multi-faith societies, secularism and education

All the countries studied here define themselves as secular, liberal, democratic states. Nonetheless, their degrees of secularism are largely debatable as in most cases, the separation between church and state is incomplete. France is perhaps the only exception, with complete institutional separation; however, the symbolic values of the dominant religion, Catholicism, even in France can be felt in public life.

In the case of France, schools are the emblems of secularism (Sala Pala and Simon 2007), while in other countries schools are largely secular but seek to accommodate the religious needs of their pupils with varying degrees of diversity in the curriculum. Thus, in Belgium, children are allowed to follow different types of religion classes in relation to their own faith, including a philosophy class for atheists (Bousetta and Bernes 2007); in Spain pupils may choose a course on the history of religions rather than religion classes (Zapata-Barrero and de Wytte 2007); while in Greece, children can be exempted from religion classes altogether if their parents wish, but there are no provisions for alternative courses (Gropas and Triandafyllidou 2007).

In fact, the varying degrees of accommodating cultural diversity are directly related to the fact that most of the countries studied recognise a specific religion as the dominant state religion, and hence religion classes at school are taught from the perspective of this specific religious tradition. Nonetheless, minority religions in each country, such as different Christian denominations or the Jewish faith, have different forms of publicly aided or semi-private schools that are affordable for parents of these minority religions, even if not completely public (and hence not completely free of fees). It goes beyond the scope of this chapter to discuss the specific statutes of these schools and the specific types of state funding they receive. What is interesting, however, is that the desire of parents and communities to establish Muslim schools, taking advantage of such provisions, has been met with notable resistance from the relevant public authorities.

Thus, the only faith-based schools that are of Muslim orientation and that are state-aided can be found in the UK and Denmark. In Denmark, the idea of 'free schools' was historically born as a protest against the church control of Danish state schools. It was driven by liberal values defending self-determination rather than aimed at protecting cultural diversity. It also established the possibility for a national (and no longer only or primarily Christian) public school to be created. The conditions for state funding of the free schools rest on the principles of a strong separation of opinions or ideologies and academic practice. This in effect means that the state and government in principle are not concerned with ideological positions as long as schools abide by the rules that define academic and administrative standards (Korsgaard 2002).

During the past thirty years, immigrants of Muslim origin have taken advantage of this status to create free schools based on their cultural and religious particularity. The first Islamic free school was established in 1978. To date about twenty free schools have been established, often based on a specific national origin, and less often on Islamic religion in general. Since the creation of Muslim free schools, the liberal right to self-determination on which free schools were based has been under political pressure. One reason is the occasionally low quality and lack of qualified teachers in certain schools – factors that have also caused non-Muslim free schools to come under scrutiny in the past. More recently, however, this picture has been partly reversed by anthropological and quantitative research indicating that pupils of many Muslim free schools perform better than Muslim students in mainstream schools. Reasons cited are a mixture of more traditional, curriculum- and test-oriented forms of teaching (strongly favoured by immigrants who see this as a means to upward mobility for their children) and the absence of the (racialised) cultural prejudice from teachers that exists in mainstream schools. The argument that such pupils may become more isolated from Danish society is a weak one, first, because these students have the default option to attend public schools which are already heavily dominated by non-Danish children, and second, because research has suggested that students in the Muslim schools are in fact more exposed to critical discussion about mutual stereotyping than they would be in mainstream schools. The reasons that have been put forward for this are twofold; first, that these students are more active and less marginalised in the Muslim schools, and second, because a large part of the teaching staff have a Danish background and actively make a point of engaging students in discussions about cultural prejudices and mutual stereotyping (Ihle 2007).

Muslim schools have been under intense scrutiny and are not actually perceived as a welcome development because of the politicisation of Islam and of Muslim migrant integration, as illustrated in the case of Denmark. The principle behind Muslim free schools simply conflicts with the chosen politics of integration, according to which any segregation is problematic and immigrants must integrate into a dominant civic culture and a dominant liberal, secular concept of citizenship. In other words, the difference represented by Islam has been seen as less acceptable than any other religious differences that have previously been accepted as legitimate aspects of Danish society and that were accommodated by the institution of the free schools.

The British debate on faith-based schooling and in particular on the setting up of voluntary aided schools of Muslim orientation has been rather similar to the debates in Denmark regarding student performance. Concerns that the wider socio-economically disadvantageous conditions of the neighbourhoods within which they are located may affect these schools' performance have been raised. In spite of this, however, recent studies appear to be suggesting high performance scores for students of these schools.[4] Moreover, many parents argue that their children cannot receive the appropriate overall education that they wish (that is beyond the standard curriculum) unless they are in a faith-based school. However, the thorny question of gender relations and in particular of gender segregation is a sensitive issue which advocates of faith-based schooling are called on to address. It should be noted, nevertheless, that the demand for single-sex schooling is neither universally sought by Muslims nor only specific to Muslims (Keaton 1999). Thus, dismissing it as simply patriarchal denies the valid pedagogical arguments in support of single-sex schooling. In fact, until a few decades ago, gender-segregated schooling was a dominant practice in most of the EU countries studied in this research. Given the changes that have taken place in the EU, driven by the desire for greater equality, women's emancipation and greater democratisation, the overall question that arises is whether gender segregation is compatible with 'what successful people aspire to in the west' (interview, quoted in Meer and Modood 2007), namely social mobility through education.

Thus, the debate over faith-based schooling is representative of the entire range of issues discussed earlier in relation to the concepts and approaches of intercultural and multicultural education and the individual vs group accommodation of cultural diversity. Faith-based schools are a prime example of the need expressed by Muslims (as well as by other minority religions) in Europe to integrate their cultural and religious traditions into state institutions and national identity and culture. The quest for states to integrate Muslim (or for that matter Evangelical or Seventh Day Adventist) schools into the core system of education means a quest for European societies to reconsider what is considered acceptable and legitimate diversity.

Minority religion schools of the major Christian denominations (Catholic, Orthodox, Protestant) and of the Jewish faith have long existed in all European countries. The current concern with Muslim or other small and new Christian minority schools seems therefore to have less to do with their specific religious traditions and values, and more to do with the fact that they have not been historically present in Europe. Hence, they have not been included in institutional arrangements that were negotiated in the different European countries between states and their dominant churches and faiths.

Faith-based schooling, although not free of contradictions and dilemmas, expresses most strongly and evidently the need to pluralise national traditions and identities by incorporating new minorities that are issued from recent waves of immigration. The question, in other words, is less one of secularism, given that all European countries practice moderate forms of secularism and most recognise religious education as part of school curricula, and more one of 'citizenship' and 'civic values'. To what extent does civic citizenship and currently advocated civic values allow for the multi-faith nature of contemporary European societies to be recognised not only in the private but also in the public domain? How can the desire for civic integration and non-segregation be effectively combined, in practice, with the desire of some parents to provide for an education that is impregnated with specific traditions and religious values?

These dilemmas are very real and certainly cannot be answered or tackled in a manner that is valid for all countries, all religions and all contexts. Rather, what our study aims to show is that the debate about faith-based schools and the type of diversity that can be accommodated in contemporary European societies is more one about citizenship values and legitimate diversity than one of secularism.

Conclusion

This chapter has discussed whether there is a common approach towards education for cultural/religious/ethnic/racial diversity and indeed whether this is best described as multicultural or intercultural education. It has also considered whether state-funded faith schooling is compatible with an approach that valorises cultural/ethnic/

religious/racial diversity in education within a secular context or whether, by contrast, it leads to segregation and even the development of parallel societies.

As regards the common attitude and how best to describe it, we have found that the major gap in the different country approaches is not really related to the pedagogical methodologies adopted or the means and programmes used for educating children of different cultural, ethnic, racial or linguistic backgrounds. The main issue at stake is whether the emphasis is on integrating the individual in full (or partial) respect of their cultural capital and of their special requests or needs, or whether the aim is to integrate the groups (that is, the collective) with their ethnic, cultural, religious or linguistic features. The former approach can more easily be accommodated within today's European societies that are essentially liberal, moderately secular and predominantly Christian. However, it is the latter approach, notably the emphasis on the group level, that can produce the necessary pluralisation of national education systems, and the related national identity constellations so that migrants and ethnic minorities can truly be integrated in the social and political fabric of a country.

As regards the second issue of state-funded faith schooling, our analysis of the different national realities shows that it is widespread across Europe but concerns mainly Christian or, to some extent, Jewish schools. It is seen as part and parcel of the liberal, civic and democratic ethos of European societies which provides individuals with the freedom to chose their own type of schooling. Only in France are schools ostensibly defined as civic and non-religious, thereby leaving no place for state-aided and church-sponsored schools. What our analysis suggests here is that the argument that faith-based schools are not secular 'enough' to be placed in the European democratic, secular and liberal environment is misleading. Rather, the question here is one defined by history: Muslims were not there when concessions to faith-based education were made in the different European countries. Also, the question at hand is not one of secularism but rather of citizenship values. Thus, to the extent that people belonging to different religious traditions, and schools that teach different faiths, abide by a common set of citizenship principles, then faith-based schooling can provide a positive school environment allowing for children to flourish, especially those children who come from minority backgrounds and who may regrettably feel stigmatised in 'mainstream' schools.

Based on the above considerations and analyses, we would like to point out some further directions for research and policy development in the field of education for diversity. On the subject of multicultural education, our empirical research leads us to reaffirm that multicultural education needs to be approached in a holistic manner, cutting across and transcending school curricula, disciplines, material and extra-curricular activities. For instance, critical reflection is required in the way subjects such as history or geography are taught and a greater diversification ought to be considered as regards religious education in terms not only of making it optional, but also of what and how students learn about the main faiths. Equally, greater flexibility in the teaching of the humanities should be encouraged regarding both the content of the courses and experimenting with new methods and approaches.

Interconnected with this and critical for its success is the role of educators. The role of educators and teachers is pivotal in actually applying the core foundations and principles of multicultural education to their everyday teaching. It makes a positive difference when educators are proactive in ensuring that different groups are not disadvantaged by ethnic, racial or religious 'difference', and that they present the positive benefits of diversity in the classroom.

To this effect, teacher training in intercultural/multicultural pedagogy is essential for all educators, as is training in teaching the language of the receiving country as a second language. Other practical measures that are relevant and necessary involve providing ongoing training for educators and teachers so that they can be kept informed of innovative teaching methods and approaches that may be more relevant and applicable to increasingly dynamic and diverse classrooms.

A necessary resource that is relevant to consider tapping into involves the existing human potential in each country's education sector. Providing recognition and incentives for educators and teachers who are interested in teaching in schools with large minority groups or students of immigrant origin, or who have specific expertise in teaching in multicultural classrooms is important. Time and again, personal involvement, drive and commitment (especially when it is rewarded symbolically and formally) are what makes the difference in transposing and applying policies to everyday practices in schools such that they have an impact which leads to results.

As regards the case of newly arrived immigrants, four significant issues have been noted in the course of our empirical research in the nine aforementioned EU countries. Learning the language of the receiving country is a priority for inclusion and participation. Thus, new teaching methods should be developed and applied, and language teaching should be approached as a task across all subjects (to include the natural sciences). In addition, reception and support classes are necessary for the students and for their parents as these facilitate the integration of newly arrived migrants and their adjustment in the host country's institutions and the society's economy and norms. As such, it is important to recognise and accommodate the linguistic diversity that exists within the immigrant population (particularly in the way the language of the receiving country is taught). Moreover, for students of immigrant background, learning the language, culture and history of their country of origin is considered valuable, and has proven to be quite necessary, for the student's social and cultural capital.

Increased employment of bilingual/bicultural teachers and social workers is also a policy option that could constitute a positive contribution, especially in areas with demographic diversity or with a high concentration of minority or migrant population groups. This leads to another practical dimension regarding the size of classrooms and teaching methods. Our research concluded that smaller-sized classrooms with two teachers and a cultural mediator appear to have better results. Whole-day schooling that offers qualified supervision to the students does not only seem to have positive results on immigrant students or students belonging to minority groups, but also has a number of potential side-effects including increased class cohesion and rendering schools attractive for the majority population, thus minimising the 'ghettoisation' of schools.

Given that there seems to be a rather wide gap between the theoretical approach to education for an ethnically diverse student body and how this is in fact implemented in everyday reality in schools, it is necessary to consider various methods of monitoring and evaluating. For instance, it is important to increase the visibility of how each school adheres to its statutory public duty of promoting social cohesion and anti-discrimination principles or good race relations. This includes having a written policy that may be monitored for effectiveness and amended as new challenges arise.

There is no doubt that today's fast-paced, highly diverse and rapidly changing globalised European societies create a very demanding reality to modern-day teachers and educators. Education has an important role to play in confronting and challenging societal attitudes and practices marked by racial and discriminatory dynamics. This is relevant not only as regards the content of the material taught or the curriculum but also practical issues, innovations and concrete actions that schools and teachers can undertake in order to apply anti-discrimination principles. Education continues to be, perhaps more than ever, the most crucial socialisation institution. Thus, principles of equality and opportunity, of societal cohesion, of respect of diversity and of social justice are particularly relevant in Europe's education policies.

Schools should continue to prioritise the need to reach out more to the parents and engage them in their children's education and in the school in general. This requires increased support and resources, including offering language courses, translation services, and so on. At the same time, schools ought to be encouraged and supported in proactively seeking communication and interaction with local communities and associations in their neighbourhood (this of course should also include migrant associations, or organisations formed on the basis of ethnic or religious affiliation). Where relevant, positive action for schools in underprivileged neighbourhoods through increased infrastructural and financial support should be encouraged as a means to try to reduce social and ethnic segregation.

Finally, education for diversity must be grounded on a solid basis of citizenship education. We argue that three interdependent elements of citizenship education should be included in school curricula and are relevant for all European societies irrespective of whether they are older or newer migration countries, or whether they have smaller, larger or growing migrant populations. Citizenship education must be based on the triptych of social and moral responsibility, community involvement and political literacy. These three dimensions are important in contributing to the societal and political human development of Europe's younger generations and to create global citizens who are civically engaged and socially responsible.

Notes

1. For more information, see the website of DG Education and Culture of the European Commission: http://ec.europa.eu/dgs/education_culture/index_en.htm and the website of the Council of Europe on Cultural Cooperation: www.coe.int/T/E/Cultural_Co-operation/education/
2. Paleologou and Evagelou (2003: 69–70) note that we need to distinguish between *culture* and *civilisation*. They define civilisation as a societal

system of values, while culture is seen as the codified system by which people make sense of the world and orient themselves within it. It is often unclear in the literature on education whether the terms 'intercultural' and 'multicultural' refer to civilisations or cultures. In reality, this distinction is blurred in much of the literature as culture is taken to mean a relatively stable set of values and mores (for instance, a concept that fits more with what Paleologou and Evagelou define as civilisation).
3. Philosophy classes in Belgium are currently available as an option instead of religion classes. Religion classes are differentiated for children of different religious backgrounds (for more see Bousetta and Bernes 2007).
4. For an analysis of student performance results from state-funded Muslim schools in the UK, see Meer, N. (2009), 'Identity articulations, mobilisation and autonomy in the movement for Muslim schools in Britain', *Race, Ethnicity and Education*, 12 (3), pp. 379–98.

References

Bousetta, H. and L.-A. Bernes (2007), 'Ethnicity, religion and social disadvantage in the formation of education policy: the case of French speaking Belgium', EMILIE Working Paper WP3. Available at http://emilie.eliamep.gr/wp-content/uploads/2009/04/belgium-wp3-final-report-revised.pdf, accessed on 23 May 2011.

Brands Kehris, I. (2007), 'Multicultural education in Latvia', EMILIE Working Paper WP3. Available at http://central.radiopod.gr/en/wp-content/uploads/2008/10/wp3_education_report_latvia.pdf, accessed on 23 May 2011.

Gmaj, K. (2007), 'Educational challenges posed by migration to Poland', EMILIE Working Paper WP3. Available at http://emilie.eliamep.gr/wp-content/uploads/2009/07/wp3_education_poland_cir.pdf, accessed on 23 May 2011.

Govaris, X. (2001), *Εκπαίδευση και Ετερότητα* ('Education and Otherness'), Athens: Kritiki.

Gropas, R. and A. Triandafyllidou (2007), 'Greek education policy and the challenge of migration. An intercultural view of assimilation', EMILIE Working Paper WP3. Available at http://emilie.eliamep.gr/wp-content/uploads/2009/07/wp3_greece_final.pdf, accessed on 23 May 2011.

Ihle, A. H. (2007), *Magt, Medborgerskab og Muslimske friskole i Danmark: Traditioner, idealer og politikker*, Copenhagen: Department of Intercultural and Regional Studies, University of Copenhagen, pp. 1–97.

Keaton, T. (1999), 'Muslim girls and the "other France": An examination of identity construction', *Social Identities*, 5 (1), pp. 47–64.

Korsgaard, O. (2002), 'Et demokratisk dilemma', *Kristeligt Dagblad*, 1 March 2002.

Leeman, Y. and C. Reid (2006), 'Multi/Intercultual education in Australia and the Netherlands', *Compare*, 36(1), pp. 57–72.

Lex, S. and P. Mouritsen (2007), 'Approaches to cultural diversity in the Danish education system: The case of public schools', EMILIE Working Paper WP3. Available at http://emilie.eliamep.gr/wp-content/uploads/2009/07/emilie_wp3_denmark_final.pdf, accessed on 23 January 2011.

Luciak, M. (2006), 'Minority schooling and intercultural education – a comparison of recent developments in the old and new EU member states', *Intercultural Education*, 17(1), pp. 73–80.

Martínez Alemán, A. and K. Salkever (2001), 'Multiculturalism and the mission of liberal education', *Journal of General Education*, 50(2), pp. 102–39.

Meer, N. and T. Modood (2007), 'The political and policy responses to migration related cultural diversity in the British education system', EMILIE Working Paper WP3. Available at http://emilie.eliamep.gr/wp-content/uploads/2009/07/uk-wp-3-final.pdf, accessed on 12 February 2011.

Miera, F. (2007), 'German education policy and the challenge of migration', EMILIE Working Paper WP3. Available at http://emilie.eliamep.gr/wp-content/uploads/2009/07/wp3-germany-formatted.pdf, accessed on 2 March 2011.

Modood, T. (1997), '"Difference", cultural racism and anti-racism', in Modood, T. and P. Werbner (eds), *Debating Cultural Hybridity*, London and New York: Zed Books, pp. 154–72.

Modood, T. (2007), *Multiculturalism: A Civic Idea*, London: Polity Press.

Paleologou, N. and O. Evagelou (2003), Διαπολιτισμική Παιδαγωγική. Εκπαιδευτικές, Διδακτικές και Ψυχολογικές Προσεγγίσεις ('Intercultural Pedagogy. Educational, Teaching and Psychological Approaches'), Athens: Atrapos.

Sala Pala, V. and P. Simon (2007), 'The political and policy responses to migration-related diversity in the French education system', EMILIE Working Paper WP3. Available at http://emilie.eliamep.gr/wp-content/uploads/2009/07/emilie-wp3-french-report.pdf, accessed on 23 February 2011.

Zapata-Barrero, R. and N. de Wytte (2007), 'Spanish approaches to the management of cultural diversity in compulsory education', EMILIE Working Paper WP3. Available at http://central.radiopod.gr/en/wp-content/uploads/2008/10/spanish_approaches_to_the_management_of_cultural_diversity_in_compulsory_education.pdf, accessed on 23 February 2011.

7

Active Immigrants in Multicultural Contexts: Democratic Challenges in Europe

Ricard Zapata-Barrero and Ruby Gropas

Introduction

International migration has reshaped societies and politics around the world in recent decades. European societies in particular have changed deeply and have been diversified further in social, cultural, economic, ethnic, racial and religious terms through various waves of migration in the post-World War II era. Migration intensified again after the end of the Cold War towards both old and newer European receiving societies. Although there are very distinct migration patterns and different migrant populations in every EU member state, all European countries face comparable challenges as multiculturalism is already a reality at the grassroots level. Within this global framework we wish to explore the democratic challenges that are posed in multicultural contexts and how these challenges affect the definition of a multicultural European democracy.

The case has often been argued in most European countries that the governance and societal systems that resulted from the nation-state building process (in the seventeenth– nineteenth centuries) have had difficulties in accommodating and managing the multicultural challenges posed by contemporary migration-related diversity. After decades of migration and the gradual naturalisation of this population, however, the diversity that characterises today's European societies is a reality that should be neither ignored nor bypassed when attempting to conceptualise European multicultural democracy (Zapata-Barrero 2002: 506).

Democracy and multiculturalism have been approached in recent literature in a rather theoretical and normative way. The focus has often been on democratic education, or on the multinational dimensions of states, citizenship and public policies (see notably Morag 2002; Marri 2003; Macedo 2003; Salili and Hoosain 2010; Van Den Bergue 2002). Yet there is still very limited context-based research that comprehensively tries to identify commonalities and differences among European states, in order to envisage a European multicultural democracy line of research. In this chapter therefore, we propose some of the main factors that are relevant in understanding the sort of multicultural democracy that is being constructed and attempted in a number of European countries.

Democracy is defined with respect to the processes through which it is exercised, its inclusiveness and its representativeness. Democratic governance is based on the principle that all members of a polity are able, directly or indirectly, to participate in the decision-making process by expressing and defending their stake. Robert Dahl (1989) argued that democracy has undergone three fundamental transformations. The first occurred with the Greek *polis* (city-state); the second took place during the construction of the nation-state; and the third, after 1989, involved the construction of a global democracy. Dahl has based his thesis on the territorial criterion: from the city-state to the nation-state, and from there to the world-state, assuming the uncontested homogeneity and constitution of the *demos*. For Dahl, the principle of inclusion is one of the defining variables of a democracy. More specifically, he posits that if an individual is part of a given society and abides by its laws, then he or she ought not to be excluded from the *demos* of this state as this would unavoidably lead to a democratic deficit (Dahl 1989: 147). In effect, democratic societies require that all affected by the decisions of the collective should have influence and opportunities for participation in these decisions. In this light, a democratic challenge is posed if some groups are excluded from, or do not participate in, common binding decisions. A dimension that is missing, however, from Dahl's description of the third transformation is a qualitative one (Zapata-Barrero 2009a: 17). Just as the shift from national to global democracy is a challenging one, so is the shift from a national democracy of a largely monocultural nature to a multicultural democracy. These issues are highly pertinent in the EU with regard to third country nationals (TCNs) legally residing in the member states, estimated at almost 20 million.[1]

Thus, in this chapter we examine this democratic challenge from the perspective of three main dimensions: participation, representation and naturalisation. Our purpose is to explore the extent to which third country nationals are able to participate in the political process in various EU member states, and the criteria according to which they are either granted political rights or are excluded from these.

The reasons for which participation is central to democratic governance are multifold, but for our purposes we can identify two. First, political participation offers individuals the opportunity to influence the outcomes of the decision-making processes and thereby defend their interests as individuals or as members of a specific interest group. Second, participation in commonly binding decisions may have a 'socialisation' function in terms of enriching citizens' feelings of belonging and shared identities (Lindekilde 2009). Both dimensions are crucial to social integration, cohesion and the development of a dynamic democratic polity increasingly characterised by diversity.

Participation and representation require the granting of formal political rights and opportunities for political participation, as well as conditions that encourage active civic engagement. Research on political participation in democratic societies suggests that formal rights and institutional opportunities for political participation are decisive as regards the nature and level of political participation and mobilisation of minorities and ethnic communities in a given context (see, for example, Tilly 1978; Ireland 1994; Layton-Henry 1990; Vogel 2007). In other words, political opportunity structures are able to shape the nature and channel claims of ethnic groups and minorities into the political system (Koopmans and Statham 1999; 2005). Some institutional contexts, for example, may foster more cooperation between ethnic groups, others may lead to more institutionalised forms of participation and others still may encourage ethnic minority participation at particular levels of governance (at the local more than the national level).

EU member states present very different political structures and opportunities, and this is reflected in the very different ways and degrees in which ethnic minorities or newer immigrant populations participate in the respective political systems. Equally important, however, is the fact that for political rights to be actively and effectively exercised and for political opportunities to be able to be translated into actual influence, resources are essential (Verba et al. 1995; see also Lindekilde 2009). Language competence, access to relevant information, social networks, financial means and education are among these key resources. Further, the extent to which these resources exist within a society's different communities may affect the level of their participation and representation. For instance, notable differences may exist among first- and second-generation immigrants, between long-time settlers and newcomers, between women and men, and between different groups of TCNs.

Finally, access to citizenship is one of the defining dimensions of political participation and representation. The EU member states' naturalisation policies largely affect the participation, inclusion and representation of migration-related minorities (Bauböck 2006). Citizenship policies constitute a core instrument that governments have at their disposal to further democratise their increasingly diverse societies (Zapata-Barrero 2009b). The fact that EU member states have different naturalisation policies (frequently characterised by selective or preferential criteria towards certain ethnic or national groups) affects the quality of democracy that is being exercised at an EU-wide level and the principles upon which European democracy is based.

Drawing from the above, this chapter provides an overview of the democratic challenges posed in seven European countries, namely Belgium, Denmark, France, Germany, Greece, Spain and the UK. In particular, it explores the political engagement of migration-related minorities by examining the remit of political rights and the extent of their political participation.

7.1 *European countries in perspective: dimensions of democratic challenges*

According to Eurostat data (2009), a quick overview of the countries analysed indicates the number and relative percentage of non-EU foreigners, and foreign-born inhabitants, including those EU-citizens born in another EU member state.

We consider two main categories related to political engagement in multicultural contexts, namely voting rights and political mobilisation. Access to full voting rights is associated with citizenship and naturalisation. Naturalisation, in turn, is conditional upon a set of basic criteria including length of residence and degree of integration (Bauböck et al. 2006), as well as certain preferential considerations (such as ethnic or historical ties) as defined by the receiving society.

The formal or informal structures through which receiving societies encourage political inclusion are just as important as migrants' own civic and political capital in determining the extent, intensity and forms of political mobilisation that they choose to undertake. Thus, it is relevant to consider migrants' participation in voluntary and self-organised associations as well as political consultation and

Table 7.1 Number of non-EU foreigners and foreign-born inhabitants in seven European countries and in the EU 27 (2009) (in thousands)

	Citizens 2008	Non-EU Foreigners 2008	%	Foreign-born 2008	%
EU 27	497,431	19,476	3.90	30779	6.20
Belgium	10,667	312	2.90	971	9.10
Denmark	5,476	205	3.70	298	5.50
France	63,753	2,391	3.80	3674	5.80
Germany	82,218	4,740	5.80	7255	8.80
Greece	11,214	748	6.70	906	8.10
Spain	45,283	3,149	7.00	5262	11.60
United Kingdom	61,176	2,406	3.90	4021	6.60

Source: Eurostat. Statistics in focus 94/2009 http://epp.eurostat.ec.europa.eu/cache/ITY_OFFPUB/KS-SF-09-094/EN/KS-SF-09-094-EN.PDF

representation structures that have been set up as compensatory systems in situations where formal political rights are not granted in order to channel immigrant claims through consultative and advisory bodies. Furthermore, the extent to which representative political bodies reflect the multicultural character of societies is equally important. The cases of Belgium, Germany, the UK and Denmark, for instance, are interesting in this issue both with regard to the composition of their national/municipal/local assemblies, but also in terms of the composition of their political parties.

7.2 Voting rights

In most European countries, full political participation requires access to citizenship; over the last decade, however, the most significant change in terms of access to political rights has been the enfranchisement of EU citizens who reside in another EU member states (established in the 1993 Maastricht Treaty). Even though there was a certain reluctance and delay on behalf of some EU member states to widen their electoral bases to include other EU nationals for local/municipal and European Parliamentary elections, the harmonisation of EU nationals' political rights across all EU member states is now an established fact; the *demos* has been widened to include all EU citizens.

There has been no similar harmonisation effort as regards the political rights of TCNs, and this will probably be rather unlikely in the foreseeable future (for reasons ranging from political constraints to the need for some member states to undergo constitutional changes and also further modify the Lisbon Treaty). Nevertheless, EU citizenship has affected the debate on democratic standards and expectations and the sort of democracy the EU and its member states wish to represent in a noteworthy manner. It has accorded intellectual and political legitimacy to the argument in favour of enfranchising TCNs, particularly in countries with a more recent migration history. In effect, a political consensus is being constructed between centre and left-wing political parties across Europe on the need to concede voting rights at the local level to TCNs. Further, a fair number of EU member states have already granted full or partial voting rights to TCNs: Belgium, Denmark, Estonia, Finland, Greece (as of March 2010), Ireland, the Netherlands, Malta, Portugal, Slovakia, Slovenia, Spain, Sweden and the UK (Triandafyllidou and Gropas 2007).

Against this background, it is interesting to consider the cases of Belgium, Denmark, France, Germany, Greece, Spain and the UK in terms of whether, in what manner and at which level they enfranchise foreign residents in order to gain an understanding of the differences that are characteristic of the EU. Each of these countries has a very different migration history, experience and population, and it approaches citizenship and TCNs' access to political rights in very different ways.

The Belgian citizenship regime is very open and liberal, offering multiple avenues towards naturalisation. As a result, significant numbers of people of foreign origin have become full citizens with full political rights since 1990. Naturalised citizens represented only one quarter of the migrant and minority population in 1991; two decades later, their share is 44.5 per cent. Moreover, all TCNs who legally reside in the country are enfranchised for local elections (without any eligibility criteria restricting this right). Since the late 1980s there has been very vivid debate on the concept of political citizenship in Belgium. Naturalisation has come to be considered as the mechanism *par excellence* for migrant integration since the early 1980s. In effect, the Belgian Nationality Code is one of the most liberal and flexible in Europe. The linguistic cleavage and conflict between the French-speaking and Flemish communities strongly influenced the debates and policies on migration and diversity-related issues and, to an extent, slowed down the process of enfranchisement resulting from the Maastricht Treaty[2] (Bousetta and Swyngedouw 1999). What is interesting to note here, however, is that while the issue of political rights for EU and non-EU citizens was framed in terms of threat to the balance of power between the Francophones and the Flemish, this has not been the case for the issue of naturalisation (see Bousetta and Bernes 2009).

In Denmark, two significant developments have gradually come into being since 2002, namely tightened rules of naturalisation on the one hand, and cuts in funding for ethnic minority organisations on the other; both have rendered political participation of ethnic minorities more difficult. Danish citizenship is a prerequisite for participation in national elections and, since access to citizenship by naturalisation has been tightened since 2002, a steadily growing group of permanent residents is excluded from national elections and politics. However, TCNs are entitled to vote and stand as candidates in local elections. Ethnic minority organisations have proven important both for channeling claims into the political system and as a basis for ethnic candidates in local elections. Although ethnic minority members tend to participate less than native Danes in local elections, when compared with other countries that have granted voting rights to non-citizens, Denmark ranks among the countries with the highest rates of participation of non-nationals in office (see Lindekilde 2009).

In France, citizenship and nationality are inseparable, and access to political rights is completely conditional upon the acquisition of French nationality. The case of EU citizenship clearly demonstrates the difficulty in separating nationality from citizenship in the French context. France has been impressively slow in enforcing Article 19 of the Maastricht Treaty regarding EU citizens' right to vote and stand as candidates in local and European elections. The European Commission had to lodge several appeals to France before they eventually adopted Article 19. Article 88-3 was added to the French Constitution in 1998, and European citizens were able to vote in local elections for the first time in 2001. Although access to political rights is restricted to French nationals, obtaining French citizenship is relatively easy compared to other countries in Europe. Foreigners can acquire French citizenship after five years' residence and it is noteworthy that since 2000, the average approval rate of citizenship applications has consistently been above 77 per cent (see Escrafé-Dublet and Simon 2009). In effect, in 2005, 40 per cent of the five million immigrants living in France were French citizens. Naturalisation is granted when applicants fulfil certain basic criteria regarding residence requirements and financial resources in addition to knowledge of the French language, loyalty and sharing of 'republican values'. A 2003 law reinforced these criteria, adding the requirement of proving sufficient knowledge about the rights and responsibilities of French citizenship, and thereby leaving substantial room for the naturalisation decision to be based on the administration employees' discretion.

In Germany, citizenship is required in order to vote or stand as a candidate in national elections. Thus, full formal political participation is linked to German citizenship that is in turn acquired at the end of a successful integration process. The 2000 Citizenship Law is considered a milestone in German integration policies, symbolising a qualitative step from ignoring to acknowledging the immigration situation by departing from the exclusivity of *ius sanguinis*, applicable since 1913. In their well-known study Koopmans and Statham (2005: 72) also testify that Germany's immigration policies have shifted from the model of ethnic assimilationism towards cultural pluralism and a more civic-territorial conception of citizenship. Nevertheless, the change has not led to a significant increase in naturalisation figures. On the contrary, naturalisation figures have steadily decreased. In 2008, the numbers fell below 95,000, compared to 187,000 in 2000, while migrants from countries with a Muslim majority tend to be less frequently naturalised. *Späte Aussiedler* (returning ethnic Germans) constitute the exception to this trend and have been granted full citizenship rights, while since 1992, all EU citizens have been entitled to participate in elections at the municipal level. All other TCNs – including so-called 'guest workers' and refugees who have been living in Germany for several years – are not allowed to vote in national or local elections. Migrant organisations have been campaigning for decades for the introduction of local franchise as a means of integration. Several initiatives attempting to introduce this right from left-wing parties have failed; notably, in February 1989 two *Länder* amended legislation in order to introduce voting rights at the municipal level. With an appeal initiated by the Conservative Parliamentary Party, in October 1990 the Federal Constitutional Court of Germany judged these amendments to be unconstitutional on the basis of a strict interpretation of the Basic Law as referring to citizens only. More recently, in 2008 the federal government examined the issue of local franchise for TCNs as part of its commitments within the National Integration Plan. The conclusion of the inquiry was that a constitutional amendment would be necessary, which would require a majority of two-thirds of the members of the national parliament (*Bundestag*) and the Senate (*Bundesrat*) of the Federal Republic of Germany. Given that a wide consensus would be needed across all parties, this initiative was deemed unfeasible and was abandoned (see Miera 2009).

One additional issue that has affected the participation of Germany's predominant Turkish-origin migrant population in particular is the principle of disallowing multiple citizenship.[3] Despite the general refusal of multiple citizenship that characterises Germany's citizenship regime, there are several bilateral agreements or tacit conventions that (reciprocally) allow multiple citizenship. Between 2000 and 2008 about 46.5 per cent of all naturalisations accepted multiple citizenship, particularly for German *Späte Aussiedler* who kept their other citizenship. The main group to which these exceptions do not refer are those of Turkish descent. This became clear in early 2000, when thousands of Turkish migrants applied for reapproval of their Turkish passports after being naturalised. As a consequence, they had their German citizenship withdrawn and also lost their permanent residence status, for which they were forced to reapply. The fact that migrants from Turkey or second-generation migrants had been denied double citizenship and automatic residency permit renewal caused huge discontent among Turkish migrants who felt that the principle of not allowing double citizenship was directly targeted against them (Miera 2009).

In Greece, co-ethnics from the former Soviet Union (Pontic Greeks) were granted preferential access to Greek citizenship upon arrival in the late 1980s and early 1990s. Ethnic Greeks from Albania (*Voreioepirotes*) did not have access to citizenship rights until 2006 but enjoyed a secure residence status and socio-economic rights equal to those of Greek citizens. Since late 2006, however, naturalisation of co-ethnics from Albania have been steadily increasing as they have been fulfilling the legal requirements which include ten years' residence for naturalisation. Greece's naturalisation process was until recently restrictive and lacked transparency, with naturalisations counted in two- to three-digit numbers per year in the period before 2006. In March 2010, however, the situation in Greece changed as the Hellenic parliament voted a new law (Law No. 3838/2010) on citizenship and naturalisation. This law introduced provisions for second-generation migrants, notably children born in Greece of foreign parents or children born abroad of foreign parents but who have completed at least six years of schooling in Greece and who live in Greece. In either case, these children can be naturalised through a simple parental declaration when they are born or when they complete their sixth year of attending a Greek school. The new law also lowers the requirement for naturalisation from ten to seven years of residence, provided the applicant has already received the EU long-term resident status, which can be acquired after five years of legal residence. The new law also introduces local political rights for foreign residents who have been living in Greece for five years or more. Law 3838/2010 has marked an impressive transformation of the concept of Greek citizenship (until recently based exclusively on *ius sanguinis*) by introducing a substantial element of *ius soli*. The same aforementioned law also grants TCNs voting rights in local elections, thereby substantially extending the *demos* at the local and regional level of governance.

In Spain, the debate on immigrants' voting rights has two dimensions (Zapata-Barrero and Zaragoza 2009). The first concerns the territorial dimension of elections. More specifically, a Spanish citizen has the right to vote in elections at four different levels: the European, the national, the regional and the local. The core debate therefore has revolved around on which level of governance non-EU immigrants should be allowed to vote. The second debate focuses on the legal criteria that should be used for granting voting rights to immigrants, for example, access to citizenship and access to political rights through the principle of reciprocity and/or permanent residence. The Spanish Constitution (Article 13.2) does not grant immigrants the right to vote and stand for election. Sole exceptions are cases where this right is established by treaty or when the law attends to the so-called principle of reciprocity. This exclusion from political participation does not affect residents who are EU citizens, who have been entitled to vote in municipal and European Parliamentary elections since the adoption of the Maastricht Treaty in 1993. The principle of reciprocity is another particularity of the case of Spain: immigrants whose country of origin grants voting rights to Spanish emigrants living in its territory receive equivalent political rights in Spain (for example, Norway and, in principle, Argentina, Chile, Colombia, Uruguay and Venezuela). This, however, leads to the differential granting of political rights to immigrants (based on their country of origin) and, therefore, to the undermining of the objective of common and indiscriminate integration. Finally, the Spanish Civil Code (Article 22.1) establishes that in order to naturalise, an immigrant has to prove continued and legal residence in the country for ten years prior to applying. This period decreases to two years for

Latin-Americans and other nationalities historically linked to Spain such as Filipinos. In other words, the Spanish Civil Code establishes a framework of 'institutional discrimination', which impacts directly on the equal access to political rights between TCNs residing in Spain (see also Zapata-Barrero 2010).

In the UK, full political rights encompassing a range of entitlements beyond voting rights are only secured if an immigrant becomes a citizen. This requires a minimum of five years' legal stay, of which at least one year must be classified as 'indefinite leave to enter or remain'. This category denotes the immigration status conferred to a person who does not hold the right of 'permanent abode' but who has been admitted to the UK without any time limit on his or her stay and thus is free to travel to and from the UK and to take up employment or study without restriction. So, while full social and political rights, including access to social welfare, are only secured if an immigrant becomes a UK citizen, people with 'leave to enter' or with 'leave to remain' in Britain are entitled to vote. These permits may cover any length of time between three months to many years, but they exclude persons who have entered the country illegally. However, the formal legal arrangements around the political participation of non-citizens are not necessarily addressed, or are inhibited by convoluted opportunity structures. This is particularly evident in the practical issues surrounding the formal political participation of some ethnic minorities and most starkly illustrated by the experiences of asylum seekers and refugees. EU nationals, irrespective of immigration status, may vote in local elections and in elections for devolved assemblies (Wales, Scotland, Northern Ireland and the Mayor of London), but not in national elections. Conversely, British citizens living abroad can register as overseas electors and are eligible to vote in the UK and European Parliamentary elections for up to fifteen years after they have left the country (Meer and Modood 2009).

In short, there exists a patchwork of different regimes regarding access to citizenship and political rights across the EU, rendering any effort to define a European multicultural democracy in formal terms rather challenging. The exercise of democracy and political participation, of course, is far from limited to the formal, institutionalised and procedural dimension of elections. There is a vast range of civic and political participation that essentially underpins the quality, inclusiveness and representativeness of a society's democracy. Therefore, it is interesting to consider also the parallel or informal channels of political participation that have been created either on the initiative of the receiving society or on behalf of the migrant communities themselves.

7.3 Political mobilisation

In Belgium there are various ways through which immigrant ethnic minorities can voice their claims. Historically, labour unions were an important platform, but their weight and role within communities of non-EU origin has eroded in more recent decades. Migrants' political participation in civil society and voluntary association is less intensive and less active than the native Belgians', and there is a growing disinterest in institutionalised forms of consultation. These are increasingly viewed as vestiges of previous decades where migration was viewed as a more temporary phenomenon and the objective was to compensate for the absence of political rights. Since individuals of foreign origin have significantly increased their political representation and can now make their voice heard within mainstream institutions, there is less motivation for setting up such consultative bodies. In effect, the electoral breakthrough of people of non-EU origin has been observed steadily in all elections since 1994 and particularly since 2004. Among the more notable examples are the appointment to a ministerial position in the Brussels regional government of a second-generation Turk from the Francophone Socialist Party, and another in the government of the French Community of Belgium of a second-generation Moroccan woman from the Francophone Socialist Party. What is important to stress here is the role institutional factors can play in encouraging and facilitating the representation of migrants and minorities in the political realm. The case of Brussels testifies to this as the notable representation of ethnic minority candidates is not only due to Belgium's liberal naturalisation regime but also the country's electoral system that includes both proportional representation and preferential voting, thereby opening the political system to the city's large migrant population (Bousetta and Bernes 2009).

Denmark was one of the first European countries (after Sweden and Ireland) to grant voting rights to foreign citizens for local elections. Nevertheless, there has been surprisingly little debate about the formal political rights of ethnic minorities in Denmark. Since the early 1990s the public debate regarding ethnic minorities has centred on how much cultural adaptation can be expected from ethnic minorities and to what extent significant value differences can be accepted.

It has also dealt with how ethnic minorities can be better integrated in the job market and the educational system, and how to address the challenges posed by existing residential segregation. Moreover, over the last decade in particular, the debate has focused mainly on Islam and its perceived non-conformity with Danish political culture and democracy. What has been largely missing from these debates is the role of ethnic minorities as political actors and active citizens in Danish society. Denmark's particularity also lies in the fact that the political participation of ethnic minorities in decision making varies significantly between the local and the national level. Ethnic minorities have little influence on nationwide political decisions but a much wider one on local political decisions. At the municipal level, many cities have well-functioning integration councils that give a voice to migrants' claims. In addition, institutional design has facilitated the election of a large number of ethnic minority candidates to local administration. The Danish voting system allows voters to support and cast their preference for specific candidates on the party ballot slip. Thus, immigrant candidates have in many cases gathered large numbers of personalised votes in municipalities with high concentrations of ethnic minorities. Furthermore, collective mobilsation and the pooling of available resources (financial, political capital, social capital) is easier at the local level, thereby resulting in overall higher rates of political participation and representation for ethnic minorities here than at the national level (which obviously requires wider coalitions and networks). An additional dimension that is interesting to note is the fact that participation in local elections varies greatly between ethnic groups. Resources such as skills in organisation building in the Danish context, contacts and language skills all affect the degree of self-organisation of ethnic groups so that groups that have been in the country longer (such as Turks, Pakistanis and Iranians) are typically better organised than the more recent arrivals (such as Somalis and former Yugoslavs).

Informal consultations between ethnic minority representatives and the national political elite take place, though rather selectively, thereby including migrant and ethnic minority claims in the public debate at the national level. Research suggests, however, that overall there exists an ineffective representation of ethnic minorities at the national level because their organisations are fragmented and lack coordination (Mikkelsen 2003; Ziadeh 2003; Mouritsen 2006). It has therefore been argued that for ethnic minorities to be able to channel their claims and influence at the national level of government, they would need to organise themselves within umbrella organisations as this would lead to the development of a larger pool of representatives. Such organisations would thereby create a sufficient critical mass to be invited to regular meetings with relevant political committees and ministers. The experience of Sweden may be useful here as the provision of financial incentives has encouraged the formation of larger unions of organisations (Lindekilde 2009). Last, the creation of local integration councils has had an important effect on political participation. In fact, 18 per cent of the ethnic minority candidates who stood for election in 2001 were prior members of local integration councils. There is a widespread view that integration councils should be made mandatory and their positions should be elected and not, as is the case in some municipalities, through governmental appointment.

In France, the situation is very different. French republican culture has translated into a solid tradition of 'ethnic blindness' that has essentially shaped the debate over minority participation in politics. Republican discourse rejects the categorisation of minority identities and consequently ethnic preference is considered as an illegitimate basis for political strategy. The risks involved in this approach are the political marginalisation of entire segments of the population and the fact that inequality between individuals of different backgrounds remains in part unaddressed. Mobilisation around foreigners' political rights and minority recognition has been consistent for over almost thirty-five years now, though results are still limited. In this context, two alternative routes of mobilisation have developed. The first involves the practice of 'cooption' through the creation of consultation bodies at different levels of political decision making and the nomination of foreigners in the political process of decision making. 'Cooption' draws from the 1970s tradition of appointing 'community leaders' to 'represent' minorities in the administrative council dealing with migration-related issues and is at present best represented by the *Conseil de la citoyenneté des Parisiens non communautaires* (Council of the Citizenship of Parisian TCNs). There are, however, two shortcomings, namely that consultation bodies do not have substantial leverage on political decisions, and that this process may attribute a disproportionate agency to associational leaders (instead of the actual constituency they are meant to represent). The second route consists of the vibrant mobilisation that has developed on immigration and anti-racism issues, which has been critical in voicing minority demands. This mobilisation took a stronger dynamic in support of diversity representation in national-level politics after the events that took place in the suburbs of French cities in November 2005, especially by organisations such as *Le Conseil représentatif des associations noires de France* (CRAN) [Representative Council for Black Associations] and the *Association Collectif Liberté, Égalité, Fraternité, Ensemble, Unis* (AC Le Feu) [Collective Association for Freedom, Equality, Fraternity – Together, United].

Germany too presents a very distinct situation regarding migrant mobilisation and participation in the political realm. Recent studies that have examined political interest and voting preferences of migrants and naturalised Germans highlight some interesting findings: migrants without German citizenship show significantly low levels of interest in German politics (Diehl and Urbahn 1998). While political interest is stronger among naturalised Germans, it still remains around 50 per cent lower than among native Germans. When further examining political mobilisation and interest among naturalised citizens, it further emerges that Turkish Germans account for the highest number of politically interested citizens, particularly in comparison with the ethnic Germans (*Späte Aussiedler*) from the CIS, Poland and Romania, who were guaranteed German citizenship upon arrival (Wüst 2003). In terms of actual representation on the political scene, however, with the exception of *Aussiedler*, the parliamentary representation of migrants in Germany is relatively new and still quantitatively low. In 2007, there were eighty deputies of Turkish origin in German parliaments, while overall the number of members of parliament with a migrant background is low, at under 2 per cent. Nevertheless, there are changes underway in the manner and extent to which migrant politicians have become increasingly visible particularly in the SPD (Sozialdemokratische Partei Deutschlands) and the Green Party. They are able to represent a diversity of viewpoints and (not only ethnic) identities, indicating that there is a trend within German politics that is taking into consideration and responding to the country's new citizenry (Miera 2009).

With regard to other institutionalised forms of participation and consultation that exist in Germany, Foreign Citizens' Advisory Councils that had been implemented in many German cities since the 1970s further to migrants' claims, constituted for quite some time the only way for non-German immigrants to have any kind of participation in institutionalised or formal politics. However, these have always been contentious since the extent of their power and influence is limited and over the past decade, there has been a steady decline in interest in these councils. More recent forms of institutionalised involvement of migrants in policy making – primarily concerning integration issues more than political representation – include involvement in round tables, integration councils such as the National Integration Summit (July 2007) and the German Islam Conference (founded in 2006).[4] These provide new forums of communication and consultation between state authorities, migrant organisations and other civic and political agents. Some of these forums have established representative procedures, but generally their composition is set by the state.

In Greece, while the public debates on the social and economic integration of migrants have been ongoing since the turn of the century, the political dimensions of integration (political representation, voting rights and participation) represent a relatively new yet steadily growing trend. Immigrant participation in public life has been hampered and affected by the long-standing undocumented or insecure status of most immigrants due to delayed and incomplete regularisation policies and efforts on the part of the public authorities. Until the early 2000s, the institutional and legal framework of migration in Greece provided immigrants with very limited opportunities to participate in public life and to be civically and politically active. Since then, however, Greece's civil society landscape has changed substantially. Immigrant, cultural and sports associations, women's associations, trade unions and other professional organisations, networks of associations of immigrant and mainstream human rights non-governmenatsl organisations (NGOs), or NGOs active in the protection of refugee and asylum seeker rights, anti-discrimination or the fight against racism and xenophobia have created a rich, active and increasingly vocal civil society. This development has benefited greatly from two separate factors. One is that EU programmes and sources of funding (such as EQUAL and INTERREG) have been fundamental in raising awareness among the public and the media on immigrant integration, multiculturalism and programmes combating discrimination, racism and xenophobia. The other is that left-wing parties in Greece, particularly from the Coalition of the Left (Syriza) and from the more centre-left Socialist party (PASOK), have been instrumental in providing human and financial resources to migrant and other organisations, helping them develop their organisational capabilities and engaging them in the public sphere. In effect, many party members have held a double role, serving on the boards of NGOs involved in migration and anti-discrimination matters.

To date, migrants' political mobilisation and inclusion in the Greek political sphere has not taken place through formal, institutionalised consultative mechanisms (such as including migrants in local/regional councils or establishing consultation and institutionalised forums of regular dialogue with migrant organisations) as in other EU countries. In the case of Greece, the inclusion of migrants in the country's political life has taken place through links with individual politicians. In effect, over the past decade, a number of parliamentarians have included immigrants in their office team of experts and associates leading to their participation as observers in party conventions and party working groups. Additionally, all main political parties have developed extensive networks and informal links with co-ethnic (mainly) and immigrant associations (increasingly). Such networks conform to the prevailing political culture in Greece of political clientelism and patronage rather than notions of civic citizenship and political inclusion (Gropas and Triandafyllidou 2009).

In Spain, since 1995 immigrant associations have had a consultative body at the national level in which they are represented and are able to claim and demand their interests: *Foro para la Integración de los Inmigrantes* (Forum for the Social Integration of Immigrants). Its composition is divided into three kinds of actors: public administration (comprising the central administration, the autonomous administration and the local administration), social organisations (where the trade unions and employers' organisations are represented) and immigrant associations. The spokespersons who are appointed to represent the associations of immigrants and refugees, and the social support organisations are assigned by the Ministry of Employment and Social Affairs. This top-down selection process has contributed to the fact that the role of immigrant associations in this forum has been rather weak. Their participation is determined by a number of factors, including, *inter alia*, their economic dependence on public authorities; the moderation of their discourse (negotiation and reform versus conflict); the extent to which they are included in official channels of dialogue; their access to economic resources (González-Enríquez, 2005: 27); and the type of political culture that develops within these associations (depending on the charismatic leadership of some individuals, the degree of participation of the wider community, representativeness and transparency, and so on) (Veredas 2003: 212). One of the commissions of the forum concentrates on the debate on the political rights and participation of immigrants in Spain. The conclusions of this commission, summarised in the *Report on the Situation of the Social Integration of Immigrants and Refugees* published in 2007, are the following:

1. The active participation of immigrants in all social spheres and public matters is key to guaranteeing equality in rights and duties with the native population.
2. Immigrant participation cannot depend on nationality but should be promoted in different ways in order to make immigrants feel part of the new urban cultural set-up and also motivate them to contribute and provide possible solutions to the problems that affect current coexistence.
3. It is necessary to establish common criteria in order to overcome the existing disparities in immigrant participation between the different Autonomous Communities.
4. To promote the participation of immigrants it is necessary to encourage a political culture and provide education on the democratic values of the social rule of law, by providing resources that encourage and strengthen associationism.
5. The visibility of migrants in the public function is essential to terminate stereotypes and to carry out political pedagogy. In this sense, access to public posts cannot be limited by nationality and there must be greater visibility of immigrants in public administration such as schools (teachers), security corps (police), hospitals, and so on.
6. The right to vote is considered as an essential right in order to achieve full integration. In order to encourage debate on this important issue, it is necessary to seek solutions to the limits that Article 13.2 of the Spanish Constitution places on granting immigrants participation rights in municipal elections. A reform of this article should take place, independently of the promotion of bilateral agreements of reciprocity.
7. Finally, the forum made a petition to the government to ratify the Convention of the Council of Europe on the participation of foreigners in public life at a local level in order to promote the voting rights of immigrants following the criteria of length of residence (permanent residence).

In the case of the UK, the political representation of migration-related minorities has occupied an important place in the public sphere. The situation is very different from most other EU member states as the UK has one of the highest levels of ethnic minority citizenry with a right to franchise in Europe (Hansen 2000). Although the proportion of minority representatives holding elected office does not sufficiently reflect Britain's ethnic diversity, ethnic minority voter registration and participation have been steadily increasing in recent years. Mainstream Muslim identity politics, by and large, appears to comprise a significant strand of this engagement and will provide an interesting dimension of the debate in the coming years. The challenge for political parties remains how to appeal to all sections of society including ethnic minorities, but specifically how to ensure the participation of ethnic minorities, and that minority candidates are selected and elected. There is widespread recognition within political parties and among the wider public of the need to address ethnic under-representation in UK politics. However, progress has been slow to the extent that the Labour Party still has only thirteen ethnic minority MPs, despite attracting the majority of the ethnic minority voters (Meer and Modood 2009). Political parties are not covered by the duty to promote equality under Section 71 of the Race Relations (Amendment) Act 2000, so it is largely up to the internal political dynamics of the main political parties to decide whether there is a need to further pursue strategies that actively promote equality in order to address ethnic minority under-representation.

Conclusion

Each EU member state has addressed and responded to the democratic challenges that arise from an increasingly multicultural society by adopting very different approaches and policies. There are different approaches to citizenship, political inclusion and representation in each member state. The most significant change in terms of access to political rights has been the enfranchisement of EU citizens living in another EU member state since the Maastricht Treaty. The introduction of voting rights for European citizens in local and European elections widened the democratic polity in an unprecedented manner. Given the current sensitive political climate on migration issues across the EU, marked by a growth in anti-immigration discourse among right-wing political parties, combined with Europe's dire economic situation that is triggering feelings of economic and employment insecurity among EU citizens and translating into immigration-scepticism, it would be difficult to expect a similar development across the EU for TCNs. Nevertheless, this expansion of the notion of citizenship has encouraged debate on the political rights of non-European resident foreigners, that is, third country nationals. What is important to note is that this has led to a vivid and dynamic discussion in both academic research and, just as decisively, in the public sphere on the traditional linkage between citizenship and nationality. It has triggered the pursuit of a more civic understanding of citizenship.

Over the past fifteen years, advocacy groups, intellectuals and proponents of a multicultural *demos* have been arguing for the need to revisit and redefine sustainable democratic forms of citizenship that are able to integrate and address the needs of minority groups and new collective identities. The redefinition of citizenship has far-reaching democratic implications. It involves expanding access to political rights to new citizens and revisiting the constitutive elements of national identity. This redefinition is being argued for on the basis of the principles of political equality, human rights and respect for diversity.

Furthermore, since the 1990s we have been able to observe a growing inclusion of migrants and minorities in the political systems of the EU member states examined. Unquestionably, there exists a significant degree of national and local variation in how multicultural political debates are structured in each EU country. Some countries have proactively pursued initiatives aimed at the political inclusion of these groups (such as Denmark, the UK and Belgium), while in others, the debate remains essentially focused on the conditions of access to political citizenship and rights (such as Greece and Spain). There has been a wider and more active engagement on behalf of migration-related minorities in older migration countries, in assemblies, across political parties and so on, although different models and levels of political participation and inclusion can be identified. In the UK, France, Denmark and Belgium, for instance, large segments of the permanent migrant population have been enfranchised either through naturalisation or through specific enfranchising legislation. These minority groups have significantly progressed in terms of electoral participation and representation over the last decade in local and national politics and in the European Parliament. In Germany, where TCNs both faced restrictive naturalisation procedures and had no formal political rights, this has not been synonymous with political exclusion from the public space. In fact, forms of consultation with public authorities have been set up (even if in some cases these are still at very elementary stages) thereby allowing these groups to express their political expectations outside the traditional channel of the vote. In newer migration countries, such as Greece or Spain, the naturalisation processes are, or have been until recently, rather long and restrictive. In most cases there are still rather limited formal consultative institutions or other alternatives to encourage their political participation in the receiving society. Nevertheless, a political consensus has been constructed between centre and left-wing political parties on the need to concede voting rights at the local level to TNCs and engage them more actively in civic and political terms.

There are, of course, a number of continuing challenges. Where data on migrant and minority voters exists, it suggests lower levels of electoral participation among them than among native nationals. Reasons are varied and may range from lack of access to relevant resources such as registration requirements in order to exercise voting rights, to objective obstacles to political participation exemplified as highly restrictive naturalisation legislation, electoral strategies of political parties or even electoral systems.

Where integration policies have attempted to encourage migrant political participation and representation through consultative and advisory institutions at the local and sometimes national levels of governance, responses have been mixed. Councils or advisory committees have been specifically set up in order to include migrants in the following countries: Spain, Germany, France and Denmark. Although this is a proactive initiative aiming at increasing participation of all groups (including disenfranchised residents) and dialogue between all actors, these have frequently faced substantial limitations and criticism in terms of effectively channelling immigrant claims. In some instances, they are reported to actually have provoked adverse effects on multicultural recognition. For instance, the Paris Consultative Council for Foreigners is considered to have marginalised ethnic demands, while in Denmark, there is a concern that the general inefficiency that characterises consultative bodies may lead to demobilisation and disillusionment vis-à-vis the migrant populations.

In short, political opportunity structures are diverse in each European country and there is scope for much to be done in terms of integrating minority communities, new citizens and permanent residents in the democratic polity. Public information campaigns and educational programmes on civic values should target the entire population, while more focused efforts should include migrant and minority populations and in particular women. At the same time, efforts to encourage voter registration across all societal groups should be intensified. Access to funding and media outlets are important for minority and migrant organisations in order to improve and support their contribution to the national debate and encourage a wider representation. In all these situations, the role of political parties is pivotal. They should be encouraged to consider the degree of their intercultural composition and membership and the levels of ethnic minority participation and representation at local, national and European levels.

As discussed above, representativeness and participation are central to democracy. Where significant portions of the population living within a constituency are excluded from formal means of political expression and representation, this translates into a democratic deficit. Democratic governance in Europe has aimed at ensuring the inclusion of all groups and segments of a polity's population in the democratic process. Moreover, in today's plural societies, strengthening the civic identity of its constitutive members is necessary for multicultural societies that are socially cohesive. Political participation and representation are therefore necessary for residents and citizens to have a stake in the community in which they live. It adds the dimensions of responsibility and obligation to that of rights. This is important for the quality of a society's democracy and development, and for the making of a European multicultural democracy.

Notes

1. According to the last data available in the EU-27 there are 499,433 million EU citizens, and 19,916 million non-EU citizens, that is 4 per cent of the EU population. Source: Eurostat. http://epp.eurostat.ec.europa.eu/portal/page/portal/eurostat/home (October 2010).
2. An institutional reform of the Belgian federal state accommodated Flemish concerns that EU citizenship would weaken the institutional representation of the Flemish minority in Brussels and in its periphery.
3. Children of foreigners acquire German citizenship if one parent has been legally living in Germany for at least eight years; these children are then allowed to hold two passports until the age of twenty-three, after which they have to opt for either the German or the other citizenship.
4. The German Islam Conference was the first national reaction, involving federal, regional and local authorities, to the relatively recent presence in historical terms of Muslims as a significant population group in Germany. Its work focuses on Muslims' integration in Germany (including among other issues establishing Islamic theological university institutions, reporting on Islam and Germany's Muslim population in

the media, introducing Islamic religious studies in German state schools, and so on) so as to counteract social polarisation and segregation.

References

Bauböck, R. (ed.) (2006), *Migration and Citizenship. Legal Status, Rights and Political Participation*, IMISCOE Reports, Amsterdam: Amsterdam University Press.

Bauböck, R., E. Ersböll, K. Groenendijk and H. Waldrauch (eds) (2006), *Acquisition and Loss of Nationality. Policies and Trends in 15 European Countries*. IMISCOE Reports, 2 vols, Amsterdam: Amsterdam University Press.

Bousetta, H. and L.-A. Bernes (2009), 'Post-immigration challenges to political citizenship. The case of Belgium', EMILIE Working Paper, Political Participation. Available at http://emilie.eliamep.gr/wp-content/uploads/2009/09/belgium-wp5-final.pdf, accessed on 30 May 2011.

Bousetta, H. and M. Swyngedouw (1999), 'La citoyenneté de l'Union européenne et l'enjeu de Bruxelles. Le droit supranational européen confronté aux réalités d'une société multiethnique et multinational divisée', *Courrier Hebdomadaire du CRISP*, 1636.

Dahl, R. A. (1989), *Democracy and Its Critics*, New Haven, CT: Yale University Press.

Diehl, C. and J. Urbahn (1998), *Die soziale und politische Partizipation von Zuwanderern in der Bundesrepublik Deutschland*, Bonn: Friedrich-Ebert-Stiftung.

Escafré-Dublet, A. and P. Simon (2009), 'From integration to diversity. The political challanges of migration-related divesity in France', EMILIE Working Paper, Political Participation. Available at http://emilie.eliamep.gr/wp-content/uploads/2009/09/emilie-wp5-french-report.pdf, on accessed on 23 May 2011.

González-Enríquez, C. (2005), 'Active civic participation of immigrants in Spain', Country Report prepared for the European research project POLITIS, Oldenburg.

Gropas, R. and A. Triandafyllidou (2009), 'Migrants and political rights in Greece. Between patronage and the search for inclusion', EMILIE Working Paper, Political Participation. Available at http://emilie.eliamep.gr/wp-content/uploads/2009/12/wp5_greece_final.pdf, accessed on 23 May 2011.

Hansen, R. (2000), *Citizenship and Immigration in Post-war Britain: the institutional origins of a multicultural nation*, Oxford: Oxford University Press.

Ireland, P. R. (1994), *The Policy Challenge of Ethnic Diversity: Immigrant Politics in France and Switzerland*, Cambridge, MA: Harvard University Press.

Koopmans, R. and P. Statham (1999), 'Challenging the liberal nation-State? Postnationalism, multiculturalism and the collective claims making of migrants and ethnic minorities in Britain and Germany', *American Journal of Sociology*, 105(3), pp. 652–96.

Koopmans, R. and P. Statham (2005), 'Configurations of citizenship in five European countries,' in R. Koopmans, P. Statham, M. Giugni and F. Passy, *Contested Citizenship*, Minneapolis, MN: University of Minnesota Press.

Layton-Henry, Z. (1990), *The Political Rights of Migrant Workers in Western Europe*, London: Sage.

Lindekilde, L. (2009), 'Organisation and representation of ethnic minorities in Denmark: Recent developments and future challenges', EMILIE Working Paper, Political Participation. Available at http://emilie.eliamep.gr/wpcontent/uploads/2009/07/emilie_wp5_denmark_final.pdf, accessed on 23 May 2011.

Macedo, S. (2003), *Diversity and Distrust: Civic Education in a Multicultural Democracy*, Cambridge, MA: Harvard University Press.

Marri, A. R. (2003), 'Multicultural democracy: Toward a better democracy', *Intercultural Education*, 14(3), pp. 263–77.

Meer, N. and T. Modood (2009), 'The impact of migration related diversity upon political participation in Britain', EMILIE Working Paper, Political Participation. Available at http://emilie.eliamep.gr/wp-content/uploads/2009/07/uk-wp-5-final.pdf, accessed on 23 May 2011.

Miera, F. (2009), 'Political participation of migrants in Germany', EMILIE Working Paper, Political Participation. Available at http://emilie.eliamep.gr/wp-content/uploads/2009/09/wp5-germany-formatted.pdf, accessed on 23 May 2011.

Mikkelsen, F. (2003), 'Indvandrer-organisationer i Danmark', in F. Mikkelsen *Indvandrer-organisationer i Norden*, Århus: Phønix-Trykkeriet A/S.

Morag, P. (2002), 'Rights and recognition: Perspectives on multicultural democracy', *Ethnicities*, 2(1), pp. 31–51.

Mouritsen, P. (2006), 'The particular universalism of a Nordic civic nation: Common values, state religion, and Islam in Danish political culture', in T. Modood, A. Triandafyllidou and R. Zapata-Barrero, *Multiculturalism, Muslims, and Citizenship: a European Approach*, New York: Routledge.

Salili, F. and R. Hoosain (2010), *Democracy and Multicultural Education*, Charlotte, NC: Information Age Publishing.

Tilly, C. (1978), *From Mobilization to Revolution*, Reading, MA: Addison-Wesley Publishing Company.

Triandafyllidou, A. and R. Gropas (2007), *European Immigration: A Sourcebook*, Aldershot: Ashgate Publishing Limited.

Van Den Bergue, P. L. (2002), 'Multicultural democracy: can it work?', *Nations and Nationalism*, 8(4), pp. 433–49.

Verba, S., K. Lehman Schlozman and H. E. Brady (1995), *Voice and Equality: Civic Voluntarism in American Politics*, Cambridge, MA: Harvard University Press.

Veredas, S. (2003), 'Las asociaciones de inmigrantes en España. Práctica clientelar y dependencia política', *Revista Internacional de Sociología*, 36.

Vogel, D. (ed.) (2007), *Highly Active Immigrants – A Resource for European Civil Societies*, Frankfurt: Peter Lang International Academic Publishers.

Wüst, A. M. (2003), 'Das Wahlverhalten eingebürgerter Personen in Deutschland', *Aus Politik und Zeitgeschichte*, B 52, pp. 29–38.

Zapata-Barrero, R. (2002), 'State-based logic versus EU-based logic towards immigrants: Evidences and dilemmas', *Asian and Pacific Migration Journal*, 11(4), pp. 505–28.

Zapata-Barrero, R. (2009a), *Fundamentos de los discursos políticos en torno a la inmigración*, Madrid: Trotta.

Zapata-Barrero, R. (ed.) (2009b), *Citizenship Policies in the Age of Diversity. Europe at the Crossroads*, Barcelona: Cidob.

Zapata-Barrero, R. (2010), 'Managing diversity in Spanish society: A practical approach', *Journal of Intercultural Studies*, 31(4), pp. 383–402.

Zapata-Barrero, R. and J. Zaragoza (2009), 'La gestión del derecho de voto de los inmigrantes en España', in R. Zapata-Barrero (ed.), *Políticas y gobernabilidad de la inmigración en España*, Barcelona: Ariel, pp. 139–63.

Ziadeh, H. (2003), 'Historien om et forudsigeligt politisk selvmord', *Information om Indvandrere*, 7(2), pp. 10–14.

8

Not a One-way Road? Integration as a Concept and as a Policy

Frauke Miera

Introduction

Chapters 2 and 3 propose the concept of multiculturalism as a theoretical point of reference for the analysis of ethnic and religious diversity in Europe. They propose this in spite of – or perhaps precisely because of – a tendency in media, political and everyday discourse in many European countries to dismiss and/or heavily criticise the idea of multiculturalism as a political programme.

In practice, for empirical research in the case of Germany,[1] this point of departure meant that approaching experts with a research project using the term 'multiculturalism' in its heading evoked an immediate and explicit expression of the experts' standpoint. Some respondents even criticised the idea of multiculturalism, deeming it inadequate for addressing problems regarding the integration of migrants today. Criticism includes the argument that multiculturalism reinforces cultural boundaries and can even legitimise cultural relativism and disguise social disparities as forms of cultural diversity. In public discourse in Germany, multiculturalism is often described as the cause of current failures in migrants' integration; for example, proponents of multiculturalism allegedly support the existence of so-called 'parallel lives'. The concept of 'parallel lives' is a term applied especially to Muslim migrants who allegedly live apart, closed off from the majority of society, lack German language skills and customs, and obey Islamic rules and educational concepts. These rules are depicted as backward, traditional, narrow-minded and oriented to principles such as honour, submission, women's oppression and male dominance (Miera 2007). In many respects, however, these assumptions are counterfactual in that multiculturalist policies have never been systematically implemented in Germany where the concept is broadly discredited.

Some of the contributors to this book have observed in several countries a similar crisis relating to the concept. Even in the UK, which serves as a model of multiculturalism, we see increasing criticism, particularly regarding the accommodation of ethno-religious minorities and specifically Muslims. More precisely, the rise of discourses around 'community cohesion' and a greater emphasis upon the assimilatory aspects of 'integration' have increasingly competed and sought to rebalance the recognition of diversity in previous dialogue and policy (Meer and Modood 2009).

At the other end of the spectrum of cultural diversity and immigration is assimilation – which is rarely overtly formulated as an objective in the policy declarations and recommendations of European countries. The term 'assimilation' implies

> bringing immigrants and refugees into society through a one-way, one-sided process of adaptation: the newcomers are supposed to give up their distinctive linguistic, cultural or social characteristics, adopt the values and practices of the mainstream receiving society, and become indistinguishable from the majority population. (Castles et al. 2002: 115f.)

It seems to be broadly acknowledged and commonly understood that 'assimilation devalues the cultures and languages of minority groups, and thus contradicts democratic principles of diversity and free choice' (ibid.).

The concept of integration seems to have won increasing acceptance among politicians and in the media in European countries and become an unquestioned legitimate objective as policies concerning integration seem to be generally popular. The term 'integration' is used in empirical research, theory and political practice with much variation in meaning that is often quite broad or unspecific. In research, 'there are as many definitions and conceptions of integration as there are writers on the subject' (Penninx and Martiniello 2004: 141). Likewise, there is a broad variety of local-, national- and European-level policies under the label of integration policies. Integration thus appears to have an inherently positive connotation, in contrast to the concepts of multiculturalism or assimilation.

Based on a British research survey on immigrants and refugees, Castles et al. (2003) conclude that integration as a concept 'is vague and slippery and seems to mean whatever people want it to' (ibid.: 112ff.). Similarly, in the German context the sociologist Karakayali (2009) observes that integration is used as a 'catch-all phrase' for a variety of political practices and policies that may follow divergent interests or objectives. In Latvia, for instance, the definition of integration officially adopted in 2001 was

> unclear enough that although the term was widely used ... divergent views on the content of the concept remain until the present time. Conflicting strands continue to coexist as policy undercurrents, ranging from a nationalistic interpretation with elements of assimilation to the recognition of the valuable contribution of all constituent ethnicities, but under the umbrella of the Latvian nation, which reserves special recognition of Latvians and Livs as the indigenous ethnicities. (Brands Kehris 2007: 5)

It is perhaps because the term is so vague or, supposedly, neutral, or at least not as politically charged as 'multiculturalism' or 'assimilation' that several initiatives and policy programmes can be subordinated under it. Nevertheless, this chapter aims to argue that in many policy programmes integration is far from being a neutral concept; this chapter intends to encourage a critical and more in-depth focus on integration as a concept and policy. To facilitate a critical review of the concept of integration in European countries we should briefly discuss some theoretical definitions of the term.

Penninx and Martiniello (2004), scholars in migration and ethnic studies, characterise integration in a variety of European cities as 'the process of becoming an accepted part of society'. They emphasise one important aspect, that is the 'processual character of integration rather than defining an end situation'. Penninx and Martiniello stress that with their definition, they do 'not specify any particular requirements for acceptance by the receiving society (in contradistinction to ... normative models)' (ibid.). Nevertheless, the authors maintain that integration 'is ... appropriate for analysing the situation of first-generation migrants and groups that are not yet familiar with the new society and need to learn in many respects how to fit in' (ibid.: 142). With the focus on first-generation migrants and their processes of 'becoming familiar with a new society' and learning 'how to fit in' they implicitly refer to a quite constrictive definition according to which newcomers must be the ones to adapt. While the authors refer to the powerful role of the receiving society and to 'inherent risks' and 'power inequalities', society is not really conceived as part of the process of change but only as a more or less open and generous provider of opportunities for individual immigrants or groups.

In their aforementioned survey Castles et al. (2003) identified two main usages of the term 'integration'. They are of the opinion that the main criterion in differentiating between integration policies is the degree of adaptation or assimilation required on the part of the migrants. In other words, the interpretations of integration as a concept differ according to whether it is conceptualised as a 'one-way-process' to be achieved by the individual migrant, or as a reciprocal or 'two-way-process' between the majority society and the newcomers concerned. Castles et al. define these two main usages of the term integration as:

> Usage 1: The process through which immigrants and refugees become part of the receiving society. Integration is often used in a normative way, to imply a one-way process of adaptation by newcomers to fit in with a dominant culture and way of life. This usage does not recognise the diversity of cultural and social patterns in a multicultural society, so that integration seems to be merely a watered down form of assimilation. Usage 2: A two-way process of adaptation, involving change in values, norms and behaviour for both newcomers and members [of] the existing society. This includes recognition of the role of the ethnic community and the idea that broader social patterns and cultural values may change in response to immigration. (Castles et al. 2003: 112ff.)

According to the second definition, 'members of the existing society' are not simply providers of opportunity structures, but are themselves potentially affected by changes in 'values, norms and behaviour'. Nevertheless, this definition should also be considered critically since it considers two parties in opposition to each other in a quite static or simplistic way: the immigrants on the one hand and 'society' on the other. This conceptualisation reifies and manifests the dualism between immigrants and society, and Muslims and society in particular. It could be argued that the aim of integration policies should be to overcome this dualism. This can be illustrated by a one-way road that is changed into a two-way road without actually widening the road; this does not allow room for a great degree of change or for opportunities to leave the given path and develop something new.

We would even go further in our critique of the idea that integration is a mutual process in which 'natives' and 'migrants' have to approach each other from a fixed point. In fact, this concept is based on the idea that natives of the majority society are already integrated because of their linguistic, ethnic and national belonging, and that this is a contained state of being (see also Krüger-Potratz 2003). According to the main definitions of integration mentioned above, the concept of integration follows the idea of a static entity – the receiving society – which is, so to speak, disturbed by immigrants.

Looking at the etymology of the word confirms this: the Latin term *integer* means 'complete' or 'consistent'. Hence integration could be translated as the remaking of an entity. In this way it is suggested that immigrants destroy an intact and functioning entity – that is, society – which should be reinstalled through integration measures. The 'receiving society' only opens up to immigrants and their needs because of political decisions based on 'goodwill' or for humanitarian reasons.

Instead, integration should be conceived as a proactive process, which follows the 'ideal aim', indentifying with the political community, constitutional values, the legal system and political institutions in a democratic constitutional state. The aim is an 'ideal' one 'because it is only ever achieved by the native citizens in different degrees of approximation and is not a static or irreversible state of being' (Oberndörfer 2001: 11). In other words, integration is a goal to which everyone has to contribute every day; it is a continuous and changing process in which the status quo is maintained and defended and that therefore entails dissent and conflict in order to produce something new (Krüger-Potratz 2003; Leggewie 1996).

If we look at integration programmes we should therefore ask what is meant by the postulated mutuality of the integration process? Who are the agents of the integration process? Who is addressed? Who has the willingness or capability to move along this road or the power to change its course? Who sets the agenda? How is the process managed on this road? Is there any space for negotiation and change? What is the institutional setting of integration and how is it reflected upon?

First, questions regarding the integration concept as it is agreed upon in the 'common basic principles for immigrant integration policy in the European Union' (Council of the European Union 2004) will be addressed below. In the second part of the chapter, some of the cases of EU countries represented in this book will be referred to. The German case will be highlighted and the substance of the integration concept will be discussed in more depth. In conclusion, practical examples will be illustrated against the background of theoretical considerations.

8.1 *The integration concept of the European Union*

In 2004, the Council of the European Union agreed on eleven common basic principles for immigrant integration policy in the

European Union (Council of the European Union 2004). According to the first principle integration is defined as

> a dynamic, long-term, and continuous two-way process of mutual accommodation – not a static outcome. It demands the participation not only of immigrants and their descendants but of every resident. The integration process involves adaptation by immigrants, both men and women, who all have rights and responsibilities in relation to their new country of residence. It also involves the receiving society, which should create the opportunities for the immigrants' full economic, social, cultural, and political participation. (Council of the European Union 2004: 19)

The mutuality of the integration process is conceived as 'adaptation by immigrants' on the one hand and, with regard to the 'receiving country', to 'create the opportunities for the immigrants' full ... participation' on the other. Integration in terms of adaptation is to be fulfilled by immigrants, while 'society' facilitates the process. Although it is stated that integration demands the 'participation not only of immigrants and their descendants but of every resident', it remains unclear in which ways 'every resident' is asked to participate. One can assume that 'every resident' is not addressed according to the ideal understanding of integration as discussed above, namely integration as involving all residents – migrants, their descendants or natives – being in a permanent process of negotiating, defending and changing the existing status quo.

The second common basic principle for immigrant integration policy in the EU states:

> Member States are responsible for actively assuring that all residents, including immigrants, understand, respect, benefit from, and are protected on an equal basis by the full scope of values, rights, responsibilities, and privileges established by the EU and Member State laws. Views and opinions that are not compatible with such basic values might hinder the successful integration of immigrants into their new host society and might adversely influence the society as a whole. Consequently successful integration policies and practices preventing isolation of certain groups are a way to enhance the fulfilment of respect for common European and national values. (ibid.)

Interestingly, the first sentence is a quite general statement and could also refer to the protection of individuals against, for instance, right-wing extremist groups or various forms of political or religious fundamentalism. The subsequent sentence draws implicitly and without further explanation on immigrants and their potentially incompatible views and opinions, which might hinder their integration. Indirectly, immigrants are suspected of not agreeing to basic existing values. Similarly, the eighth common basic principle for immigrant integration policy in the EU mirrors a general scepticism regarding whether migrants, particularly Muslims, hold values compatible with democracy. While it first underlines the guarantee of the practice of diverse cultures and religions and the role that the cultures and religions 'that immigrants bring with them' plays in the integration process, the principle also elaborates on the threat that cultural or religious practices may pose on individual migrants:

> However, Member States also have a responsibility to ensure that cultural and religious practices do not prevent individual migrants from exercising other fundamental rights or from participating in the host society. This is particularly important as it pertains to the rights and equality of women, the rights and interests of children, and the freedom to practice or not to practice a particular religion. (ibid.: 23)

Here again, one could ask why these principles are explicitly related to migrants and not to all members of society in general. By emphasising the 'rights and equality of women, the rights and interests of children, and the freedom to practice or not to practice a particular religion' it is assumed that these rights are especially called into question by immigrants, while they are common assets in the entire 'host society'. Another central aspect of the integration discourse is the emphasis on the necessity of learning the host society's language, history and culture. The fourth common basic principle for immigrant integration policy in the EU states:

> Basic knowledge of the host society's language, history, and institutions is indispensable to integration; enabling immigrants to acquire this basic knowledge is essential to successful integration ... Acquiring the language and culture of the host society should be an important focus. Full respect for the immigrants' and their descendants' own language and culture should be also an important element of integration policy. (ibid.: 20)

There is no doubt that proficiencies in the language and procedures of the host society facilitate the opportunities, social contacts and career chances of non-native language speakers.[2] However, the phrase 'enabling immigrants to acquire this knowledge' is important as it refers to the role of the host society in facilitating this learning process. Still, the high priority of the 'language and culture' of the host society together with the rather vague statement that 'full respect for the immigrants' . . . own language should be also an important element of integration policy', suggests that something contradictory to the idea of an open, multilingual society with evolving cultures is operative. Beyond that, cultures are depicted as static and self-contained, which becomes even more obvious in the first part of the seventh common basic principle for immigrant integration policy in the EU:

> Frequent interaction between immigrants and Member State citizens is a fundamental mechanism for integration. Shared forums, inter-cultural dialogue, education about immigrants and immigrant cultures . . . enhance the interactions between immigrants and Member State citizens. (ibid.: 22)

Notions of certain self-contained cultures appear to apply both to immigrants and to member state citizens. Integration should be facilitated through dialogue and learning about the immigrant's own culture. Migrants and their descendants are ascribed to their cultures – there is little space for hybrid, context-bound or changing cultural practices and expressions.

Finally, the issue of discrimination and the role of institutions of the host society is explicitly or implicitly raised in several of the common basic principles for immigrant integration policy in the EU. For instance, the sixth principle states:

> Access for immigrants to institutions, as well as to public and private goods and services, on a basis equal to national citizens and in a non-discriminatory way, is a critical foundation for better integration . . . Conversely, uncertainty and unequal treatment breed disrespect for the rules and can marginalise immigrants and their families, socially and economically. The adverse implications of such marginalisation continue to be seen across generations. Restrictions on the rights and privileges of non-nationals should be transparent and be made only after consideration of the integration consequences, particularly on the descendants of immigrants. (ibid.: 21–2)

Here, the potentially exclusionary role of institutions and the need for equal access for immigrants is raised. Still, it remains unclear how extensively forms of institutional discrimination are reflected upon. Is there consideration for the role of institutions in shaping a normality that may marginalise those individuals who do not know the unspoken rules, routines and habits? Further, this principle of equal access is directly modified as it is emphasised that non-nationals may be restricted in their rights and privileges. Interestingly, the restrictions should be made only 'after consideration of the integration consequences, particularly on the descendants of immigrants' as these restrictions may cause marginalisation across generations. It seems that the reason for scrutinising these restrictions is directed more at the aim of social cohesion than at the democratic principle of equal rights.

8.2 *Integration policies in European countries*

8.2.1 LANGUAGE AND CULTURE

One major feature of integration policies – as has already been made clear in the EU principles on integration – is the high priority given to knowledge of the language and culture of the host country. In a growing number of European countries, language and citizenship tests are required in order to acquire citizenship; additionally, however, newcomers are obliged to undertake language or integration courses in some countries with the threat of potential sanctions if they don't (see Chapter 4).

Positively read, on the one hand these approaches provide an infrastructure for migrants to learn about the conditions of the host society and to improve their opportunities to participate in society. In fact, such an infrastructure has only recently been created in Germany. The fact that the courses are obligatory reflects a general 'integration imperative'; learning the language is not understood simply as a reasonable aim for most migrants, but rather as an obligation. One reason behind this is the practical objective to have 'employable' residents.

A second reason is the fear of dispersion of the host country's 'own' language and culture. Citizenship tests often reflect the suspicion that migrants, especially Muslims, would not understand or respect the norms and values of the host society. In that sense, the integration policies follow thoroughly political aims of making adaptation to language and allegedly clear-cut norms and values obligatory to immigrants, while the state simply provides the infrastructure for this process. Infrastructural measures for multilingualism or change of cultures are secondary or not on the agenda at all.

Language skills are a central issue in educational policy, especially since international comparative surveys on students' academic performance have shown the competitive disadvantages of not being proficient in the host country language (for example, German and Danish). In countries with a relatively young immigration history and a strong mono-ethnic and mono-religious conception of the nation, such as Greece and Spain (despite the latter's strong regionalism), the policy and discourse adopted so far with regard to the integration of non-mother tongue pupils has been one of implicit assimilation. In Greece, intercultural concepts that not only involve intercultural exchange and knowledge of other cultures, but also encompass a reconsideration of the 'in-group' culture through the interaction with culturally diverse pupils remain marginal within education policy (Gropas and Triandafyllidou 2009b).

Elsewhere, the German National Integration Plan (NIP) (2007) sets out that the importance of educational integration was 'to meet future needs of skilled personnel and to stay competitive on an international level' (Bundesregierung 2007: 65). The NIP has maintained, therefore, that the most important requirement is good German language skills. Intercultural competence is regarded as a specific potential in migrant children, rather than a general educational aim. In contrast to earlier recommendations made by the Standing Conference of the Ministers of Education and Cultural Affairs of the *Länder* (1996), which include a quite elaborate agreement on intercultural education, in terms of education the NIP does not include any real acceptance of, or approach to, difference and cultural heterogeneity.

In Denmark, meanwhile, not only citizenship but also the status of permanent residents is tied to effective integration which must be proven, beyond the self-support requirement, by a language and a multiple-choice knowledge test. Conspicuous cultural or religious difference, whether or not it is a real barrier, is represented as a handicap, as unwillingness to integrate and, above all, as a need to 'learn Danish values' – in order to function in Danish society (Mouritsen et al. 2009).

There are other conceivable approaches that may overcome the dualistic view of immigrants as having deficits in citizenship knowledge and skills versus a native's irreproachable democratic beliefs and capacities. Against the background of a web of political clientelism and patronage in Greece, Gropas and Triandafyllidou (2009a) recommend strengthening 'civic citizenship in Greece among migrants and natives alike. This can be pursued through encouraging civic classes on constitutional values, democratic governance and human rights for all population groups within Greece' (ibid.: 24). In the UK, meanwhile, beside citizenship tests for naturalisation applicants, the introduction in 2002 of citizenship education – with the purpose of promoting 'active citizenship' – may overcome the addressed dualism. Still, indepth analysis of the contents of such courses is necessary in order to assess to what extent these overcome the idea of the deficit Muslim or immigrant 'other'.

Citizenship tests generally mirror the idea of an identifiable and testable curriculum on a nation's culture and history. In Germany, the implementation in September 2008 of a nationwide citizenship test, as well as its predecessors that existed in some *Länder* from 2006, reflect the notion in the German debate that integration and its final achievement of German citizenship points to something beyond formal rights of participation or commitment to the constitution. Citizenship is 'about the feeling of belonging' and commitment to the values underlying the constitution (Schiffauer 2007; see also Peter 2010).

While the broadly criticised citizenship test in Baden-Wuerttemberg, especially in its first incarnation from January 2006, quite explicitly infers that Muslim applicants do not share the norms and values of German society (Miera 2009), the nationwide citizenship test is regarded as being more fact-based. Nonetheless, some of the questions reveal the underlying aim of testing the 'real' appropriateness of (Muslim) migrants becoming part of the nation. Although they do not openly target an allegedly Islamic way of thinking, they implicitly reify Islamic beliefs as a potential threat to security and/or the democratic order and liberal gender relations. For instance, several of the questions in the test are as follows:

> Which right is one of the basic rights in Germany?
> (a) The right to possess a weapon (b) The right of the strongest (c) Freedom of opinion (d) Self-administered justice
> Which of the following statements is part of the German law?
> (a) Smoking on the street is not allowed (b) Women must wear skirts (c) Beating children is not allowed (d) Women are not allowed to drink alcohol (Gesamtkatalog 2008: nos. 4, 242)

A further example, which on the one hand presumes that applicants favour polygamy and on the other construes as German 'normality' liberal views about a variety of ways of living, in particular same-sex partnerships, we have the question, 'Which way of living is not allowed in Germany?' The possible answers are as follows: '(a) Man and woman are divorced and live together with new partners (b) Two women live together (c) A single father lives together with his two children (d) A man is married to two women at the same time' (ibid.: 272).

Moreover, the test quite explicitly gives us the idea of the prevalence or even exclusive relevance of Christianity in German and European culture. A prime illustration is the following question, in which appplicants can only choose one (that is, the second) of the given answers: 'Which religion has shaped European and German culture? (a) Hinduism (b) Christianity (c) Buddhism (d) Islam' (ibid.: 295).

What Amir-Moazami writes with regard to the implications of the German Islam Conference test also holds true for the national citizenship test; she says that

> the process of requiring identification with the values behind the law ... precisely [uncovers] the non-neutral, i.e. ethical character of the constitutional principles themselves. The demand to also subscribe to an ethical substance of the constitutional principles, indeed, itself unveils the particularity of allegedly universal constitutional norms. (Amir-Moazami 2009: 10)

8.2.2 Dialogue and consultation structures

An important element of recent integration policies in some European countries is the involvement of immigrants in the debate on integration issues on both a national and local governmental level. Increased participation could be interpreted as an indicator of the mutual and process-related character of the integration programmes. There are different types of forums and dialogue structures granting different degrees of participation to immigrants. The purpose of these forums is in fact ambivalent, being a symbol of recognition and an institution of (restricted) participation on the one hand, and an instrument of pacifying or disciplining on the other. On the national level, in the case of Germany dialogue structures symbolise a sort of acknowledgment of immigrants as part of society; however this is still not the case in some EU countries.

In Denmark, as Mouritsen et al. (2009) explain, while the experience with local consultative networks has often been positive, the cooptation of ethnic minority organisations at the national level has not. The creation of local consultative networks did not offer any special power of representation nor did it give recognition to immigrants.

In Spain in 1995, the Forum for the Social Integration of Immigrants was established as a consultative body with the capacity to issue reports and policy recommendations and to adopt agreements on its own initiative, or by a non-binding consultation with the public administration (Zapata-Barrero and Zaragoza Cristiani 2009). The forum is composed of thirty representatives from public administration, social organisations and immigrant associations who are appointed by the Ministry of Employment and Social Affairs. The selection criteria actually restrict accessibility to immigrants who wish to participate in the forum and limit their power to define the modality of dialogue within it. As Zapata-Barrero and Zaragoza Cristiani (2009) show, the participation of immigrants is conditioned by their economic dependence on public authorities, the moderation of their discourse – negotiation and reform versus rupture and conflict – and the expectations of the institutions that the immigrants will behave 'appropriately', that is cooperate and assist the authorities rather than engage in hostile behaviour (ibid.: 21f.).

The German case also exemplifies the restricted power of immigrants in setting the agenda in such dialogue structures. In July 2006, German Chancellor Angela Merkel of the Christian Democratic Union (CDU) invited migrant organisations and representatives of other relevant social groups to take part in the National Integration Summit (NIS). This was the first governmental initiative in German immigration history to acknowledge the reality of immigration and to involve migrants in an institutionalised debate.

In the run-up to the second NIS in July 2007, the legislator passed an amendment to the Immigration Law that included the requirement of new immigrants from non-EU countries to have basic German language skills and the introduction of a minimum age of eighteen for immigrating family members. Moreover, these amendments referred to regulations concerning the reunion of spouses and introduced a differentiation between Germans born in Germany with single citizenship and individuals with dual citizenship, or those having lived abroad for a longer period before being naturalised as Germans. The amendment predominantly affected German-Turks, as it generally questioned the potency of German citizenship with regard to naturalised migrants.

The fact that a discussion of these amendments was not included in the Integration Summit was sharply criticised by several migrant associations and other organisations. The representatives of three Turkish and/or Islamic organisations boycotted the NIS in protest. The migrant associations argued that there was a discrepancy between the official use of rhetoric and symbolic policies and the simultaneous propagation of unequal and restrictive immigration policies. This criticism pointed to the limits of the politics of 'toleration' in the sense of 'symbolic recognition' (Galeotti 2002) without substantially providing for participation and equal opportunities.

Further, the new legislation was criticised as discriminating against Germans of Turkish decent in comparison to German-born Germans. The German leadership, however, did not see it that way; in fact Chancellor Merkel declared to the protesting migrant associations, 'one cannot simply give the government an ultimatum'.[3] Having said that, she offered an olive branch by saying that she would host the NIS and that 'my hand is outstretched' (ibid.). The Federal Integration Commissioner Maria Böhmer (CDU) argued that one should not only pay heed to 'those with the loudest voices' and the integration process should not be dominated by the 'Turkish-Islamic question'. Chancellor Merkel insisted, 'We don't talk about migrants but with them', thus accusing the boycotting organisations of making any dialogue impossible.[4]

This example illustrates the nature of the dialogue at the NIS. The government takes the role of the host offended by the guests who have rejected its generous invitation. As soon as migrant representatives dare to criticise publicly the government by contesting its modes of dialogue and asking for a different agenda, they are sharply rebuked and described as being too immature or unwilling to take part in a democratic procedure. The criticism itself – that there was a discrepancy between the rhetoric of dialogue and the factual involvement of migrants – was ignored by the government. Nevertheless, in retrospect, both parties – the government and the migrant associations – stress the positive outcome of the whole NIS process (Miera 2009). This could be seen as a sign that migrants have taken on state targets as their own. Another interpretation might be that they have in fact achieved relevant influence and that new fields of activity and opportunity structures for migrants and cultural groups are opening up either within – or despite – the disciplining nature of the integration project.[5]

8.3 *Change of institutions and routines?*

If integration is a 'two-way process' – irrespective of the critique of the notion of linearity implicit in this approach – the contribution of both parts within this process should be apparent. We have already seen the demands made of immigrants to learn the language and the culture of the host country. We have discussed the dialogue structures through which the host society takes the concerns of immigrants seriously, while at the same time holding the power to set the agenda, define the modes of dialogue and take decisions. Nevertheless, the analysis has shown that on the side of society, a willingness to open up or to make decisive steps towards the acknowledgment of cultural and religious diversity is quite restricted. One instrument in this sense could, in fact, be a substantial anti-discrimination policy which we will discuss in the following paragraphs.

EU member states have implemented anti-discrimination legislation, along the lines of national traditions as in the UK and the Netherlands, or because of EU requirements, as is the case in most other EU member states. Certainly, legislation to prevent and sanction discrimination and effective institutions to enforce this legislation is a democratic instrument and a central feature of equal rights and of the protection of vulnerable individuals or groups. It may also be an instrument of raising consciousness within society and of developing a 'culture of non-discrimination' or of equal recognition. But is the implementation of an anti-discrimination legislation already an indicator of 'a two-way adaptation, involving change in values, norms and behaviour for both newcomers and members of the existing society'? Is it also a sign of integration as a common enduring process?

The process of transposing the EU directives in the countries under study in this volume has been met by general resistance against such legislation. Nearly all country reports document a low awareness of discriminatory practices and perceptions, and insufficient measures to raise consciousness and knowledge in institutions and among legal experts, employers and individuals potentially subject to discrimination. Discrimination is often regarded as a problem of individual behaviour or even as legitimate (Gropas and Triandafyllidou 2009b). In the UK, anti-discrimination policies have been implemented since the 1960s; nevertheless, as in other countries policy responses to discrimination on the grounds of religion, and Islamophobia in particular, face greater opposition to traditionally conceived (colour-based) discrimination (Meer 2010).

Interestingly, one rationalisation of anti-discrimination policies that is increasingly gaining relevance is an economic argument rather than an ethical one. Principles of equal rights and protection against racism, sexism and Islamophobia take a back seat. In France the recognition of group or minority rights would contradict the republican idea of the equal individual and non-distinction of citizens. In fact, this view has led to colour blindness and double standards in citizenship (Lepinard and Simon 2008). In France one can observe a slow change in the anti-discrimination paradigm due to the issue of ethnic discrimination and demands of group recognition by non-governmental organisations (NGOs). With the implementation of an independent authority in charge of monitoring all types of discrimination, anti-discrimination policies are now encapsulated by a concept of diversity. The term is easier to communicate, since it is not connected to a broader framework of values. It replaces a worn-out expression of integration – in France this is interpreted in the sense of assimilation – which became unpopular and ineffective in addressing issues such as ethnic relations and discrimination. On the other hand, the concept of diversity and discrimination is more prevalent in the human resources side of business and has yet to be deployed or appropriated in a broader sense.

Similarly, in German official anti-discrimination policies diversity is only appreciated in the limited sense of being a means of economic progress. The Federal Anti-Discrimination Authority focuses mainly on business and argues that diversity management is economically advantageous, seeing 'equal treatment as added value'. This is accompanied by a human rights approach without any convincing reflection upon the potential conflict between these two focal areas. NGOs frequently criticise the fact that in practice, the Federal Anti-Discrimination Authority does not significantly engage in the development of an encompassing support infrastructure. Furthermore, NGOs and some trade unionists point to the limitations of the diversity management approach as being more oriented towards economic benefits than equal rights.

It is doubtful whether this strategy alone is sufficient to achieve the aim of effectively implementing anti-discrimination legislation, embedding an anti-discrimination culture and equal rights in society. Alongside this strategy, the Federal Anti-Discrimination Authority does not significantly engage in the development of an encompassing support infrastructure for (potential) victims, which could indicate a step forward on the two-way integration road.

More generally, the effects of anti-discrimination legislation are restricted as this legislation does not offer the possibility to tackle structural discrimination. The law does not provide real instruments to help the increasing numbers of employees in insecure employment, or in small firms where employees are not represented by working councils or trade unions, let alone address the situation of undocumented workers. As a respondent in the German case study reported, firms acting outside this framework would not implement required procedures and practices, and employees would not dare complain for fear of losing their jobs. The pressure to keep their jobs and earn money is far greater than the importance of making a stand against discrimination, something that is especially relevant to undocumented migrants (Miera 2008).

Similarly, the issue of institutional discrimination resulting from routines, habits and established practices in an organisation are barely reflected upon in integration policies. For example, in the case of schooling, Gomolla and Radtke (2002) show that headmasters, teachers and administrations would often inadvertently act in a discriminatory way simply by following the organisational conventions of the system, for example primary schools choosing which type of secondary school pupils would move on to, principally taking into account the places available in the secondary schools in the neighbourhood rather than the skills and talents of the children. Ignoring or not considering the effects of structural or institutional discrimination contradicts the idea of a mutual process of integration, for the migrants alone are deemed responsible for their success or failure in adapting to society.

Conclusion

Taking into consideration EU principles on integration policies alongside examples from particular national contexts, especially that of Germany, this chapter has offered an analysis of the contemporary meaning of integration as a concept and political practice in Europe. In contrast to the concepts of multiculturalism and assimilation, integration appears at first to be less politically charged as well as a positive, unquestioned objective. In several political programmes, integration appears as a concept somewhere between multiculturalism and assimilation, which therefore would ask of immigrants a certain degree of adaptation to existing social norms and conventions without demanding that they give up their cultural specificities. This programme is often illustrated with the picture of the 'two-way path', one of integration as a mutual process.

The theoretical discussion illustrates that inherent to the concept of integration as a 'two-way path' is the concept that migrants disrupt an existing coherent order, which then has to be re-established through integration measures. Conceiving integration as something to which all members of society would permanently contribute is not really part of the common idea of integration. What does the 'mutuality of the integration process' or 'two-way path' of integration mean exactly in the political integration programmes of contemporary European countries? The analysis shows that in the first instance, migrants are viewed within the integration process as needing to fulfil certain integration requirements – above all, learning the language and adapting to the culture of the host society. Apparently, the mutuality of the process only means that the host society facilitates the process by providing the infrastructure (or improving the existing structures). Respect and recognition of the 'other culture' are often claimed as missing in concrete measures.

Significantly, culture is often conceived in these policies in terms of a firm, static entity, which can and has to be learned. Here, the mutuality of the integration process means that residents should learn something about the 'other' culture in the form of intercultural festivities or forums – a concept that does not leave much space for change and mutual influence. It is indirectly assumed that respecting the migrant culture and religion entails a possible disrespect of human rights, liberal rights and democratic values by migrants. For instance citizenship tests have, as a matter of course, an insinuated assumption that migrants and especially those of Muslim faith are not able to, or do not want to, respect democratic values.

According to the dualistic image of the 'two-way path', migrants and 'society' oppose each other; migrants, and Muslims in particular, are referred to as the 'other'. The 'other' is associated with deficits that potentially threaten democratic order on one hand, and that are intact and are civically capable in society on the other. Beyond that, an analysis of institutions that are supposed to translate this idea of mutuality in the integration process, through the creation of dialogue forums between government and migrants, has shown the limitations of these projects. Access to these forums, agenda setting as well as the modes of negotiation are all defined by the state. The state appears as the generous host who also reprimands its guests when they do not conform to its norms and habits.

Finally, the analysis illustrates that even approaches that could be appropriate for reflecting upon and changing exclusionary mechanisms in society are still very restricted. Legislation on anti-discrimination in several European countries provides instruments for combating discrimination and raising consciousness about discrimination in society. Interestingly, the economic rationalisation to acknowledge anti-discrimination measures is gaining much relevance. It is doubtful whether this standpoint can adequately encompass the role of structural and institutional discrimination in society and facilitate concrete steps toward integration.

This critique should not negate the importance of anti-discrimination legislation or the acknowledgment of mechanisms to support migrant rights through state dialogue structures. The aim of this chapter is to foster a critical reflection on the extent to which such measures actually contribute to a mutual process of integration and which political programme is in fact followed by the allegedly neutral postulate of integration.

Notes

1. Refer to the empirical study on the German case as part of the EU project, *A European Approach to Multicultural Citizenship. Legal, Political and Educational Challenges* (2006–9). The theoretical framework of this empirical study is described in Chapters 2 and 3 by Tariq Modood and Nasar Meer.
2. There is more expectation for non-Western Europeans or non-US English speakers to learn the language of the host country.
3. *Frankfurter Allgemeine Zeitung* (2007), 'Merkel: Der Regierung stellt man keine Ultimaten', 12 July 2007. Available at www.faz.net/artikel/C30923/integrationsgipfel-merkel-der-regierung-stellt-man-keine-ultimaten-30025450.html, accessed on 12 August 2009.
4. 'Boykott sorgt für Ärger', *Tagesspiegel*, 12 July 2007.
5. See also the German Islam Conference, Amir-Moazami 2009 and Peter 2010.

References

Amir-Moazami, S. (2009), 'Islam und Geschlecht unter liberal-säkularer Regierungsführung. Die Deutsche Islam Konferenz', in J. Brunner and S. Lavi (eds), *Juden und Muslime in Deutschland*, Göttingen: Wallstein, pp. 185–205.
Brands Kehris, I. (2007), *Citizenship and Multiculturalism in Latvia: Public and Political Discourses*, report for the EMILIE project. Available at http://emilie.eliamep.gr/emilie-reports-on-multiculturalism-debates/, accessed on 13 July 2010.
Bundesregierung (ed.) (2007), *Nationaler Integrationsplan: Neue Wege – Neue Chancen Bonn*. Available at www.bundesregierung.de/Content/DE/Artikel/2007/07/Anlage/2007-08-30-nationaler-integrationsplan,property=publicationFile.pdf, accessed on 25 March 2010.

Castles, S., S. Vertovec, M. Korac and E. Vasta (2002), *Integration: Mapping the Field*, Report of a Project carried out by the University of Oxford Centre for Migration and Policy Research and Refugee Studies Centre, contracted by the Home Office Immigration Research and Statistics Service (IRSS), Home Office Online Report 28/03.

Council of the European Union (2004), 'Common basic principles for immigrant integration policy in the European Union', Press Release, 2618th Council Meeting, Justice and Home Affairs, Brussels, pp. 19–24.

Galeotti, A. E. (2002), *Toleration as Recognition*, Cambridge: Cambridge University Press.

Gesamtkatalog (2008), *Gesamtkatalog der für den Einbürgerungstest zugelassenen Prüfungsfragen*. Available at www.bmi.bund.de/cae/servlet/contentblob/123028/publicationFile/13216/Einburgerungstest_Allgemein.pdf and http://oet.bamf.de/pls/oetut/f?p=514:30:800670263286528::NO, Berlin: BMI, accessed on 13 July 2010.

Gomolla, M. and F. O. Radtke (2002), *Institutionelle Diskriminierung. Die Herstellung ethnischer Differenz in der Schule*, Opladen: Leske + Budrich.

Gropas, R. and A. Triandafyllidou (2009a), *Immigrants and Political Rights in Greece. Between Patronage and the Search for Inclusion*', report for the EMILIE project. Available at http://emilie.eliamep.gr/emilie-reports-on-immigrants-political-participation-in-europe/, accessed on 13 July 2010.

Gropas, R. and A. Triandafyllidou (2009b), *Migration, Identity and Citizenship: Approaches for Addressing Cultural Diversity in Greece*, report for the EMILIE project. Available at http://emilie.eliamep.gr/emilie-comprehensive-country-reports/, accessed on 13 July 2010.

Karakayali, S. (2009), 'Paranoic integrationism. Die Integrationsformel als unmöglicher (Klassen-)Kompromiss', in S. Hess, J. Binder and J. Moser (eds), *No Integration? Kulturwissenschaftliche Beiträge zur Integrationsdebatte in Europa*, Bielefeld: transcript, pp. 95–103.

Krüger-Potratz, M. (2003), 'Sprachförderung und mehr ... Integration von (Neu-)Zuwanderern – politische, konzeptionelle und didaktische Notwendigkeiten, *Werkstatt Weiterbildung, Sprachförderung und mehr – Herausforderung zur Integration von Neuzuwandern*. Available at www.lzz-nrw.de/docs/DOKU_WW2001.pdf, accessed on 3 June 2010.

Leggewie, C. (1996), 'Ist kulturelle Koexistenz lernbar? Multikulturalismus und Erziehung', in P. Kalb, C. Petry and K. Sitte (eds), *Werte und Erziehung. Kann Schule zur Bindungsfähigkeit beitragen?*, Weinheim: Beltz, pp. 158–69.

Lepinard, E. and P. Simon (2008), *From Integration to Antidiscrimination... to Diversity? Antidiscrimination Politics and Policies in French Workplaces*, report for the EMILIE project. Available at http://emilie.eliamep.gr/reports-on-the-discrimination-in-the-labour-market-in-europe/, accessed on 13 July 2010.

Meer, N. (2010), 'The impact of European equality directives upon British anti-discrimination legislation', *Policy & Politics*, 38(1), pp. 197–215.

Meer, N. and T. Modood (2009), 'The multicultural state we're in: Muslims, "multiculture" and the "civic re-balancing" of British multiculturalism', *Political Studies*, 57(1), pp. 473–9.

Miera, F. (2007), *Multiculturalism Debates in Germany*, report for the EMILIE project. Available at http://emilie.eliamep.gr/emilie-reports-on-multiculturalism-debates/, accessed on 14 July 2010.

Miera, F. (2008), *Labour Market Discrimination and Legal Challenges in Germany*, report for the EMILIE project. Available at http://emilie.eliamep.gr/wp-content/uploads/2009/02/labour-market-discrimination-and-legal-challenges-in-germany2.pdf, accessed on 14 July 2010.

Miera, F. (2009), *Political Participation of Migrants in Germany*, report for the EMILIE project. Available at http://emilie.eliamep.gr/wp-content/uploads/2009/09/wp5-germany-formatted.pdf, accessed on 14 July 2010.

Mouritsen, P., S. Lex, L. Lindekilde and T. V. Olsen (2009), *Immigration, Integration and the Politics of Cultural Diversity in Denmark: Political Discourse and Legal, Political and Educational Challenges*, report for the EMILIE project. Available at http://emilie.eliamep.gr/emilie-comprehensive-country-reports/, accessed on 13 July 2010.

Oberndörfer, D. (2001), 'Integration der Ausländer in den demokratischen Verfassungsstaat: Ziele und Aufgaben', in K. Bade (ed.), *Integration und Illegalität in Deutschland*, Osnabrück: Rat für Migration e.V., pp. 11–29.

Penninx, R. and M. Martiniello (2004), 'Integration processes and policies: State of the art and lessons', in R. Penninx, K. Kraal, M. Martiniello and S. Vertovec (eds), *Citizenship in European Cities. Immigrants, Local Politics and Integration Policies*, Aldershot: Ashgate Publishing, pp. 139–53.

Peter, F. (2010), 'Welcoming Muslims into the nation: Tolerance politics and integration in Germany', in J. Cesari (ed.), *Muslims in the West after 9/11. Religion, Politics and Law*, London: Routledge, pp. 119–44.

Schiffauer, W. (2007), 'Der unheimliche Muslim – Staatsbürgerschaft und zivilgesellschaftliche Ängste', *Soziale Welt*, 17, special issue, pp. 111–33.

Zapata-Barrero, R. and J. Zaragoza Cristiani (2009), *Political Rights of Immigrants in Spain*, report for the EMILIE project. Available at http://emilie.eliamep.gr/emilie-reports-on-immigrants-political-participation-in-europe/, accessed on 14 July 2010.

9
Ethnic Statistics in Europe: The Paradox of Colour-blindness

Angéline Escafré-Dublet and Patrick Simon

Introduction

Trying to assess the multicultural dimension of European societies by portraying the diversity of their population can seem awkward, if not impossible. Most population data in Europe is 'blind' to ethnic diversity, providing desegregated information by gender, age, citizenship or place of birth, sometimes by ethnicity, but never by race. This 'statistical blindness' is a legacy of the strategy to dismiss race and ethnicity from all legal texts and collective representations in the post-war period. However, the ban on ethnic statistics has recently been challenged by the implementation of equality policies, where data on the situation of ethnic and racial minorities is required to assess and monitor discrimination, increase awareness and design policies (Goldston 2005; Simon 2005). As stated by the European Commission against Racism and Intolerance (ECRI) in its first General Policy Recommendation of 1996, 'it is difficult to develop and effectively implement policies ... without good data'. The ECRI recommended collecting, 'in accordance with European laws, regulations and recommendations on data-protection and protection of privacy, where and when appropriate, data which will assist in assessing and evaluating the situation and experiences of groups which are particularly vulnerable to racism, xenophobia, anti-Semitism and intolerance' (CRI, (96) 43 rev). The same holds for the CERD (Committee for Elimination of Racial Discrimination) and for most of the international organisations, including the European Commission, striving to tackle racism and discrimination.

The production of ethnic statistics remains contentious, however, and, in the context of the anti-discrimination legal framework put in place by the EU Race Directive of 2000, member states have had contrasting responses. While the UK had already been producing ethnic statistics in the census as part of its equality policies since 1991 and has continued to do so (Ni Brochlain 1990; Coombes 1996; Stavo-Debauge 2005), other countries have been reluctant to pursue the idea or have simply ignored the matter. Although ethnic groups or minorities are mentioned in multicultural and anti-discrimination policies in Scandinavian countries and the Netherlands, the categories are in fact referring to data on the second generation of immigrants. France and, to a certain extent, Belgium have had contentious debates on the production of ethnic statistics deemed to foster racism by numerous social actors (anti-racist organisations, policy makers and some social scientists). In other cases, such as Germany, the collection of ethnic data has not been mentioned until recently in the process of implementing anti-discrimination policies. Finally, in countries that have started experiencing (or acknowledging the experience of) immigration, such as Italy, Greece, Poland and Spain, the issue is absent from the debate.

Official statistics result from national historical paths and reflect the structural divisions of societies. The designs by which states classify and categorise individuals vary depending on their immigration patterns, historic minorities and colonial legacies. Classification also changes according to the states' understanding of inequality and represents an assessment of their positioning on the debate over multiculturalism: the higher the commitment, the stronger the data. It does not mean, however, that countries with low levels of group recognition do not categorise or operate distinctions among individuals, but rather that they focus on what they consider a legitimate basis of distinction, such as nationality and legal status. In their production of statistics they also reinforce boundaries, between nationals and non-nationals, citizens and non-citizens.

With a view to charting the different stages at which each member state stands in its implementation of anti-discrimination policies, this chapter will analyse how countries take up the challenge of measuring diversity. First, it explores how the official production of statistics reflects the process of differentiation at play in each national context. Second, it investigates the implementation of anti-discrimination policies and the opportunity to collect ethnic data as introduced by European policies. Third, it discusses why debates on ethnic data have emerged in some countries and why they are absent in others. We will examine one of the strongest criticisms against ethnic data, which maintains that it stigmatises individuals and encourages racism. This chapter argues that the various processes of differentiation at play in each country pre-existed the debate on ethnic statistics. The construction of comprehensive monitoring systems to measure diversity does not constitute a return to past occurrences of racial prejudice, but rather a move forward. It provides new methods against discrimination as well as new opportunities for the empowerment of minority groups.

9.1 The making of the 'other' through official statistics

European societies have different levels of ethnic and racial diversity depending on their nation building, colonial legacy and migration history. Beyond the 'concrete' diversity of populations,[1] these various historical paths have also resulted in the construction of contrasting representations of diversity. How societies describe and characterise diversity varies according to media coverage, political discourses and the construction of national narratives. These 'depictions' of diversity may become embodied in institutional practices and modes of governance (Vertovec 2010). We would like here to focus on official statistics as a relevant medium to highlight processes of 'othering' in European societies.

Population statistics may well be designed to analyse demographic trends and to benchmark public policies; they are, however, also crucial venues for the construction of nation-building and the (re) production of national identity (Anderson 1991). Official and scientific statistical categorisations both reflect and affect the structural divisions of societies, as well as mainstream social representations. The existence of any kind of categories and variables in official statistics – ethnic and racial categorisation being the most prominent example – should therefore be analysed according to historical developments and political contexts. Moreover, the absence of ethnic and racial categorisation should also be regarded in this perspective. The decision to avoid ethnicity as a salient category is a choice in the *repertoire* of identity politics and boundary making: it favours citizenship over ethnicity and distinguishes citizens from non-citizens. These processes of making groups visible and invisible through statistics account for the heterogeneity of data collection across Europe, despite a general trend towards standardisation.[2]

Looking at the wide variety of practices of ethnic and racial categorisations in time and space, Rallu et al. (2006) have suggested a basic yet comprehensive typology of four types of 'data collection regimes': type 1: counting to dominate; type 2: not counting in the name of national integration; type 3: counting in the name of multiculturalism; type 4: counting to implement positive action in the name of equality. The first type, 'counting to dominate', has been used by most imperial and colonial states that have asserted an ethno-cultural supremacy. Very widespread in the past, it still exists in some newly independent countries and neo-imperial states. The second type, 'not counting in the name of national integration', relates to states where the process of nation building is based on the homogenisation of the population and this indistinctiveness among individuals is conceived as a condition for national cohesion (Gellner 1983; Hobsbawn 1990). Distinctive ethnic identities are regarded as undesirable markers of fragmentation, bound to disappear in the assimilation process. If anything, their expression might be kept in the private sphere. The producers of official statistics refrain from using ethnic categories for the same reason that ethnic identities are kept outside of the public sphere – because this is perceived as a threat to national cohesion.

The third type, 'counting in the name of multiculturalism', relates to states that have an increasing appreciation of the ethnic and racial diversity in their population. Contrary to the first type of this typology, states do not operate distinctions among individuals according to principles of racial hierarchy in order to assert a position of superiority. Their attempt to identify groups pertains to an acknowledgement of diversity from a symbolic and organisational point of view. This type applies to multinational states where the process of nation building has kept national minorities within the nation-state. The fourth type, 'counting to implement positive action for equality', has appeared only recently. It is a complete reversal of the first type in the typology. It may resort to categories that have been produced in times of imperial or colonial rule, but it is aimed at correcting past inequalities. In this fourth type, the process of data collection is embedded in a broader equality policy. Classifications are defined in equality laws and fit the legal standards that protect specific minority groups (Simon 2004).

How does this typology apply to European countries? Out of the forty-two countries of the Council of Europe, twenty-two collect data on ethnicity (even though they use the terminology of 'nationality' that does not refer to the actual legal status of the individuals), twenty-four on religion by denomination or belief (or by affiliation, more rarely both) and twenty-six on language (most commonly mother tongue, but other information on the language spoken is also collected). A closer look at the countries, however, reveals a clear divide between countries of Central and Eastern Europe that follow type 3 of the typology ('counting in the name of multiculturalism'), and countries in other parts of Europe, which have no such tradition of recording ethno-cultural characteristics and follow the second type ('not counting in the name of national integration'). Only two countries of Western Europe, UK and Ireland, follow type 4 and collect data on ethnicity with the aim to implement positive action (Simon 2007).[3]

More precisely, the following table identifies the types of data collection for the nine countries under scrutiny in this book. It distinguishes collection of data through census and population registers.

One series of countries describe their population with reference to citizenship and country of birth: France, Germany, Greece and Spain. Statistics mainly distinguish citizens, aliens and immigrants. The combination may vary depending on their history and nationality codes.[4] Those are countries that follow type 2 of the typology ('counting in the name of national integration'); they are 'state-centred' in the sense that the state is the main criterion they use to distinguish individuals from one another.

A second series of countries, such as Poland and Latvia, place the emphasis on language and 'nationality' (understood as ethnicity). These are the countries that emerged from the wreckage of the former Austro-Hungarian and Soviet empires. They are 'mosaic' countries in the sense that the legacy of a national minority's policy that characterised these empires and regions explains the attention given to ethno-cultural questions. Moreover, the tradition to collect data on ethnicity has been recently supported by the implementation of the 'Framework Convention for the Protection of National Minorities' (1995), which encourages the use of statistics.

An intermediate type of country defines 'ethnic minorities' according to the country of birth of the immigrants' parents. Even though this category has not been featured to implement anti-discrimination policies, it meets most of the anti-discrimination objectives and corresponds to a low level of commitment to multiculturalism – a soft version of multiculturalism. Sweden and the Netherlands are the most prominent cases of countries using this category. Regarding the countries under scrutiny in this book, it would fit the description of Denmark and Belgium.

Finally, the UK is the only country in this group to define itself officially as multicultural. Its approach to population diversity has led it to operate certain classifications that are designed to reflect

Table 9.1 Data collection in a selection of countries

Countries	Censuses Year	Censuses Variables	Censuses Comments	Population Registers
Belgium	2001	Semi register-based census. Population statistics have been mainly collected through the population register since 1991. Questions on language are considered sensitive in view of its position in the political organisation of the country. In addition, the information gathered varies according to the community concerned: in the Flemish-speaking part of the country 'ethnic' data is collected (in the category of *allochtone*), but not in the Walloon part.		Country of birth Citizenship Country of birth and citizenship of parents
Denmark		Interconnection of administrative files with the population register	In education, languages spoken by children at home are collected to build categories.	Country of birth Citizenship Country of birth and citizenship of parents
France	1999, yearly since 2004	Country of birth Citizenship	Former citizenship for French by acquisition is also collected. Place of birth of parents in an equivalent of Microcensus and in surveys.	
Germany		Interconnection of administrative files with the population register and a Microcensus	Specific register for aliens (*Ausländerzentralregister*, AZR). A Microcensus collects information about *Migration Hintergrund* by combining citizenship and place of birth of parents.	Country of birth Citizenship Religion (affiliation)
Greece	2001	Country of birth Citizenship	Greek citizenship applies also to the Greek diaspora so that 'return migrants' can be considered as Greek nationals.	Population register

	Censuses			Population Registers
Countries	Year	Variables	Comments	
Latvia	2000	Citizenship Nationality Language (mother tongue and proficiency)	Nationality, religion and language are collected by ticking a box in a pre-coded list.	Population register
Poland	2002	Country of birth Citizenship Nationality Language (spoken)	Questions on citizenship and nationality use a binary format: Polish/Other	
Spain	2001		Semi register-based census. Population statistics are collected mainly through the population register (*Padrones*).	Country of birth Citizenship Language
United Kingdom	2001	Country of birth Ethnic Group Religion Language (mother tongue)	Questions on ethnic group and religion use a pre-coded list. Questions on religion are optional.	Diffusion of standards of classification (ethnic group), reproduced in a large number of administrative files and employers' records

the recent history of immigration, whether originating from labour migration or post-colonial flows. The categories that are used to reflect on 'ethnic diversity' combine direct references to ethnicity and to immigration background.

To what extent does the case of the UK foreshadow the future practice of other states in comparable situations? The recent implementation of an anti-discrimination legislation has provided a strong impetus for European countries. It is likely, though, that countries with a high level of diversity related to post-war migration flows will follow a different path. Since the place of birth of the parents is used as a proxy for ethnicity, the focus on the so-called 'second generation' in Europe provides an alternative to the 'ethnic question'. In this respect, it is revealing that Eurostat added a migration module to the 2008 EU-wide Labour Force Survey and that they chose to collect information on the parents' place of birth. There are different reasons for this predictable choice that we will further investigate.

9.2 Implementing anti-discrimination policies: the challenge of collecting ethnic data

The strong impetus given by international human rights bodies to the collection of ethnic statistics – including official ones – may resonate as a paradox. Historically, the collection of data on ethnic, racial or national origin, religion and even languages has been used to exclude, discriminate against and even exterminate groups and individuals who have been identified as undesirable minorities (Seltzer 1998; Kertzer and Arel 2002). Moreover, not only have ethnic and racial statistics been used for ill purposes, but their mere existence reflects a misconception of human nature. It fosters the reification of ethnic and racial identities and encourages the perpetuation of ethnic and racial hierarchies. In this context, one can hardly expect a positive use of ethnic and racial statistics.

9.2.1 A NEW GENERATION OF ANTI-DISCRIMINATION POLICIES

For a long time, the key explanation for the relative absence of statistical data on race and ethnicity in continental Europe was twofold. First, it was linked to data protection laws which define ethnic and racial origin as 'sensitive data' and therefore banned their collection (Kriszan 2001; Simon 2007; Ringelheim and De Schutter 2009). Second, this data was considered inadequate to describe inequalities that were mainly perceived as resulting from differences in social status. As a consequence, ethnicity was deemed irrelevant to describe and analyse European societies. Moreover, this framing matched the anti-racist creed that race – ethnicity being understood as a proxy for race – is a scientific fallacy. What we may refer to as the UNESCO compromise was settled by two statements in 1950 and 1951, which dismissed the use of race and considered it a political danger (UNESCO 1975 [1956]).[5] Even though the ban on race coexisted with institutional racial segregation in the US and in South Africa, and there was an extensive use of racial classification in colonial empires, the consequences of this compromise have been – and still are – highly influential on the use of categorisation in statistics. They provide a justification against any (re)introduction of race into the official statistical apparatus.

However, the political framework is changing in the aftermath of mass migration to Europe, where immigrants are coming from parts of the world that have been heavily racialised and 'orientalised' – if we can borrow this neologism from Saïd (Saïd 1978). Race and ethnicity are no longer exotic categories referring to pre-modern groups (Modood 2007) or restricted to the post-slavery 'American dilemma'. They are everyday realities in multicultural European societies, even though the concepts are missing in non English-speaking areas.[6] The idea that colour-blindness is the best way to blur (artificial) ethnic and racial boundaries in order to achieve equality is challenged by academics and policy makers who try to forward the anti-discrimination agenda. The wide reappraisal of equality laws and policies set by two equality directives enacted in 2000 has put the issue of data collection back on the agenda[7] (Ringelheim and De Schutter 2009). The implementation of a 'new generation' of anti-discrimination policies is based on a positive use of ethnic and racial statistics (Simon 2004; Manila 2005; Makkonen 2007; Fredman 2008). The development of evidence-based policies has revealed the overall absence of consistent statistics linked to race or ethnicity in most European countries. The need to monitor unfair treatment has exposed the lack of information on the experience of ethnic and racial minorities. The concept of 'indirect discrimination' that was introduced by the Race Equality Directive goes beyond the condemnation of blatant discriminatory practices and seeks to apprehend discrimination from a systemic point of view. The objective is to scrutinise apparently neutral regulations, procedures and practices, and to identify differential impacts on individuals or groups according to their ethnic or racial origin, gender, religion, disability or age. One of the main consequences of this new approach is that it renders reactive policies outdated and it requires proactive actions. Anti-discrimination policies no longer add up to a set of condemnations over racist discourses and explicit prejudices; they now imply acting proactively through the implementation of positive action and diversity management. EU countries are now facing two linked challenges: to rethink the framing and construction of 'ethnic statistics' and to overcome the lack of statistics to implement effective equality policies.

9.2.2 Statistics to render visible the invisible

How, then, should we proceed to implement positive action when discrimination is so subtle, even invisible, a phenomenon? How can the invisible be made visible? This requires defining and collecting indicators that will reveal the discriminatory processes without waiting for potential victims to react. For this matter, statistics are a crucial, if not indispensable, tool. Statistical reasoning allows for the exposure of indirect discrimination because an implicit bias can be proven to be discriminatory when it affects an entire group. It consists of identifying the negative effect of an ascribed characteristic (such as race or ethnicity) on one element or action. Producing statistics on a large range of processes, selections or trials allows for a third party to monitor differential outcomes. Disparate impact is regarded as discriminatory only if it is significant, in other words not reducible to odds and if it is not justified by relevant criteria, such as social status or education level. The level of significance is assessed by designing indicators to which more or less sophisticated statistical tests are applied.

Statistics play a central role in anti-discrimination policy because each selection procedure can be assessed by statistical techniques. In the case of employment, for instance, scoreboards are set up to examine recruitment, promotion, access to training, salaries, dismissals, positions held, exposure to dangerous or unpleasant work and so on. The same data can be collected on education or access to housing to assess differential treatments in selection processes. In that sense, 'measuring discrimination' goes beyond the mere counting of discriminatory acts or the quantitative assessment of unfavourable treatment. What is referred to as 'measurement' covers a wide range of statistical tools to evaluate the equal treatment of individuals. They can include the exposure of discrimination in every domain of social life, through social science surveys to raise awareness among public opinion and policy makers; the observation of persistent differences in survey records or census data that reveals the existence of systemic or indirect discrimination; or the setting of quantitative targets for policies and the measurement of progress made each year. Finally, statistics may be useful to frame the sociological context of a court case and assess the credibility of the plaintiff's case.

Such statistical measurements are already used to assess gender inequality and implement policies of gender mainstreaming. Yet, the Racial Equality and the Employment Equality Directives did not make the establishment of monitoring systems compulsory. With no legal incentives to collect ethnic data, the policy of positive action is thus like a car without petrol.

The fact that collecting information on ethnic and racial origin is considered 'sensitive' from a legal point of view only reinforces states' resistance to collect such data. Interestingly enough, the collection of data considered as sensitive is actually conditioned to a series of legal impediments that guarantee the protection of individuals. In many countries, the collection of 'sensitive data' is formally prohibited unless certain conditions are fulfilled. This conditional prohibition implies that 'sensitive data' can have harmful effects on the people concerned and require extra-cautious handling when processed. To ensure such vigilance, the law gives power to data protection authorities to review the proposed operation beforehand, while imposing a general prohibition. Sensitive data may thus be collected within a predetermined regulatory framework.

9.2.3 The opportunity to waive the legal impediment

From a legal point of view, the collection of sensitive data is not prohibited; it merely requires specific precautions. However, policy makers and public opinion have interpreted 'precautions' as a ban on collecting sensitive data such as ethnic data. The assertion that these laws make it hard to collect such data is partly true. The collection of 'ethnic' data has to meet at least one of these three conditions: (1) the collector must obtain the explicit consent of the person involved; (2) the survey must be carried out for public interest; or (3) there should be a legal obligation to run such a survey. The first two conditions give control to the data protection authority. But empirical experience shows that 'ethnic' data is rarely processed when the data protection authority is the authorising body, essentially because data producers anticipate a refusal from this institution and engage in self-censorship. The third condition of the legal obligation to collect 'ethnic data' represents the main practical option to break through the legal restrictions and set up a monitoring system.

Since anti-discrimination and minority protection laws require the creation of monitoring systems, the restriction attached to the law should be lifted, thus rendering the processing of 'ethnic' data a routine matter. It would then be backed – as in the case of most statistical operations – by guarantees of confidentiality, informed consent and methodological rigour. The system would be based on voluntary self-identification and in no circumstances should individuals be assigned to one specific ethnic group with which they do not wish to identify. The collection of ethnic data would, to some extent, become commonplace and lose its special status. Moreover, it would reflect the otherwise generalised use of 'ethnic' labels in social interactions to describe individuals.

The lack of explicit regulation on the role of statistics in the implementation of equality policies, however, limits the production of ethnic data in European countries (Makkonen 2007). Neither Article 14 of the European Convention on Human Rights nor Protocol No. 12, which contains a general non-discrimination clause, tackles the question of 'ethnic' data. Directive 2000/43/EC has remained deliberately vague on the role of statistics in legal action. This role is mentioned only in Recital 15, and then in a relatively non-binding form, where it is cited among other legal proofs of the existence of indirect discrimination. By bringing indirect discrimination into community law and the law of member states, the Directives make it logically essential to produce statistics that give a picture of the extent and characteristics of racial discrimination, assess the impact of policies and facilitate legal proceedings (De Schutter and Ringelheim 2009). Yet they leave member states to decide whether to use these statistics and to define the form they are to take.

The downside of this new generation of equality policies and their extensive use of statistics is that they require the implementation of an extensive system of data collection and monitoring processes that can be referred to as a new 'bureaucracy of diversity'.[8] In addition to the collection of ethnic data through censuses and a large array of files in every domain of social life, such bureaucracy comprises 'diversity and equal opportunities officers' located in big firms, who compile massive amounts of information to monitor processes and comply with regulations. Beyond the assessment of the efficiency of such a system, these 'politics of documentation' (Ahmed 2007) reinforce ethnic and racial labelling in collective representations. As such, the decision to implement a comprehensive system of data collection and monitoring processes has different consequences whether it has to be implemented in a society that has a long history of ethnic and racial classification, or in a society where it has to be created from scratch.

Looking at the wide range of practices and ways in which statistics are used against discrimination, one can discern some indicators for devising a coordinated European strategy. However, there is no tried and easily copied recipe for the collection of 'ethnic' data. Each country devises its own nomenclature, which reflects its own history, and the system in the UK has no equivalent in other European countries. Moreover, the link between collecting data and using it for anti-discrimination policies can vary greatly. While nearly half the European countries collect 'ethnic' data in their official statistics, very few really use them to combat ethnic and racial discrimination.

9.3 Public debate on data collection and classification: minorities and majority

The scale of the debate on the collection of ethnic data varies greatly from one country to another. In some countries, such as France and Belgium, the issue resonates with older conflicts on the matter that are developed below. While in other countries (such as Germany and Denmark), although there might be resistance towards the collection of ethnic data, governments have hardly made the connection between the passing of anti-discrimination legislation at the European level and the necessity to collect ethnic data. In countries such as Spain, Greece or Poland, the identification of specific groups likely to be discriminated against does exist, but it is far from systematic and only concerns specific groups such as the Roma people, national minorities or illegal migrants. In this section, we will review the situation in some of the countries studied in this book (Belgium, Denmark, France, Germany, Greece, Latvia, Poland, Spain and the UK) and focus more specifically on the debate on the collection of ethnic data in France.

9.3.1 European countries with a low investment in the debate over ethnic data

The impetus of the European directives to implement anti-discrimination policies has not always been connected with the collection of ethnic data. Some countries have hardly made the link between the political objectives and the statistical instrument. In Germany, the organisation in charge of monitoring anti-discrimination policy, *Antidiskriminierungstelle des Bundes* (ADS), does not work in collaboration with the Federal Agency for Migration Refugees and Integration (Atzamba 2007: 9). Though the ADS launched a consultation on data collection on discrimination in 2010 (Peucker and Lechner 2010), the issues connected to immigration are overwhelmingly understood in terms of integration rather than discrimination. The public debate in Germany focuses on the 'failure of integration' and the so-called '*MultiKulti*' (multiculturalism) model. In a speech delivered in Potsdam in October 2010, Angela Merkel stated that 'the approach [to build] a multicultural [society] and to live side-by-side and to enjoy each other ... has failed, utterly failed', urging immigrants to integrate and, more specifically, to learn German. Critical views against the alleged excess of multiculturalism in Germany had been popularised a few months before by Thilo Sarrazin, in a highly controversial book violently attacking immigrants and Muslims who are accused of spoiling the genius of the German *Volk* (Sarrazin 2010).[9] In Denmark, despite the passing of anti-discrimination legislation, there was little acknowledgement that such a policy should be monitored through the collection of numerical information. For instance, in 2010 the ECRI deplored the fact that there was no systematic record of complaints about racism or discrimination (ECRI 2010).

Countries also frame the issue of anti-discrimination legislation in an old anti-racist paradigm, that racism is a product of imprudent individual behaviours and victims of racism are migrants who are exploited and have limited access to rights because of their legal status. This paradigm makes little acknowledgement of the formation of minority groups resulting from generations of immigrants who are exposed to discriminatory practices. In Germany, the collection of information concerning racist crimes targets mainly foreigners and in official statistics only the nationality of the individuals is recorded.

However, since the Nationality Act of 1 January 2000 was passed, which gives the children of foreigners born in Germany an automatic right to German nationality,[10] the superposition of nationality and minority changed. Currently with a 'third Turkish generation' born in the country and a large group of *Aussiedler*, Germany encompasses a large population of nationals with an immigrant background. Alongside the terms 'migrants' and 'aliens' (*Ausländer*), we see the new category of 'Germans of immigrant origin' (*Deutsche mit Migrationshintergrund*)[11] being used in public discourse, official statistics and research. Moreover, the question of the parents' country of birth, introduced by the Microcensus in 2005, has brought about a considerable change in the statistical approach of integration. Whether based on combining nationality and individuals' country of birth, or directly on information concerning parents, the concept of *Migrationshintergrund* (immigrant origin) is beginning to take hold.

The language spoken at home is used in surveys carried out in schools, and is included in the data collected by the Ministry of Education. The ministry has recently published studies that contain data on 'children and young people of immigrant origin',[12] generating discussion on the pros and cons of extending the observation of pupils beyond their current nationality. The statistical tables in the Berlin Senate's report on migration and integration are now using three categories. Alongside aliens (*Ausländer*), a category of 'Germans of immigrant origin' (*Deutsche mit Migrationshintergrund*) was added. The category paired with the latter is no longer 'Germans', but 'Germans not of immigrant origin' (*Deutsche ohne Migrationshintergrund*). In fact, problems of terminology are just as acute for minorities as they are for the majority. In 2009, the population with an immigrant background was counted at 16 million and the population without an immigrant background at 66 million. As a result of steady growth since 2005, the population with an immigrant background comprises 20 per cent of the total population of Germany.

It is interesting to note that representatives of minority groups in Germany were reported to be against the collection of data on people by reference to their ethnic group (ECRI 2010). This is an indicator of the obstacles that might be encountered in trying to set up a systematic collection of ethnic data. Similarly, Denmark only records individuals on the basis of personal citizenship or the origin of parents. As for Spain, discrimination issues have been mainly understood with regard to the situation of illegal workers in the labour market; thus discrimination is framed in relation to the legality/illegality of immigrants' status. There is little acknowledgement of Spain as becoming a multicultural society; however, Catalonia is becoming an outlier in this respect.[13]

Those European countries that do not reflect societal change in their official records are resistant because their approach to discrimination is restricted to the dichotomy between nationals and foreigners, or legality and illegality. They limit the issue of discrimination to an external problem (applied to foreigners) outside the nation, when the EU understanding of discrimination as laid out in the 2000 directives is a provision for European citizens.[14] Moreover, with a general trend to grant citizenship to immigrants who have been legal residents after a certain number of years (Germany in 2000, Greece in 2010) there is a risk that official statistics conceal the reality of diversity when they only record nationalities. The fact that the ECRI repeatedly urges national authorities to improve their monitoring system by collecting relevant information broken down into categories such as religion, language and national or ethnic origin shows that the current state of official data is not sufficient and that countries tend to lag behind in this respect.

In countries where there has been a tradition of recording the population in the name of multiculturalism, and historical minorities have been recorded via official statistics, the ECRI has already issued recommendations that the system encompass all ethnic groups (for example immigrant communities) and not only historical minorities. In Greece, the Roma population is identified with a view to monitoring housing policies when a broader system should include Muslim minorities and immigrants. In Poland, the recording of data should be comprehensive and include groups with immigrant backgrounds. However, the debate in Poland has focused in the past year on the very concept of the implementation of an anti-racist policy and the national authorities have yet to shift to the stage of monitoring discriminatory practices.[15]

In countries where there has been a tradition of not counting in the name of integration, authorities have been generally colour-blind and have implemented anti-racist policies according to an approach that is now characterised as outdated. The outdated modes, however, have not been challenged by the passing of the Race Directive at the European level. In countries where the possibility of collecting data has emerged in the public debate, controversial discussions have followed, as is the case for Belgium (Jacobs and Rea 2005) and France, where a constant debate has now raged since around 2000 (Simon 2008).

9.3.2 European countries with controversial debates: Belgium and France

In Belgium, the implementation of an anti-discrimination policy has been linked to the necessity to monitor the policy and to evaluate the existence and the persistence of discrimination in the labour market (Bousetta 2008). Anti-discrimination policy was institutionalised through the creation of the Center for Equal Opportunity and Opposition to Racism (CEEOR). The debate that followed has mainly been about the danger of stigmatising the population through the identification of ethnic groups. The CEEOR undertook a series of consultations on the subject of data collection as related to country of origin with representatives of minority groups and specialists.

Tensions arose from the consultations, as some parties argued against the collection of such data for fear that it would stigmatise ethnic groups and that information could be used negatively by extreme-right parties. The consultation also showed the negative perception associated with questions dealing with ethnic origin and brought to the fore the concern that this would overshadow other grounds for discrimination such as gender, social origin, age or religion. Finally, the collection of ethnic data was criticised for being associated with a multicultural understanding of society that prioritised groups over individuals that was in contradiction with a country such as Belgium. The general understanding of the 'instrument' of collecting ethnic statistics in connection with a 'model' shows the difficulty for such a country as Belgium to adopt the new anti-discrimination paradigm.

In France, the debate has mobilised numerous social actors to include policy makers, social scientists, anti-racist NGOs and public media. The official invisibility of minorities plays a pivotal role in the French political and legal framework. If we were to summarise the republican strategy into a slogan it would be 'equality through invisibility'. The credo of indifference to differences, the French colour-blind approach, leads to promoting what could be called the 'choice of ignorance' by removing any reference to ethnic or racial origin from policies or laws (in compliance with the Constitution[16]) as well as from statistics. Nevertheless, such a strategy reaches its limits with the growing spread of the categories of 'race' and ethnicity in public debates, political speeches, representations conveyed by the media and social reports. No one would contest the fact that the absence of the official use of ethnic or racial categories fails to curb the spread of prejudice and stereotypes. The main result of the social and statistical invisibility of 'race' and ethnicity may well be to conceal the extent of discrimination.

In this context, the issue of statistics has emerged to crystallise conflict in the discourse. Initially a confidential topic confined to the circles of demographers and statisticians, the debate over what type of statistics to use to analyse discrimination has rapidly moved into the public sphere where it has evolved into a violent controversy. The 'controversy of the demographers' began in 1998–9 in what turned out to be only the first phase in a cycle of emotionally charged confrontations (Stavo-Debaude 2005; Spire and Merllié 1999). In the short term, the status quo was preserved, but the debate recently picked up again with the development of new initiatives to combat discrimination. When the controversy resumed in 2004, the political context had changed completely from the late 1990s. Discrimination had found its way onto the political agenda (Fassin 2002), where references to skin colour or to 'visible minorities', an expression borrowed from the Canadian debates, had become omnipresent. While the need to fight against discrimination achieves a large consensus, the role of statistics in policy and policy making is still a contentious issue.

The recent developments in the continuing controversy illustrate the imbroglio. Faced with repeated and growing pressures, the French Data Protection Authority (*Commission Nationale Informatique et Libertés*, or CNIL) issued two series of formal recommendations on the 'measurement of diversity', in July 2005 and September 2007. In these recommendations, the authority leaves it to the legislature to decide whether 'nationwide ethno-racial nomenclature' ought to be created, while acknowledging that statistics referring to origins are legitimate in the context of the fight against discrimination. The ten recommendations issued in 2007 open the door to a well-thought-out collection of 'ethnic and racial' data as part of carefully supervised surveys, as well as to the collection of data that might be useful in analysing how people 'experience discrimination'. The CNIL also conveyed that it was open to introducing the country of birth and nationality of parents into the census. To the surprise of many, these recommendations inspired the filing of an amendment in a legislative bill on immigration control, which parliament examined in September 2007. Several anti-racist associations and the Parti Socialiste criticised the amendment, either for its content or for its insertion in a bill on immigration which was acutely discriminatory in itself. The Constitutional Council accepted the claim put forward by a large number of left-wing members of the parliament that the provision in the law authorising the collection of data on race and ethnicity was unconstitutional. That provision, whose *raison d'être* was paradoxically to strengthen the power of control of the data protection agency, was nullified as a result, primarily on the ground that it was a rider devoid of any connection with the object and purpose of the law into which it had been inserted (regulating immigration and redefining the conditions under which foreigners could reside in France). Yet, in what appears to most commentators as a cryptic statement, the Council also added a statement on the unconstitutional nature of any data collection processes that would rely on race or ethnic origin, understood as a violation of Article 1 of the 1958 Constitution.

It should be underscored that the controversy has not been about the nature of the findings that studies have presented on the situation of immigrants or their descendants in French society. Most of the critics were less concerned with the production of knowledge and the empirical basis for research on discrimination than with a desire to flag political and moral dangers. The consequences of these scientific and political controversies are quite sizable when it comes to data collection on discrimination. First, it has been impossible to change the census on the matter (no modification has been applied for seventy years). Second, any attempt by social scientists to launch a survey on issues pertaining to discrimination is put under public scrutiny. As such, the main collateral effect of the decision of the Constitutional Council has not been to ban 'ethnic statistics' from the census or administrative files, where they simply do not exist, but to exert censorship on the content of the biggest survey ever made on immigrants and second-generation individuals in France, the Trajectories and Origins survey. Two questions addressing the skin colour of respondents that were asked in the pilot survey have been deleted from the final version of the questionnaire to comply with the Constitutional Council statement. Colour-blindness in the Constitution has thus to be replicated in the representation of society.

Conclusion

The collection of ethnic data as an indispensable tool in the implementation of anti-discrimination is a problematic statement when considering the low level of investment in collecting such data among countries of the European Union (with the exception of the UK and Ireland), regardless of whether these countries have been members of the EU for a long time or whether they have taken part in the negotiations of the directives of 2000. In some countries, anti-discrimination legislation has not been fully implemented and independent equality bodies have not been created to monitor discrimination (Poland, Spain and Greece, for example). In these countries, the issue lies in their limited understanding of the formation of minority groups resulting from immigration. In Spain, discrimination is exclusively understood in connection with illegal immigrants and in Greece in connection with foreigners. Finally, in countries such as France, Belgium and, to a certain extent, Germany, the formal reluctance to establish ethnic data is associated with a belief that it does not match their national model and understanding of diversity.

The establishment of official ethnic statistics depends on each country's level of understanding and commitment to multiculturalism. Spain and Greece have a low understanding of their society as a multicultural one in the sense that they are composed of various minority groups including regional minorities, historical minorities and migration-related minorities. Multiculturalism as a political model for their society, however, is not acknowledged. For France, Belgium and Germany, there is a general distrust of multiculturalism as a model of governance that involves formal arrangements with groups. It is true that the exposure of discrimination practices according to ethnicity might lead to the mobilisation of ethnic groups, but this should not be feared in a democratic society.

Moreover, contested on political and methodological standpoints, statistics involving ethnicity or 'race' are troublesome because they are subjective and fragile; they are rooted to a history made up of slavery, colonisation, xenophobia, exploitation and domination, and they have the power to reveal historically crystallised relationships of power. The irony is that these contestations are not backed up by public opinion. Two polls have recently been carried out that surveyed the reaction of Europeans to data collection on ethnicity. In 2007, a Eurobarometer on 'Discrimination in the European Union' found that 75 per cent of respondents supported the idea of providing personal information on their ethnic origin in a census, 'if that could help to combat discrimination' (Eurobarometer 2007).[17] This endorsement made by the general population was confirmed in the EU-Midis survey made in 2009 by the Fundamental Right Agency, targeting two minority groups in each of the twenty-seven EU countries (EU-Midis 2009). Among the surveyed minorities, the support was significant in Ireland and Sweden (74 per cent), intermediate in France and Germany (around 60 per cent) and lower in Denmark (45 per cent). In most cases, positions in favour of data collection on ethnicity are more frequent than opposition to it.

Finally, by looking at the terminological pitfalls that beset the Francophone world, it is clear that while the terms 'race', 'ethnic group' and 'ethnicity' could not be more commonly used in English-speaking countries, their connotations in the non-English speaking world prevent their use in public and scientific discourses. Could we therefore use other signifiers instead of 'ethnic' and 'racial' that would still preserve the meaning that has been attributed to them? Using geography, 'culture' or national origin as a proxy for ethnicity of race raises some delicate issues. The notion of 'culture' is scarcely more consistent (and less controversial) than that of 'ethnicity', since using it tends to attribute explanatory power to the most obvious 'cultural' features (notably language and religion) at the expense of the more political and social dimensions of ethnicity.[18] As for geography, which postulates the primacy of a territorial relationship and sees migration as the founding event of ethnicity, its relevance – already debatable but plausible with respect to immigrants – is more than doubtful with respect to second generations. For the latter, ethnicity has less to do with a continuous tie to a territory or national origin than with an individual's socialisation in the family and in the broader ethnic community. It is a matter more of history than of geography. Indeed, the debate over 'ethnic statistics' is itself best understood in light of the very special relationship the European countries have with their history and their recognition of their diversity. The difficulty in taking into account, let alone overcoming, colonial history as well as the way immigration has been managed remains at the core of the controversy over statistics.

Notes

1. The gradual incorporation of immigrants to the mainstream population conceals the diversity of population to observers and analysts. Economic integration, nationality acquisition and intermarriage are processes that render diversity less visible. This challenges the demographic analysis of subgroups that created diversity in the first place.
2. The United Nations published recommendations for censuses and household surveys which have contributed to harmonised census-taking (United Nations 2008).
3. In her review of ethnic classification in the course of the '2000 census round', Morning found that only 44 per cent of European countries (that is, sixteen out of thirty-six) use ethnic enumeration, compared to more than 80 per cent in North and South America and Oceania (Morning 2008).
4. In countries where the nationality codes follow the principle of *ius soli* (a person born of foreign parents automatically or after a number of years acquires the nationality of the country of birth), second-generation immigrants fall into the category of nationals. Official statistics may record the country of their parents' birth to identify them as nationals with an immigrant background.
5. 'Statement on race', Paris, 1950; 'Statement on the nature of race and race differences', Paris, 1951. Even though the first statement proposed switching race for ethnicity as a more appropriate category, the second statement did not further support this. The first statement stated clearly

that 'National, religious, geographic, linguistic and cultural groups do not necessarily coincide with racial groups: and the cultural traits of such groups have not demonstrated genetic connection with racial traits. Because serious errors of this kind are habitually committed when the term "race" is used in popular parlance, it would be better when speaking of human races to drop the term "race" altogether and speak of ethnic groups'. Introducing the second statement one year later, L. C. Dunn, rapporteur of the commission that issued the second statement, highlights the difficulties in finding a substitute to racial categories: 'Since race, as a word, has become coloured by its misuse in connection with national, linguistic and religious differences and by its deliberate abuse by racialists, we tried to find a new word to express the same meaning of a biologically differentiated group. On this we did not succeed.'

6. One should emphasise here that language conveys specific representations, since 'race' as a commonly used word to refer to populations has survived only in English. In no other European language does the word still have this neutral connotation, thus making it harder to use it to refer to a social construction in the European context. The same holds true for 'ethnicity', even if its meaning is not as loaded as that of 'race'.
7. Directive 2000/43/EC on 'implementing the principle of equal treatment between persons irrespective of racial or ethnic origin' and Directive 2000/78/EC on 'establishing a general framework for equal treatment in employment and occupation'. The Council of Europe Article 14 of the European Convention on Human Rights (ECHR) prohibits discrimination in enjoyment of the rights and freedoms set forth in the text, and Protocol No. 12 to the ECHR contains a general non-discrimination clause.
8. See, among other references, Dobbin (2009) and Fischer (2008).
9. Chistian Geyer, 'So wird Deutschland Dumm', FAZ, 26 August 2010.
10. Staatsangehörigkeitsgesetz, StAG, Act of 1 January 2000.
11. For more information on the content of these categories, see Bevölkerung mit Migrationshintergrund – Ergebnisse des Mikrozensus 2009 – Fachserie 1 Reihe 2.2 – 2009, Statistiches Budesamt, Wiesbaden, 2010.
12. Arbeitstelle Interkulturelle Konflikte und Gesellschaftliche Integration (AKI) (2005) Migrationshintergrund von Kindern und Jugendlichen: Wege zur Weiterentwicklung des amtlichen Statistik, Bildungsreform Band 14, Bonn, Berlin, Bundesministerium für Bildung und Forschung.
13. But even in Catalonia where 'interculturalism' is an official creed, the consequences of the recent massive immigration are framed as an issue for newcomers (Zapata-Barrero 2010). Second-generation migrants are in fact not identified in registers (*padrones*) or censuses.
14. That the 2000 directives draw a boundary between European citizens and Third Country Nationals has also been a matter of criticism,

namely because the directives do not extend to expelled refugee or illegal migrants from outside Europe (Guiraudon 2009).
15. In 2007, the Supreme Court of Poland decided that holding a placard reading 'We shall liberate ourselves from [among others] Jews' did not amount to an offence under Article 256 of the Criminal Code. To reach this conclusion, the court referred to Article 54 §1 of the Constitution that protects the right to express opinions. According to the court, the meaning of 'liberate' and the use of the indicative, as opposed to the imperative, showed that there was no intention to incite hatred : 'ECRI considers that allowing the holding of such a placard to go unpunished falls foul of its General Policy Recommendation No. 7 on national legislation to combat racism and racial discrimination' (ECRI 2010: 14).
16. Article 1 of the Constitution of 1958 stipulates that 'France is an indivisible, secular, democratic and social Republic. It ensures equality before the law of all citizens regardless of origin, race or religion'. The question whether, with this phrase, the Constitution prohibits the creation of statistics referring to origin is not cut and dried. See the discussion later in this chapter on the recent decision by the Constitutional Council regarding the use of 'ethnic statistics'.
17. Variations across countries were relatively small, despite the differences in the framing of the issue. Spain had the lowest level of support with 68 per cent in favour of disclosing personal information on ethnicity in censuses, while France and Belgium had a high level of agreement with 78 per cent, close to the UK (80 per cent) and behind Greece (88 per cent).
18. See Modood et al. 2002 for a debate on the issue of the reference to ethnicity in social science.

References

Ahmed, S. (2007), 'You end up doing the document rather than doing the doing': Diversity, race quality and the politics of documentation', *Ethnic and Racial Studies*, 30(4), pp. 590–609.

Anderson, B. (1991), *Imagined Communities: Reflections on the Origins and Spread of Nationalism*, New York: Verso.

Atzamba, H. (2007), 'La lutte contre la discrimination et la promotion de légalité: comment mesurer les avancées réalisées', Rapport pays Allemagne pour la Commission européenne, DG Emploi, affaires sociales et égalité des chances. Available at http://ec.europa.eu/social/BlobServlet?docId=2642&langId=fr, accessed on 30 May 2011.

Bousetta, H. (2008), *In Search of an Anti-Discrimination Strategy*, for Work Package 4 of the EMILIE Project, 6th Framework Programme of the European Commission.

Coombes, M. (1996), 'Monitoring equal employment opportunity', in V.

Karn (ed.), *Ethnicity in the 1991 Census. Vol. 4, Employment, Education and Housing among the Ethnic Minority Populations of Britain.* London: OPCS.

De Schutter, O. and Ringelheim, J. (2009), *Ethnic Monitoring. The Processing of Racial and Ethnic Data in Anti-Discrimination Policies: Reconciling the Promotion of Equality with Privacy Rights*, Brussels: Bruylant.

Dobbin, F. (2009), *Inventing Equal Opportunity*, Princeton, NJ: Princeton University Press.

ECRI (2010), *ECRI Report on Denmark*, Report of the European Commission against Racism and Intolerance.

Eurobarometer (2007), *Discrimination in the European Union*, Eurobarometer 263/65.4, European Commission.

EU-Midis (2009), *European Union Minorities and Discrimination Survey: Main Report*, Vienna: Fundamental Rights Agency.

Fischer, M. (2008), 'Diversity management and the business case', in K. Kraal, J. Roosblad and J. Wrench (eds), *Equal Opportunities and Ethnic Inequality in the European Labour Markets*, Amsterdam: University of Amsterdam Press, pp. 94–116.

Fredman, S. (2008), *Human Rights Transformed: Positive Duties and Positive Rights*, Oxford: Oxford University Press.

Gellner, E. (1983), *Nations and Nationalism*, Oxford: Basil Blackwell.

Goldston, J. (2005), 'Ethnic data as a tool in the fight against discrimination', in S. Mannila (ed.), *Data to Promote Equality. Proceedings of the European Conference*, Helsinki: Finnish Ministry of Labour, European Commission, pp. 124–37.

Guiraudon, V. (2009), 'Equality in the making: Implementing European non discrimination law', *Citizenship Studies*, 13 (5), pp. 527–49.

Hobsbawm, E. (1990), *Nations and Nationalism since 1780: Programme, Myth, Reality*, Cambridge: Cambridge University Press.

Jacobs, D. and A. Rea (2005), 'Construction et importation des classements ethniques. Allochtones et immigrés aux Pays-Bas et en Belgique', *Revue Européenne des Migrations Internationales*, 21(2), pp. 35–59.

Kertzer, D. and D. Arel (eds) (2002), *Census and Identity. The Politics of Race, Ethnicity and Language in National Censuses*, Cambridge: Cambridge University Press.

Kriszan, A. (ed.) (2001), *Ethnic Monitoring and Data Protection: The European Context*, Budapest: CEU Press INDOK.

Makkonen, T. (2007), *Measuring Discrimination: Data Collection and EU Equality Law,* Report for the European Network of Legal Experts in the non-discrimination field, Luxembourg: European Commission.

Manila, S. (ed.) (2005), *Data to Promote Equality: Proceedings of the European Conference*, Helsinki: Edita.

Modood, T. (2007), *Multiculturalism: A Civic Idea*, London: Polity Press.

Morning, A. (2008), 'Ethnic classification in global perspective: A cross-national survey of the 2000 census round', *Population Research and Policy Review*, 27(2), pp. 239–72.
Ni Bhrochlain, M. (1990), 'The ethnicity question for the 1991 Census: background and issues', *Ethnic and Racial Studies*, 13(4), pp. 542–67.
Peucker, M. and C. Lechner (2010), *Machbarkeitsstudie Standardisierte Datenerhebung zum Nachweis von Diskriminierung!? Bestandsaufnahme und Ausblick*. Report for the Antidiskriminierungsstelle des Bundes (ADS), Berlin.
Rallu, J. L., V. Piché and P. Simon (2006), 'Demography and ethnicity: An ambiguous relationship', in G. Caselli, J. Vallin and G. Wunsch (eds), *Demography: Analysis and Synthesis. A Treatise in Population Studies*, vol. 3, Amsterdam: Elsevier Academic Press, pp. 531–49.
Saïd, E. (1978), *Orientalism*, New York: Pantheon.
Sarrazin, T. (2010), *Deutschland schafft sich ab*, Munich: DVA.
Seltzer, W. (1998), 'Population statistics, the Holocaust, and the Nuremberg Trials', *Population and Development Review*, 24(3), pp. 511–52.
Simon, P. (2004), *Comparative Study on the Collection of Data to Measure the Extent and Impact of Discrimination within the United States, Canada, Australia, the United Kingdom and the Netherlands*, Luxembourg: EU Commission, DG Employment and Social Affairs, Fundamental Rights and Anti-discrimination.
Simon, P. (2005), 'The measurement of racial discrimination: The policy use of statistics', *International Journal of Social Science*, 57 (183), pp. 9–25.
Simon, P. (2007), *'Ethnic' Statistics and Data Protection in the Council of Europe Countries*, Strasbourg: ECRI, Council of Europe.
Simon, P. (2008), 'The choice of ignorance: the debate on ethnic and racial statistics in France', *French Politics, Culture and Society*, 26(1), pp. 7–31.
Spire, A. and Merllié, D. (1999), 'La question des origines dans les statistiques en France. Les enjeux d'une controverse', *Le Mouvement social*, 188, pp. 119–30.
Stavo-Debauge, J. (2005), 'Mobilising statistical powers for action against discrimination: the case of the United Kingdom', *International Journal of Social Science*, 57(183), pp. 43–55.
United Nations (2008), *Principles and Recommendations for Population and Housing Censuses: Revision 2*, New York: Department of Economic and Social Affairs, Statistical Papers Series M, no 67/Rev2.
Vertovec, S. (2010), 'Introduction: Depicting diversity', *Diversities*, 12(1), pp. 1–3, UNESCO.
Zapata-Barrero, R. (2010), 'Dynamics of diversity in Spain: Old questions, new challenges', in S. Vertovec and S. Wessendorf (eds), *The Multiculturalism Backlash. European Discourses, Policies and Practices*, London: Routledge, pp. 170–89.

Index

anti-discrimination, 12, 17–18, 20, 24, 41, 52, 53, 61, 63–4, 66, 71, 73–4, 80–1, 83–4, 89, 106, 163–4, 182–3, 206–7, 209–10, 213–14, 217, 219–23, 225–6, 228–9, 231
assimilation, 1, 3–4, 6, 22–3, 39, 42, 52, 53, 70, 73, 76, 79, 83, 89–90, 109, 116, 193–5, 201, 207–8, 216
assimilationist, 21, 36, 47–8, 62, 73–5, 118, 147, 149, 156, 174
associations, 4, 35, 42, 44, 70

Belgium, 12, 14–15, 22, 56, 62, 67, 74–8, 82, 112, 126, 135, 146, 148, 151, 154–5, 157, 165, 170–2, 178, 186, 214, 217–18, 225, 228–9, 231–2, 235
Britain, 7, 35, 46, 57, 65, 67, 105–7, 109–10, 112, 155–6, 165, 177, 185

census, 213, 217–19, 222, 224, 226, 230–5
citizenship
  banalisation of, 90
  civic, 160, 183, 201
  consequentiality of, 90
  dual, 37, 40, 95–9, 204
  European, 11
  good, 20, 89–90, 95, 102, 105
  multicultural, 10–12, 14, 18–19, 33, 49, 52–3, 64–5, 71–2, 75, 78, 84, 111
  social, 11, 41, 56, 91, 94, 105, 107
  test, 35, 70–1, 99–101, 103, 106, 200–3, 209

civic integration, 20, 62, 67, 76, 88–9, 97–8, 100–2, 104, 106, 109, 111, 160
claims-making, 5, 7–8, 12–19, 63, 116–18, 123–5, 137, 148, 169, 171, 173, 178–9, 181, 183, 187
classification, 214, 216–17, 219, 221, 224–5, 233
cohesion, 6, 18–19, 46, 47–8, 57, 61–5, 67–9, 72, 74, 76–8, 82, 106, 113, 118, 149, 163–4, 169, 193, 216
  social, 1, 3, 11, 18, 21, 52, 61, 84, 88, 104, 111, 145–7, 155, 163, 200
  value, 90
consultation, 18, 62–3, 66, 77, 170, 178–83, 186, 203–4, 225, 228–9

data collection, 215–17, 221, 224–5, 228, 230–2
Denmark, 1, 9, 12, 14–15, 19–20, 22, 35–6, 38, 62, 67–8, 72–4, 84, 88, 91, 93–107, 109–12, 126, 135, 146, 148, 154–5, 157, 159, 170–3, 178–9, 186–7, 201, 203, 217–18, 225–7, 232
diversity
  cultural, 4, 14, 19, 21, 35, 42, 44–5, 47, 65, 71–2, 75–6, 77, 79, 84, 127, 143, 146, 148, 150–1, 153, 156–9, 192–3
  ethnic, 2, 12–13, 21, 35, 65, 69, 73, 75, 146, 185, 213, 219
  linguistic, 149, 163
  religious, 1, 12, 14–15, 20, 34, 62, 70, 145–6, 148, 154, 192, 206

239

education (multicultural/intercultural), 21, 79, 83, 146, 148–56, 159–60, 162, 201
equality, 6, 12, 19, 24, 38–41, 43–6, 52, 54, 62–3, 65–8, 73–4, 80, 104–5, 116, 121–5, 127–9, 134, 136, 145, 151, 153, 159, 164, 181, 184–6, 198, 213–14, 216, 221–2, 224, 229, 231, 235
　inequality, 80, 96, 109, 153, 156, 180, 214, 222
ethnic group, 38–9, 42, 52, 76, 108, 169, 179, 214, 219, 224, 227–9, 232, 234
Europe, 3, 5, 7–14, 16–20, 22, 33–8, 42, 46, 52, 61, 78, 81, 85, 96, 98, 105, 107–9, 111, 117–18, 124–5, 129–30, 133–7, 146, 148, 150–1, 156, 159, 160–1, 164, 167, 172–3, 184–5, 188, 192, 208, 213, 215–17, 220–1, 234–5
European Union, 2, 17–18, 23, 35, 40, 72, 94, 126, 196–7, 231–2
Europeans, 117, 133, 210, 232
　non-Europeans, 35, 99

faith-based schooling, 21, 147–8, 159–61
France, 1, 7, 9–10, 12, 14–15, 18, 22, 24, 38, 44, 47, 61–5, 67–8, 72, 84, 112, 118, 122–4, 126–7, 129, 132, 134–6, 138–9, 146, 151, 154–5, 157, 161, 170–3, 180–1, 186–7, 206–7, 214, 217–18, 225, 228–2, 235

Germany, 1, 9, 12, 14–15, 18, 20, 22, 24, 35–6, 38, 40, 47, 62, 67–9, 71, 84, 88, 91, 93–107, 109–12, 146, 151, 154–5, 170–2, 174–5, 181, 186–8, 192, 200, 202–4, 208, 214, 217–18, 225–7, 231–2
Greece, 1, 12, 14–16, 22, 39, 56, 79–82, 83, 112, 146, 151, 155–7, 170–2, 175–6, 182–3, 186–7, 201, 214, 217–18, 225, 227–8, 231–2, 235

identity, 4, 8–12, 17, 19, 38, 41–2, 46, 48, 54, 61–2, 67–8, 73, 78, 79, 82, 84, 103, 105, 110–11, 116–17, 119, 124, 126, 134, 145–6, 148, 150–1, 165, 185, 188, 215
　European, 118, 148
　national, 3–4, 6, 11, 15, 18, 21, 35, 37–8, 41, 44–5, 52, 54, 61–2, 65, 68, 74, 78, 80–1, 105, 110, 134, 146, 155, 159–61, 186, 215
integration requirement, 95, 97, 100, 107, 209
interculturalism, 12, 48–52, 78–9, 82, 85, 151–3, 156, 234
Islam, 7–8, 19–20, 35, 52, 71, 73, 77, 85, 89, 103, 108, 110, 116–17, 119, 121–2, 124–6, 128–129, 131–9, 154, 158–9, 179, 182, 188, 202–6, 210
　education/schools, 158, 188–9, 192
ius sanguinis, 67, 85, 95, 97, 102, 112, 174, 176
ius soli, 18, 36, 69, 84, 91, 97–100, 176, 233

Latvia, 14–15, 17, 146, 148, 156
liberalism, 6, 37–8, 52, 88–9, 109, 117–18, 127, 134

monitoring, 24, 37, 63–4, 66, 163, 207, 215, 223–5, 227–8
multicultural democracy, 21–2, 167–8, 177, 188
multiculturalism, 1–13, 16–17, 19–22, 33–4, 36, 39, 48–50, 52, 67, 75–6, 82, 83, 88, 109, 116–19, 126–7, 129–31, 136–7, 145, 151–3, 155–6, 167, 182, 192–4, 208, 214, 216–17, 226, 228, 232
Muslims, 2–3, 5–10, 12–16, 19–20, 23, 36–8, 52, 63, 65, 67, 71–2, 77, 85, 88, 105, 107–10, 112–13, 116–19, 121–2, 124–5, 127, 129–30, 133–9, 148, 153–4, 157–61, 165, 174, 185, 188, 192–3, 195, 198, 200, 202, 209, 226, 228

INDEX

naturalisation, 4, 16–17, 22, 54, 62, 67, 69, 79, 82–3, 88–9, 91, 93, 97–100, 102, 105–6, 108, 167–8, 170, 172–6, 178, 186–7, 201
normative models, 42, 194

official statistics, 214–16, 225–8, 233
origin, 40, 62, 64, 66, 76, 84, 93, 97, 103, 105, 117, 125, 131, 133, 148, 150, 158, 162–3, 172, 175–6, 178, 181, 219–21, 223, 226–35
othering, 215

participation
　civic, 61
　political, 14, 22, 169–71, 173–4, 176–80, 186–8, 197
permanent residence, 91–5, 98–101, 106, 112, 175–6, 184
Poland, 14–17, 56, 146, 156, 181, 214, 217, 219, 225, 228, 231, 235
political parties, 171–2, 183, 185–8
political rights, 22, 83, 106, 168–73, 176–8, 180, 184–6
post-national, 19, 37, 90–3, 107

racism, 23–4, 72, 75, 118, 134, 139, 149, 152–3, 182, 206, 213–14, 221, 226, 228, 235
　anti-racist, 21, 147–8, 150, 153, 156, 180, 214, 220, 226, 228–30
representation, 4, 12, 17, 21–2, 44, 55, 65, 93, 110, 116, 121, 135, 146, 168–71, 178–9, 181–2, 184–8, 203, 213, 215, 224, 229, 231, 234

secularism, 1–2, 7–10, 14, 20, 118–19, 129, 135, 150, 157, 160–1
self-identification, 127, 224
social integration, 47, 145, 169, 183–4, 203
Spain, 1, 12, 14–16, 22, 24, 29, 56, 78, 80–4, 112, 117, 146, 151, 155–7, 170–2, 176–7, 183–4, 186–7, 201, 203, 214, 217, 219, 225, 227, 231–2, 235

voting rights, 82, 93, 170–4, 176–8, 182, 184–5, 187